how to write
SALES
LETTERS
THAT SELL

how to write SALES LETTERS THAT SELL

LEARN THE SECRETS OF SUCCESSFUL DIRECT MAIL

2nd edition

DRAYTON BIRD

KOGAN PAGE

First published in 1994
Reprinted 1995
Paperback edition published in 1997
Reprinted 1997, 1999
Second edition 2002
Reprinted 2004, 2005, 2006

Kogan Page Limited
120 Pentonville Road
London N1 9JN
www.kogan-page.co.uk

© Drayton Bird, 1994, 2002

British Library Cataloguing in Publication Data

A CIP record of this book is available from the British Library.

ISBN 0 7494 3876 2

Typeset by Jean Cussons Typesetting, Diss, Norfolk
Printed and bound in Great Britain by Antony Rowe, Chippenham and Eastbourne

Contents

Acknowledgements

Thank you to all those people who helped with the book, in particular my secretary Denise Rayner, and to those who supplied material, especially:

Stan Winston
David Tetther
Christian Brann
Roger Millington

Introduction

'No man but a blockhead ever wrote, except for money.'
Dr Johnson

LETTERS THAT MAKE MILLIONS

Few informed people would dispute that the art of writing sales letters is practised better in the US than anywhere else. And for some years over there one man was generally recognized by his peers as *the* outstanding practitioner.

He worked from a beautiful home in the California wine country with his partner, who designs their mailings. Their fame is such that they were profiled in the *New York Sunday Times Magazine*.

They only worked for publishers and helped launch no less than 37 leading American magazines. They had a waiting list several months long. They never need to go and visit their clients, who have to call on them – and were very happy to pay them what you may think is a remarkable amount of money.

Fifteen years ago one of their direct mail shots could cost you as much as $40,000 – that's just for the writing and the design: artwork and printing extra. People in the know thought this quite a bargain. The reason was that they got *results*.

The right direct mail piece can have an extraordinary effect on your business. For instance, one produced by my friend and his partner apparently saved one of America's most famous magazines from going broke. They were able to persuade a sufficient number of people to subscribe when all other attempts had failed. Even at $40,000, this is an excellent investment.

There are plenty of other examples I can call to mind where one writer's ability to persuade other people to the writer's point of view has had the most dramatic effect you could imagine.

About 20 years ago someone else I know wrote a 2-page letter which began with the words: 'Quite frankly, the American Express Card is not for everyone...' You may even have received this letter yourself. It was used by American Express for over a decade in many countries around the world to persuade people they ought to become Cardmembers. To this day, the idea behind it is still employed.

American Express – like any other business – depends for its success upon recruiting sufficient customers at the right cost. This letter, then, was largely responsible for providing an essential ingredient in a company that for years was the fastest growing business in the world and remains a powerful force in international finance. Not bad for a little sales letter.

You will notice I say 'letter', as opposed to 'mailing'. The reason for this is that among the elements which make up a mailing 'pack', the critical ingredient is rarely, as many imagine, the brochure. It is the letter. A simple, inexpensive letter on its own, with nothing else – apart from some means of reply – can work wonders.

ONE OF YOUR BEST INVESTMENTS

So the first point I would like to make to you is that the time you spend learning to write a letter that *sells* could be one of the best investments you ever make.

I learned this the best way. A four-page letter helped *me* succeed more than I ever expected. It was to persuade people they ought to employ the services of myself and my partners in a new business, in 1977.

As you can imagine, I laboured long and hard on it. We only sent out 25 copies. My partner rang up the recipients on the telephone afterwards. We got 12 jobs. Within three years we were the leaders in our field in Britain.

Seven years and eight months later – my partners having gone their

AMERICAN EXPRESS TRAVEL RELATED SERVICES COMPANY, INC
AMERICAN EXPRESS PLAZA, NEW YORK, NY 10004

Diane Shaib
Vice President
Marketing

Dear Mr. Penberthy:

Quite frankly, the American Express® Card is not for everyone.
And not everyone who applies for Cardmembership is approved.

However, because we believe you will benefit from Cardmembership, I've enclosed a special invitation for you to apply
for the most honored and prestigious financial instrument
available to people who travel, vacation, and entertain.

The American Express Card is the perfect example of the old
adage, "You get what you pay for."

For example, you get a truly impressive array of extra
privileges, all designed for your convenience and security:

. <u>A Worldwide Network of Travel Service Offices* is
at your Service</u>. Enjoy personal attention at any
of the nearly 1,000 American Express Offices --
your "homes away from home" -- around the globe.

. <u>Cash your Personal Check at Thousands of Locations</u>.
Cash up to $250 at participating hotels and motels,
and up to $1,000 at most American Express Travel
Service Offices all over the world. (Subject to
cash availability and local regulations.)

. <u>Card Lost or Stolen? You'll Get a Quick Replacement</u>.
If the Card is lost or stolen, an emergency replace-
ment will be provided at any Travel Service Office in
the world, usually by the end of the next business day.

. <u>Obtain Emergency Funds Instantly</u>. Once you've en-
rolled in this convenient service, our network of
automated Travelers Cheque Dispensers lets you obtain
up to $500...in 60 seconds or less!

. <u>Carry $100,000 of Travel Accident Insurance</u>. Just
charge your tickets to the Card, and you, your spouse
or dependent children under the age of 23 are automatically covered when traveling by common carrier
on land, sea, or in the air. It's underwritten by
Fireman's Fund Insurance Companies, San Rafael,

(over, please)

*Of American Express Travel Related Services Company, Inc , its affiliates and Representatives

Original written by Bill Trembath.

California, for approximately 35¢ of the annual Cardmembership fee.

. <u>Your Hotel Reservations are Assured</u>. As an American Express Cardmember, if you request, your hotel room will be held for you until check-out the following day, at nearly 8,000 participating hotels.

. <u>Enjoy Special Express Hotel Service</u>. Speedy check-in and check-out is available to Cardmembers at more than 1,000 hotels, including Hilton, Hyatt, Marriott, Sheraton, and more.

Extras like these only begin to tell the story of American Express Card security, emergency protection, and convenience. You'll also enjoy:

. <u>Unequalled Mobility</u>. The Card is welcomed by the world's major airlines, car rental agencies, railroads, and cruise lines. Plus it pays for auto parts and servicing at thousands of locations nationwide.

. <u>A Worldwide Welcome</u>. Fine restaurants, hotels, resorts, and a host of other establishments around the world, and right in your hometown, recognize the Card and welcome your patronage.

. <u>Purchasing Power</u>. No need to carry large amounts of cash. The Card takes care of shopping needs, whether you're choosing a wardrobe, buying theater tickets, sending flowers, or hosting a dinner (even if you can't be there!)

. <u>Financial Freedom</u>. Unlike bank cards, the American Express Card imposes no pre-set spending limit. Purchases are approved based on your ability to pay as demonstrated by your past spending, payment patterns, and personal resources. So you are free to make your own decisions about when and where to use the Card.

In a few words, American Express Cardmembership is the most effective letter of introduction to the world of travel, entertainment, and the good life yet devised. Yet surprisingly, these benefits are all yours to enjoy for the modest fee of just $35 a year.

Why not apply for Cardmembership today? All you have to do is fill out and mail the enclosed application. As soon as it is approved, we'll send along the Card, without delay.

Sincerely,

Diane Shaib
Vice President

P.S. Apply today, and enjoy <u>all</u> the benefits of Cardmembership. Those listed here are just a handful of what's available. A full listing is included in the <u>Cardmember Benefits</u> book you'll receive along with the Card.

way – I sold that company, at which point I could, if I had so wished, have retired.

So the fate of nations may not depend on whether you do or do not write a good sales letter. But it is unquestionably true that many successful businesses have been fuelled by such letters. To give just one more example, the *Wall Street Journal* has, it is calculated, attracted well over $1 billion worth of subscribers' money with a letter (shown on pages 29–30) that has run without change for over 20 years.

The letter is increasingly being recognized as one of the most powerful, if underrated and misapplied, business tools. Indeed, the use of direct mail is growing faster than that of any other significant medium apart from the telephone. There are many reasons for this.

SPEAK DIRECTLY TO THE RIGHT PEOPLE

By using direct mail you can isolate those individuals you wish to speak to and not waste money talking to the whole world – as you do in mass advertising. What is more, you can speak to them directly, without intermediaries getting in the way.

Managements have been writing directly in an effort to reach their work forces over the heads of the unions. Companies – and predators – have written directly to shareholders to persuade them they should or should not sell their shares. Even governments have woken up and use direct mail more and more to reach clearly definable audiences.

Moreoever, management thinkers have come to realise that the purpose of business is not simply to make sales, but to make customers – customers you need to keep as long as possible; for making that first sale can be expensive.

Once customers have become yours, though, it is much cheaper to sell to them than it was to get them originally. In fact, the evidence shows it is anywhere between three and eight times as easy to sell something to your existing customer as to somebody similar who is not, which is a good reason for writing regularly to those who already deal with you.

From your own experience, you know this is true. The restaurateur makes enormous effort to cultivate good spenders. The hotel groups create loyalty schemes to bind customers more closely to them, as do airlines or petrol companies, when they offer savings stamps or award schemes.

In that process of keeping customers with you longer, a persuasive letter is an essential – perhaps the most versatile – weapon at your disposal. It requires no elaborate photography or artwork: it is simply you speaking as one human being to another, just as you would if you came to see somebody in their offices.

Letters work for *every* kind of organization. There is certain to be some aspect of what you do – probably many aspects – where a well-judged campaign of persuasive letters will do the trick.

All this may be quite apparent as you read it. But think of the sales letters you receive. How many *do* sell? How many do you glance at and discard, or read, only to be appalled at how poorly they understand you and how often they actually put you off?

Clearly, although many people know well-planned and written letters can be powerful, few realise how powerful – certainly not enough to invest sufficient time and thought on them.

MONEY SQUANDERED BY THE LAZY

A prodigious amount of money is spent on sales letters that don't sell. And I have no hesitation whatsoever in saying that most is squandered by people who don't know what they're doing and are too lazy to find out. Why?

Well, for a start, we all write business letters every day. We take it in our stride; part of the daily grind – as mechanical as brushing our teeth. We see a sales letter as little more than a variation on this simple chore. How could such a trivial thing require much art or planning?

One measure of the lack of interest or appreciation of the importance of persuasive letters is simple. Look in your local library or bookshop. There are very few good books on the subject. Until recently, I could wholeheartedly recommend only one – an American one now out of print – called *The Robert Collier Letter Book*. If you ever stumble upon it in a secondhand bookshop, buy it.

Even now there are only two others I can seriously recommend to the non-professional.* There are others – but they are mostly aimed at those whose trade is direct marketing. This book is aimed at everyone; and I hope even those of you who are professionals will pick up the odd useful thought.

---

* *The Greatest Direct Mail Sales Letters of all Time*, edited by Richard S Hodgson (The Dartnell Corporation, 1986); and *Million Dollar Mailings* by Denison Hatch (Who's Mailing What, 1992).

THE PERSONAL TOUCH MAKES THE DIFFERENCE

I do not propose to give you – as some books on business letter writing do – a series of prefabricated form letters you can adapt to fit your own needs. This is more useful if you require a series of letters for ordinary business situations, eg telling somebody you can't extend them any more credit or that you have received the goods and you want to complain etc.

These are not really personal subjects and a form letter will often do. Unfortunately, though, it will not and cannot contain that *personal* touch which makes the difference between a good letter and a bad one. In fact many such letters would do better with a little more humanity added – as I shall show later.

Clearly, I cannot be exhaustive in a relatively brief book like this. However, even if your own type of business or the exact problem you face now is not covered, the examples shown, together with the guidelines and the practical advice, should be enough for you to be able to go away and write a good letter immediately. It may not be a great work of art. But I imagine that is not why you are reading this. You just want something that gets results.

HOW TO PLAN; QUESTIONS ANSWERED

Happily, the principles you should follow to write a good letter vary surprisingly little from business to business. If you have read my last book,* you will see that I touch upon them in the chapters on the subject of creativity. Naturally, there is some overlap, but this book goes into much greater detail.

First, you will discover what you should do before you start writing: how to plan your letter; what you need to consider about your product or service and how it relates to your prospective readers; and how to ensure you have the right information before you start.

I will give you the tested formula that ensures your letters incorporate all the ingredients for success: how to structure; how to begin the letter; what the 'guts' of the letter should contain; the best way to end – the way that will give you most replies.

---

* *Commonsense Direct Marketing* (1993) Kogan Page, London.

There are other things to bear in mind. How should your letter be laid out to attract the eye? How do you write so that others will enjoy reading? There are many techniques professional letter writers have found add interest to your writing. I shall cover these for you, too.

For many years now I have lectured and conducted seminars around the world on letter writing. A surprising number of the same questions come up constantly.

Do I need a brochure? How long should the letter be? Should there be a message on the envelope? How should I order the elements of the letter? When should I use headings? What about a second colour of ink? Should I use a stamp on the envelope? What should I ask the reader to do? Who should sign the letter? And there is more.

Does it pay to offer a reply-paid service to my readers? Should I give my phone number; and if so should it be an 0800 number? Should I keep sending letters if people don't reply? How many replies can I expect? How long does it take for them to come in? All these and others are covered.

STUDY WHAT WORKS AND WHAT DOESN'T

I believe one example is worth a ton of theory when it comes to learning. Studying what works and why, and what doesn't and why not: that is by far the best way to discover what makes letters sell.

So you will find the book contains many good and bad sales letters to illustrate the points I am making. In some cases I shall ask you to look at them and form your own opinion before reading what I think. This will help you to remember the points made better.

These letters fall into three types. Some are generally recognized as outstanding by those who write such letters for a living, having in some cases, as I have pointed out, persuaded people to part with millions over the years.

Some are letters which are unusual for one reason or another – like the letter from a tailor in Chapter 14. Others are fine demonstrations of the abysmal. But most are neither: they are just the kind of letters you and I receive every day. The kind you have to send out yourself. Most are a mixture of good and bad, and thus probably have more to teach.

Some I wrote myself. I show them not for vanity's sake – it is ludicrous to be vain about such a mundane activity. There is nothing remarkable about them, as you will see, except that they all worked. I chose them because I am the only person who can tell you exactly how and why they were conceived – what my thinking was.

That is what you want, I think: to be able to sit, as it were, next to someone who does this for a living, then study how they plan and write. This is the closest I can get to helping you learn on the job. Any expert can tell you the rules for writing a good letter, but very few can tell you how to *apply* them and how they have been applied.

I suggest you read all the examples carefully – and not just once. This field is no different from any other. Those who write the best letters are those who spend the most time analysing the letters they receive. You should do the same.

USE YOUR IMAGINATION

What is more, those who take the most away from such analysis are those who bring the most to it. To get best value from these pages, use your imagination. Reflect as you note each point or review each example: how does this relate to me and my business? Is there something here I could apply? Is there something I'm obviously doing wrong?

To encourage you to make that effort I have done my best to make the book interesting. Although the sales letter is not something that has the same dimension of importance as world peace or life after death, I find the subject fascinating. Maybe it's because I've got a very trivial mind.

Anyhow, I hope you'll find the book valuable, engrossing and that occasionally it may draw from you a quiet smile. If I succeed in these three objectives, I will be very happy.

If I don't, please write and tell me so. Tell me where I am going wrong. Tell me how you think the book could be improved.

If you like it – well, like all authors, I thirst for praise. So by all means write and tell me that, too.

1

Why It's Hard to Write a Good Sales Letter

'I believe he's downstairs in the cloakroom, preparing his impromptu remarks'

Said one evening by F E Smith of Winston Churchill

A class of students was being taught by the well-known American direct marketing expert Bob Stone. 'How many of you', he asked, 'have written a sales letter?' Nobody responded. He then asked 'How many of you have ever written to your parents for money?' The point was made.

I have spent my entire career writing, starting as a trade journalist at 19. I have tried most forms of writing – and enjoyed them. I still recall my delight when my first book was published, which was almost matched by my surprise and disappointment when it didn't make me famous.

I have to conclude I am just a journeyman. However, most of what I've written, from a gripping piece on the design of the Bugatti motor car engine to some exhilarating stuff about the life of the American cowboy has actually been printed. So it may surprise you to know that I have found a good sales letter one of the more difficult things to write.

We all use letters to sell, sometimes without knowing it. Unless you are a transcendent genius whose talents are so instantly apparent to all you meet that they hurry to do your slightest bidding, you have to learn how to persuade other people to do what you want – often in writing.

When you write a memo and stick it on your office notice board to encourage your employees to come in on time, or stop wasting money, or work harder – you are trying to sell them an idea.

When you write to your shareholders to persuade them you are doing a good job with their money – you are selling your company. Sometimes you may write a letter which simply makes your customers feel good – and this too will generate sales. An excellent example is shown on page 13.

The first and perhaps the most important sales letter you ever write will be to get a job. So I shall discuss it at the end of this, the first chapter.

THE WRONG POINT OF VIEW

When I do so, you will see that letters to get job interviews – like most others designed to sell – suffer from one big fault. They are written from the point of view of the writers, who believe everybody should be interested in them (or what they want to sell), rather than the readers, who have the identical feeling – but from the opposite perspective. Why is this?

One of the first things you ever learn is to write letters. Once you've learned the alphabet, how to spell a few simple words and can write legibly, you start scribbling little messages to your parents – and then letters. At the age of seven, when I was sent to boarding school, I was required twice a week to write a letter to my parents.

I often think that nearly all those who write sales letters have a subconscious hangover from this youthful experience. These early letters are written to people who are intensely interested in what we are doing. When we get older this is so far from being true that the opposite is the case.

Coping with that is quite an adjustment. Some of us never adjust. A good example from someone who ought to know better runs as follows:

Dear Friend:

I agreed to chair the New York Festivals because:

– The show is international. It's known and respected everywhere I travel.
– They publish a sumptuous Annual of Advertising presenting
  the medalist and finalist work for all to admire and study.
– The organizers want to make the show even better. They're
  open to comments and criticism from folks like us who design
  and write.

The 1994 'call for entries' for print and radio is enclosed. If
you want to compete in a relevant, highly regarded international show, consider The New York Festivals.

I wish you success.

Regards

That was written by a very experienced advertising bigwig, who
should know the rudiments of selling, but it doesn't show here. He
starts by talking about himself and ends with the reader.

So if you gain nothing else from this book, as long as you learn that
a good letter is written for the benefit of the reader, not the writer, you
will know more than most people who write letters know. Indeed, let
me state flatly that your investment may already have paid for itself.

HOW DO YOU MAKE IT INTERESTING?

When you are writing to sell, for reasons I shall go into, entertainment
is pretty irrelevant. People don't read sales letters for fun. What you
are writing about, though fascinating to you because it is your livelihood, is not necessarily so to your reader.

You have to write in a way so engaging that what you have to say
becomes interesting to those who receive it – who will be, more often
than not, strangers with no desire to read what you write. Moreover,
almost invariably, you will not know as much as you would like about
those readers.

Dear Virgin Atlantic Passengers,

        I am sorry that we are not flying you on our aircraft today. Last night our 747 that flies to Miami had a small problem with the landing gear, so we had to charter a plane and a crew at short notice while the plane is being fixed. In the two years we have been servicing New York this has never happened to us and we are only sorry it's happened to us so soon after we've started flying to Miami and that this has happened to you personally.

        Although we should love to have shown off to you all Virgin's 747 and our very special hospitality we believe we should still get you to your destination on time. I am personally flying with you today with my family, and if any of you have any problems please do not hesitate to contact me. I will be in the front row of the aircraft.

        Sorry to disappoint you. We'll make it up to you on your next flight on Virgin Atlantic Airways.

Regards,

Richard Branson
President Virgin Atlantic Airways

P.S. DRINKS WILL BE ON US TONIGHT TO HELP COMPENSATE SOMEWHAT.

VIRGIN ATLANTIC AIRWAYS LTD.
MIAMI INTERNATIONAL AIRPORT, P.O. BOX 3518 A.M.F., MIAMI, FLORIDA 33159-3518
TEL

Here is a message many would not consider a sales letter. It was placed on the seat of a plane my wife was travelling on some years ago. I bet the people who received it were more likely than not to choose Virgin on their next flight.

Suppose you're writing to a list of customers. The odds are that just about the only thing you know about them is that they *are* customers. You may be able to deduce certain things about them from this fact, eg, they are interested enough in your widgets to have bought one. And, assuming they haven't complained, they may well think you make pretty good widgets.

But that isn't much to go on when you are trying to write in a personal way. And a letter *is* an intensely personal form of communication. Apart from a conversation, either in person or on the telephone, it is the most personal communication you can imagine. To succeed, as I have already indicated, it has to have a personal character.

TWO ROADS TO DISASTER

So let's sum up the challenge this book is designed to overcome. *How do you write in a personal way to people you don't know and who don't want to read what you've written, about something they are probably not very interested in?*

The two most common approaches lead to certain disaster.

The first is that of someone who gives the matter no thought at all. Someone who sits down and wants to communicate as briefly as possible that the product or service in question is wonderful. Many letters are not even that ambitious. They adopt the minimalist approach and settle for merely announcing the existence of whatever is on offer.

People who do this are so blindly convinced of the merits of what they are selling that they think everyone else will be. They are intimately familiar with every detail of what they are writing about. Indeed, if you are an enthusiast you may be downright infatuated with what you sell.

This is particularly true if you have founded and run your own company. People start with their own businesses generally because they think they have something special to offer. They believe profoundly in what they are selling. They *live* with it. This admirable enthusiasm leads them to believe its virtues are self-evident – so much so, they hardly feel it necessary to explain why anyone should buy it.

The second approach, equally fatal, is that of writers I would categorize as half-smart: they have given the matter a little thought – but not enough. They decide people probably see far too many letters, commercials, posters and advertisements, and rarely pay attention.

Therefore, they feel they must be original, clever and entertaining, luring prospects into the letter before springing the sales message upon them.

In this case, the premise, that people get far too many sales letters already and don't read them, is false; which leads inevitably to the wrong conclusion – that entertainment and novelty are called for.

Now you may rightly respond that the interests of your audience, which I stressed earlier, are equally paramount when writing a film script or a novel, and in those instances entertainment certainly works.

But in such cases your audience *want* to be entertained. That means you can put in any element – odd, funny, dramatic, tragic – that will hold their attention. The purpose of a sales letter is much more mundane and focused: to *sell*.

Elsewhere in this book I have illustrated letters which, with rare ingenuity, manage to fall into both the traps described above. They are written entirely from the writer's perspective, and they try, very unsuccessfully, to be clever or funny. Both these roads to disaster are pursued by people who simply haven't given thought to what they are doing. They have not spent enough time preparing.

THE GOOD NEWS: PEOPLE DO READ AND REPLY

Certainly people are exposed to more selling messages than they would like. Despite this, they remain responsive. In America, for instance, people receive six times as much direct mail as people in England; in Germany about two and a half times as much. But there is no evidence to suggest sales letters are ceasing to work in any of these countries. Far from it.

Over a six-year period up to 1989 there was a 60 per cent increase in the number of Americans who responded to direct mail. This was in an article in *Time attacking* direct mail.

Other facts that came out were that 56 per cent of all the direct mail received in America is opened *and read*. In fact, although Americans receive so much more direct mail than the British, a recent study by the UK's Direct Mail Information Service suggests that response levels in the US are twice as high – which I believe is because the American direct mail industry is much better at it than we are.

The research reported in *Time* revealed that no matter what people feel about receiving an enormous volume of mail, 60.3 per cent said they were happy about it because they sometimes found something interesting.

This is very significant, for the truth is not that people receive too many sales letters, but that they receive too many *irrelevant* ones. When people say they hate junk mail, this is what they really mean. They don't like receiving things that don't interest them.

NO NEED TO BE CLEVER: JUST RELEVANT

On the other hand there is ample evidence that the reverse is true. Any letter which talks to the right person about the right subject at the right time, and appeals to that person's self-interest, will succeed. And it does not have to be clever to do so.

Of course, if it *is* also ingenious it may well succeed even more. But that touch of originality is far less important than being relevant to the reader. Indeed, unless you are a very talented writer, any attempt you make to be clever could well frustrate your purpose, because the cleverness will get in the way of the message. Moreover, what you may find original, funny or diverting is often of no interest whatsoever to the reader.

If people want to be entertained, as I have already pointed out, they watch television, read novels or go to the cinema. And very few people who write sales letters are as good at entertaining as those who do it for a living – who *are* entertainers.

What is more, although there must be some people who enjoy reading clever sales letters, they can only represent a tiny and very eccentric group among the population; and such people are not statistically likely to be the same as those you wish to sell to.

A further problem is that an approach selected because of its wit or novelty may have little relevance to the subject at hand. It is not easy to move adroitly from a good joke to explaining why someone should buy a life insurance policy.

In fact, as John Caples, one of the great pioneers of the mail order industry, discovered from years of research evaluating the differences between advertisements that got lots of replies and those that didn't, what usually works best is not ingenuity but *news of benefits*.

ALLOCATE YOUR TIME CORRECTLY

I was once talking to a colleague about a common acquaintance who gives the most wonderful, relaxed speeches. Making any speech is terrifying. I was unable to do so until I was 41, so great was my fear. Those who are not nervous are generally awful windbags.

What was this man's secret? He spends two days getting ready to make a half-hour speech, my colleague told me. After that he knows exactly what he wants to say and can concentrate on how he is going to say it.

A sales letter is such a deceptively simple object that it hardly seems worthy of elaborate preparation. And it is true that you do not need to be elaborate – indeed, the simpler the better – but to succeed you must apply much the same approach as my speechmaking friend.

I told you in the introduction about the celebrated American writer who was paid so much for his direct mail pieces. His name is Bill Jayme.

Bill was once asked how he divided his time when working. How much on writing and how much on preparation? He replied that he spent 90 per cent of the time preparing and only 10 per cent writing. This did not surprise me, because it is the approach I take and that of most of the good writers I know.

This relative division of time is common, I believe, to all forms of art, not just commercial writing. You need a good period of research and reflection before you sit down to the final job. You must examine the problem from every angle; find out all you can about the product or service; speculate about the people you are writing to.

Every minute you spend thinking about what you're going to do will be worth ten minutes spent later trying to fix something which is wrong – wrong because you didn't give it sufficient fore-thought.

FIVE ELEMENTS IN SUCCESS

I believe five elements make up a successful letter. The first two, *evaluating your product or service* and *thinking about your prospects*, are perhaps the most important.

That is because these are the two things you are trying to draw together: the product and the prospects. If you want to find out how what you sell can be relevant to those you wish to persuade, you have to know as much as possible about both. Only thus can you hope to arrive at that benefit or combination of benefits most calculated to appeal to those prospects.

The next thing you must do is see if you can construct some *offer or incentive* which will overcome people's reluctance to reply to somebody they usually do not know, but who – even if they do know them – is not sitting in front of them and able to exert the full power of personal persuasion.

Next comes *technique*: understanding how to construct an argument which is likely to persuade people; knowing the various ploys and stratagems which work; and how to write and lay out a letter in a way that will start and keep people reading.

The fifth element (the one most people often imagine to be most important) is *talent*. Quite clearly, if you have a natural talent for writing and for persuasion you'll find it easier to produce letters that sell than if you haven't. But the good news I have for you is that because so many people get everything else wrong, this is far less important than you might imagine – assuming you can write to begin with.

But, as you can see, the first three of those five elements have little to do with writing, while the fourth is only partly concerned with writing. In fact this division of resources is pretty well reflected in the arrangement of this book. Even when you look at the examples I give, you will see I say very little about the words, style or grammar but a great deal about the content.

Success in this field, as in most others, comes mostly from thinking and planning, not from doing. Please never forget that. To show what I mean, let's look at how you should write to get a job – as I promised earlier.

THE MOST IMPORTANT LETTER YOU MAY EVER WRITE

As many of us have learned the hard way, it is not easy to get a job nowadays. But your chance of doing so may well depend upon writing a good letter.

By cruel paradox, those who have to write such letters are often ill-equipped to do it well. Most are young people with little experience to guide them; many others are older people who may have been made redundant and are often demoralized, besides having forgotten those skills that got them their first job years earlier.

I am well placed to know how bad most of these letters are, having received hundreds over the years. Yet the principles of writing a good letter to sell yourself are identical to those required to sell anything else, and you will find them mentioned – and repeated – throughout this book. The most important was exemplified by the most famous job application letter ever written: from Leonardo da Vinci to the Duke of Milan.

You may think of Leonardo as a pretty nifty painter and sculptor, but those skills were not what he focused upon when writing to the duke. He concentrated on two things he knew the duke was more interested in: grandiose display and war.

So Leonardo touted himself as an expert in designing bridges and palaces, good at siege engineering, well versed in manufacturing cannon, ships and armoured vehicles, and a master at hydraulics. As an afterthought he mentioned he could sculpt and paint.

In other words, he looked at it from the customer's point of view, not his own. He started by asking himself what the duke wanted, then told the duke he could deliver it.

Now clearly I can't give you a precise idea how you, with your particular skills, should write to the employer you have in mind, for everyone has different talents. But let's look at the principles involved.

Only go for jobs you think you can handle

First, you must *select* properly. You can't write to everyone for every job. Go to the right person for the right job.

Never apply for jobs you may not be suited for. It's no use getting a job if you can't do it or learn to do it very quickly. Find out who you should write to. Writing to an anonymous 'managing director', 'human resources' or 'personnel officer' is not the best way. Addressing the person by name shows you have some initiative.

In my view, you should write to someone senior, personally. Then it has some chance of reaching whoever is really involved with an endorsement from their senior: 'she sounds interesting – what about the so and so job?'

The boss may know more about what's available than the personnel people, and might see possibilities for you that would otherwise be missed. This doesn't mean, though, that you write to the chairman of a vast organization for a beginner's job.

You must do your homework – your research.

Let me tell you about a letter which did not get me a job, but certainly obtained me an interview which is the purpose of the letter itself.

In 1966, I conceived the desire to go and work for an advertising agency, Ogilvy, Benson & Mather in New York. I had done about as well as I could in England; the US was generally seen as the advertising Mecca; and that agency was one of the two or three best. If I wanted to improve myself, that sounded like a very good place.

I found out all I could about that firm and the skills they valued. This was easier because their founder, David Ogilvy, had written a book I had read several times. In it he made it very clear that he believed advertising should sell, rather than merely entertain.

This seemed to make them a good prospect for someone with my talents. I had considerable experience in writing advertisements with coupons, and were run by people who counted their replies to see what they got for their money – just as you should with the replies to your sales letters. Many of my ads had been very successful.

I had written advertising for a wide range of companies, several in the travel field. This was relevant because I knew Ogilvy, Benson & Mather had accounts such as the French Tourist Board and the British Travel Association, for whom I had worked in Britain.

What went into a successful letter

If I'd known that years later I was to write this book I would have kept the letter – but I didn't. However, I can tell you the main ingredients and structure – even the words I used at the start.

I wrote to Mr Ogilvy himself. I seized his attention by pointing out that 'Although you have never heard of me, I have a quality I know you prize. I know how to make people buy.'

I told him some of the clients I had worked for, pointing out that they all depended upon measurable results. I believed this would interest him and make him want to find out more. I knew it is very hard to get good writers, and every intelligent senior advertising executive is always on the look-out for them. Mr Ogilvy, being one of the two or three best in the world, would surely be no exception.

However the problem as with anything else was: would he believe me? To overcome that I did two things. First, I sent him five pieces of work I thought displayed my talent. I sent five because I had seen an advertisement for creative people he had run some years previously. In it he specifically requested respondents send in five pieces of work. I told precisely the circumstances and the results of each advertisement, to heighten his interest.

To convince him I really was a good bet, I got two people who had previously worked for his agency in New York to write brief testimonies to my ability.

I rounded off the letter by saying that I had read his book *Confessions of an Advertising Man* (Atheneum, New York, 1984) several times, and always wanted to work for him. These statements were both true, as well as being mildly flattering. And, of course, I included a resumé of my career.

As a result he wrote to me suggesting I meet his senior international executive who was visiting London. So the letter did the trick. In fact, for personal reasons I never went to New York, but years later by a happy coincidence I sold my business to his firm and got to know him quite well.

Simple principles

The principles involved in that letter were, as you can see, very simple. I'll recap them, because they apply to any letter – indeed, they summarize much of what you will learn in this book.

1. Only approach the right people – the ones you think you can do a good job for; those for whom your 'product' – you and your talents – is right.
2. Conduct reconnaissance. Learn as much as you can about the people you want to work for. This will enable you to speak to the right people and address their needs.
    It also shows you have been keen enough to learn about them. Every time I get a letter from a job applicant which refers to something my company or I have done, I read with quickened interest. Like everyone else I am interested in people who are interested in me.
3. Following that, talk about the interests of your prospect, not your own (nearly all job application letters I see talk about what the applicant wants rather than what's in it for me).
4. Then move on to your special skills, which you must relate to the needs of your potential employer, just as you must relate the needs of your customer to your product or service.
5. Put in some impartial proof that what you say is true. Hardly any letters do. Almost invariably when somebody writes to me for a job, I write back and ask them for comments from previous employers, as well as samples of their work.
6. Include a resumé which gives every reason why you should be hired.
7. Make it abundantly clear that you're *eager* to work for the people you're writing to and say why.

What else should you do to get a reply – apart from asking for one?

Here I'll make a last suggestion; one you will come upon many times in this book. *Make an offer.* It could make all the difference when people are not sure.

One young man offered to work for my company for nothing just to learn the business. We weren't looking for anyone – but what could we lose? We took him on and paid him a pittance – we were too embarrassed to pay nothing – then a little more. Today he runs a very successful business selling shirts.

I once told a prospective employer to take me on for a month – then fire me if I was no good. It was the making of my advertising career.

If you do all these things, I promise you will have done more – a lot more – than about 95 per cent of the people who write looking for jobs.

2

Why Some Letters Fail, While Others Succeed

'If a man write a better book, preach a better sermon, or make a better mouse-trap than his neighbour, tho' he build his house in the woods, the world will make a beaten path to his door.'

Ralph Waldo Emerson

When I read the famous statement above, I sometimes wonder if Emerson was drunk when he wrote it. How many bankruptcies, divorces and suicides might it have caused among those who took it seriously?

Examples are legion of people who had brilliant ideas but never made enough money because they didn't understand how to market them, ranging from the inventor of the tubeless tyre to the original begetters of the McDonald's hamburger.

The truth is that if nobody knows that your product or service exists, what makes it better and why it suits them, you won't sell any.

There are many ways of accomplishing the first objective – letting people know about you: advertising, packaging and public relations, for instance. A campaign of letters to the right people is one way of doing so.

But how do you convey the other two – what makes you better and more suitable – in a way that persuades people to act? Failure to do so is the main reason why most of the millions of sales letters that go out every week do so badly. This is often because the writers have neglected to determine the purpose of the letter – what they want the reader to do. It is obviously impossible to reach an objective you have not defined.

WHY ARE YOU WRITING?

Your letter may have three purposes and these will determine the weight of persuasion you are going to need to get a reply. Let's take three likely objectives in order, with the hardest to achieve first.

1. *You wish to sell something in exchange for money paid in advance.* You not only have to make somebody want what you offer, but make them trust you enough to believe you will deliver what you have promised. This will be particularly true if you want people to pay in full. If you offer easy terms your job will be much easier: they are not so committed.
2. *You wish to get your prospect to try your product without obligation to buy.* This will clearly be easier than getting them to buy it.
3. *You wish them to come into your premises and just look at what you offer.* This will be easier still. They will feel much more in control of the situation.

In all three cases, the better known you and your product are to that prospect, and the stronger the relationship, the easier your task will be – and vice versa. Thus, getting one of your current customers who buys regularly from you to act will be infinitely easier than persuading somebody who has never heard of you.

Whatever your aim, in every case you are trying to build a bridge between the person you are writing to – your prospect – and the product or service you are selling. What does this call for? You must spend time analysing, first, what is special about what you are selling and, second, what is special about the people you are selling to.

DESCRIBE WHAT YOU ARE SELLING

Logically, then, the first step in preparing your letter is to define what

Limited

OTMA

Management & Training Consultants

Victoria House, Southampton Row, London WC1B 4DH
Telephone: 01-405 4730/5644
Telex: 21792 Ref. 3378

Registered Office: 22 South Audley Street, London W1.
Incorporated in London. Registered number 1022417

21 May 1984

Dear Mr Thomas

Communication Skills for Marketing Staff

You may remember* that earlier this year I wrote to you about this training
course. From then on it was "good news/bad news" all the way. Thus

Our February course was a great success (good)

However client companies came rather than agencies (good for
us, bad for you)

But agency interest resulted in a good deal of in-house training
rather than bookings on our central courses (good for them, good and
bad for us, not so hot for you)

So we still have places on our forthcoming central
courses (rotten for all the able executives who
could get even better with training, good for you
because you can still send some of your people).

I offer three good reasons why you should take up places on this course. The
first, we send back your staff equipped to do their jobs much better. The
second, to give the lie to all those pieces in Campaign about agencies not
taking training seriously enough (what do the people who write them do about
it?). The third is that we could all do with some more good news.

Yours sincerely,

Peter Whyborn
Director

*On the other hand, you may have forgotten completely, or passed the letter to
some hapless minion who has failed to act on your behalf. Rather than hold it
against you, I will repeat the brief details. But if you would like to see a
full syllabus, ring me and I will lash the carrier pigeon out of its loft.

Communication Skills for Marketing Staff
Course duration: 5 days
Forthcoming dates:
4 - 8 June
24 - 28 September
26 - 30 November
Fee per delegate: £350.00 plus VAT £52.50

Directors: Lord Bedwood (Chairman) K R Maylock (Deputy Chairman) P E Mophey (Chief Executive and Managing Director) T Wheedon R A Harden K F T Jeffery R G A Whybornt

**A letter that fails to explain what is being sold because it wrongly assumes the
previous offer has been read.**

you are selling. Somewhere in your letter, though not necessarily at the start, you must make it clear exactly what you have to offer. The only exception would be if all your readers know it very well already.

After that you can explain why it's so wonderful. Sounds obvious? Read the letter on page 25 and try to work out exactly what is being sold. My colleagues and I had no idea. Clearly the writer thought we would. That's because he made the error of thinking we would remember his previous letter. Never make that mistake.

So, make sure you have written down a very clear exposition of whatever you're talking about in language anyone can understand – not just an expert. Unless, of course, you're writing only to experts, who love jargon. More on that subject later.

Don't just be satisfied in your own mind that this is clear to other people. Find somebody who knows nothing whatsoever about the subject and show it to them. See if they can understand clearly what you're offering. And remember: write it from the customer's point of view, not yours.

Now, as I say, the writer of the letter shown above did have the excuse that he thought I would remember his previous effort – though if the tone was as smug as that of the follow-up, no wonder I didn't. But many writers who have no excuse fail in this way.

How many times have you had people write to you about products – especially financial ones – and not understood what they were talking about – though they clearly did?

What is term life assurance, for instance, as opposed to endowment life or whole life? What is a unit linked policy? Not all of us know the difference. Take something very simple: what is a premium? To insurance companies it is a payment. To ordinary people, research revealed a few years ago, it means something special.

Later in this book I show a letter in which a company writes about giving me an 'illustration'. What that means to me is a picture. To them it means an example.

WHAT IT IS VERSUS WHAT IT DOES

Once you have described your product or service clearly, you must make it attractive to your prospect. You have to translate the features of the product into the benefits it gives. Here are two examples.

A few years ago I came into some money. I bought my wife a Lotus sports car. Its features were that it was bright red, long, low, very beautiful and went from 0–60 mph in 5.2 seconds. It had a fibreglass body that made it very light, which was one reason why it went so fast.

But the *benefits* to her, I suspect, were rather different. Everybody looks at an attractive woman in a sports car. And if the car in question is rarely seen, they look even harder. I imagine she got a tremendous feeling when she put her foot down and shot ahead of everyone else when the lights changed. On a practical level, she could accelerate quickly when overtaking or to get out of trouble.

She still misses the car. Its only disadvantage was revealed when an eager Frenchman followed her all the way on the autoroute from Calais to Cannes one summer.

Let's look at how this difference between what something is and what it does translates into writing a good financial proposition. A life insurance policy has a £4 monthly premium and pays £50,000 if you die. In terms of benefit, this is better expressed as: 'There'll be £50,000 waiting for your family if anything happens to you – yet you pay less than £1 a week.'

If you really want to see just how spectacular the effect can be if you isolate the right benefit, read *The Wall Street Journal* letter on pages 29 and 30.

As you see, the fact that the newspaper gives you the news is far less important to the selling argument than the benefit revealed in the story at the opening of the letter, which tells how one person had a much more successful career than another because of reading *The Wall Street Journal*. This, written by Martin Conroy, may well be the most successful sales letter ever.

COMPARE STRENGTHS AND WEAKNESSES

Let me give you another, perhaps even more appropriate, example. I am writing this on a laptop. But I could use any number of other tools.

Let's take a quick look at some of them and what they offer me, the customer. We shall also look at what they don't offer – because obviously you must evaluate relative weaknesses as well as strengths.

This little exercise will show you how to assess what you have to offer. At the same time it will show you how to do something very important, which is to translate what something *is* into what it *does* for the customer. Because that is all your reader wants to know. Not what its features are, but what benefits they will get. In the process we can see how these various alternatives appeal to a particular customer – me.

I could write in longhand using a pencil

Some writers still prefer to. I never have, because my writing is dreadful; it is hard work if you have to write a book – rarely less than 60,000 words; the writing comes out grey; the lead keeps breaking and even if it doesn't you have to keep sharpening the pencil. What's more I sometimes make copies and fax things from my home to my secretary in the office. Pencil doesn't reproduce well.

On the other hand, pencils are cheap, easy to carry around and you can rub out your mistakes.

I could use a fountain pen

I have many of the objections to a pen that I have to a pencil. Of course, you don't have to sharpen a fountain pen: you just have to fill it – which, being maladroit, I find a challenging chore. In addition I find fountain pens leak when I get them, and even if they don't I usually smudge the words and get ink on my hands. Moreover, fountain pens cost more than pencils.

Again, many writers like this method. It is a distinctly elegant way of writing and even my scrawl looks better. No problems with reproduction either. And very portable, if they don't leak.

Also, some seem to gain satisfaction from the rather formal feeling it gives: 'I am writing something significant', one feels when unscrewing the top. Rather like signing a peace treaty.

I could use a manual typewriter

Indeed, for many years I did. Unfortunately, you have to learn to type. This take some time. If you are typing a lot, it is hard on the hands and shoulders. You have to change ribbons – which I could never do without becoming covered with whatever they put on them. Making corrections on a manual is a pain. I'd be much better off with an electric typewriter – you can buy them very cheaply – and they're no harder to carry around.

However, you can pick up really cheap manual typewriters for next to nothing – maybe for less than a posh fountain pen. Typing gives you some idea of how words look on the page, too. It looks professional and is easier for my secretary or publishers to read. And you don't need to plug into electricity.

THE WALL STREET JOURNAL.

World Financial Center, 200 Liberty Street, New York, NY 10281

Dear Reader:

On a beautiful late spring afternoon, twenty-five years ago, two young men graduated from the same college. They were very much alike, these two young men. Both had been better than average students, both were personable and both—as young college graduates are—were filled with ambitious dreams for the future.

Recently, these men returned to their college for their 25th reunion.

They were still very much alike. Both were happily married. Both had three children. And both, it turned out, had gone to work for the same Midwestern manufacturing company after graduation, and were still there.

But there was a difference. One of the men was manager of a small department of that company. The other was its president.

What Made The Difference

Have you ever wondered, as I have, what makes this kind of difference in people's lives? It isn't a native intelligence or talent or dedication. It isn't that one person wants success and the other doesn't.

The difference lies in what each person knows and how he or she makes use of that knowledge.

And that is why I am writing to you and to people like you about The Wall Street Journal. For that is the whole purpose of The Journal: to give its readers knowledge—knowledge that they can use in business.

A Publication Unlike Any Other

You see, The Wall Street Journal is a unique publication. It's the country's only national business daily. Each business day, it is put together by the world's largest staff of business-news experts.

Each business day, The Journal's pages include a broad range of information of interest and significance to business-minded people, no matter where it comes from. Not just stocks and finance, but anything and everything in the whole, fast-moving world of business...The Wall Street Journal gives you all the business news you need—when you need it.

Knowledge Is Power

Right now, I am reading page one of The Journal, the best-read front page in America. It combines all the important news of the day with in-depth feature reporting. Every phase of business news is covered, from articles on inflation, wholesale prices, car prices, tax incentives for industries to major developments in Washington, and elsewhere.

(over, please)

And there is page after page inside The Journal, filled with fascinating and significant information that's useful to you. The <u>Marketplace</u> section gives you insights into how consumers are thinking and spending. How companies compete for market share. There is daily coverage of law, technology, media and marketing. Plus daily features on the challenges of managing smaller companies.

The Journal is also the single best source for news and statistics about your money. In the <u>Money & Investing</u> section there are helpful charts, easy-to-scan market quotations, plus "Abreast of the Market," "Heard on the Street" and "Your Money Matters," three of America's most influential and carefully read investment columns.

If you have never read The Wall Street Journal, you cannot imagine how useful it can be to you.

<u>Save $30 On Your Subscription</u>

Put our statements to the proof by subscribing for a full year right now and <u>save $30</u> off the regular subscription price. That's right, order now and you can receive The Journal for an entire year for only $99.

Or if you prefer, a 13-week subscription is only $34. It's a perfect way to get acquainted with The Journal. Either way—one year or 13 weeks—we pay the delivery costs!

Simply fill out the enclosed order card and mail it in the postage-paid envelope provided. And here's The Journal's guarantee: should The Journal not measure up to your expectations, you may cancel this arrangement at any point and receive a refund for the undelivered portion of your subscription.

If you feel as we do that this is a fair and reasonable proposition, then you will want to find out without delay if The Wall Street Journal can do for you what it is doing for millions of readers. So please mail the enclosed order card now, and we will start serving you immediately.

About those two college classmates I mention at the beginning of this letter: they were graduated from college together and together got started in the business world. So what made their <u>lives</u> in business different?

Knowledge. Useful knowledge. And its application.

<u>An Investment In Success</u>

I cannot promise you that success will be instantly yours if you start reading The Wall Street Journal. But I can guarantee that you will find The Journal always interesting, always reliable, and always useful.

Sincerely,

Peter R. Kann
Publisher

PRK: eu
Encs.

P.S. It's important to note that The Journal's subscription price may be tax deductible. Ask your tax advisor.

How to successfully dramatize a story plus a comparison of the benefits of a product.

I could dictate to my secretary

I do, for short pieces. But for anything really long, her shorthand is not able to cope with my frenzied fancy. And often what I think I said doesn't emerge at the other end, because I have the infuriating habit of walking up and down when I dictate – usually with my head facing away from her. Also, I mumble. In any case, she has better things to do with her limited (and, in my view, ludicrously expensive) time.

On the other hand, she's there already – and paid for. And it's a wonderfully lazy way of doing things. What's more, I can be sure that whatever she produces will look good.

I could use a dictating machine

Not only could I: I still do. Unfortunately to write anything at all complex requires an enormous effort of will – first, to organize and get fixed in my mind what I am going to say in advance; second, to remember in what sequence I plan to make a series of points; third, to avoid sloppy, repetitive language as I dictate.

This is difficult enough when writing something one can see – but when one can't, it's extremely hard. In fact I spend far more time editing than dictating; maybe it would be better to write the stuff out in the first place.

However, if you are very busy and not so concerned to get your writing perfect first time – if you have lots of letters and memos to send out each day – a dictating machine is perfect.

I can dictate things the minute they occur to me, night or day, wherever I am. And dictating means the original draft retains the rhythm and feeling of face-to-face speech – important, as you will see later in this book. Also, you can buy a pocket dictating machine for just a few pounds. A good fountain pen could cost much more.

I could use a desk top computer

This has the problem that I have to learn how to use it – daunting, because I'm the kind of person who needs a map to change a plug and can't do anything technical. Also, it's expensive. And a fairly hefty piece of machinery, too. I can't use it without electricity.

To add to that, I have to learn a new language. An icon will no longer mean a Russian religious artefact, but a sign on my screen. A window will have nothing to do with my house, but some device I have to get into or out of – and so on.

On the other hand, the look of what I produce will be superb. And I can see what it would be like when printed. Indeed, I can even move type around to see how different arrangements will look. With the right software I can insert pictures. I can create documents, reports, advertisements, I could fire my art director and do my own layouts (sorry, Chris: hard times). And because I do lots of speeches and presentations I could use it to create my own slides. I could save a fortune.

Or I could get a laptop

It has all the disadvantages of the desk top computer and costs much more.

But I will put up with these things because I travel; I work in the train, in planes, at home – anywhere. This machine has a built-in battery. Now I can do all the things I have to do, with all the advantages of a desk top computer – on the move. This compensates all the questions of cost, learning and the associated exasperation. For *me* it works. For *me*, the need for this particular product has overcome the misery of paying for it.

If they would only produce a battery that lasted longer after each charge, write their instructions in English and provide a decent after-sales service, I'd be ecstatic.

And, that, dear reader, is what a sales letter begins by calculating; why people should choose you. Can you find an argument so persuasive as to impel sufficient individual readers to pay the price or make the effort you want?

FEW CUSTOMERS CARE ABOUT TECHNICALITIES

Notice that in assessing the various options open to me I hardly mentioned the technical things – the features – that the manufacturers probably think important and usually prattle on about in their advertising. I don't care how many bytes, or is it bits, or RAM a machine has. A ram to me is one of the sheep I used to keep in Somerset. I just want to know what it *does* for me.

I probably missed out, too, some of the relevant factors and certainly will have made misstatements of fact. It is not my job as a customer to know all about the various options; it is the seller's job to tell me.

Fortunes are lost every year because people confuse *what* they are selling with *why* should people buy it. They confuse the attributes of the product or service with its benefits, what it is with what it will do for you. They forget to find out how what they are selling is better than the alternative. And, just as important, they forget to check how it might be worse.

The differences can be very obvious or very subtle. But in my experience they are always very important, because simply explaining to somebody what something is won't sell it. What they want to know quite simply is: What's in it for me? Even more: What's in it for me that's *better*?

Just so that you don't forget this point, here's a little rhyme to memorize:

> *Tell me quick and tell me true*
> *What your product's going to do*
> *Or else, my love, to hell with you.*

In the next chapter we shall go a little bit more into the matter of what we mean by 'better'. We're going to talk about your competition.

3

Who is Your Competitor?

'The object of the game is to win' said Vince Lombardi, the great American football coach, when somebody asked him what the aim of the sport was.

The purpose of your letter is simple. It is to make your prospect *choose*. To choose between what you are asking them to do, and any number of alternatives – which include doing nothing at all.

Let's dwell on that third possibility for a while, because the easiest choice for your customer may be exactly that – do nothing. Either because what you suggest is not appealing enough or because it is not appealing at all.

A man once came to me with what he thought was a brilliant idea for a product. It was the sort of wheelbarrow which could carry two dustbins at once. When people come up with an idea they often think they are brilliant. I don't blame them. After all, it isn't easy to come up with an idea at all.

It certainly had not occurred to him that there might be no need for his idea, so he was quite put out when I pointed out to him that in the two residences I then occupied, it was completely unnecessary. In my London flat, the dustbins were in the basement and even if I had two (which I didn't) you couldn't wheel them anywhere. Apart from that it was unnecessary, since the dust collectors did the job themselves.

In my house in the country, much the same situation applied – we didn't have to wheel anything anywhere. This man was starting from his own situation and generalizing to assume that everyone was the same. What's more, he was quite unmoved by my argument.

Another man – a tragic case I thought – had spent all his own money, his family's savings, everything he could borrow and quite a number of years putting together a beautiful audio version of the Bible, employing well-known actors. Unfortunately, as one cynic I knew who was experienced in such matters put it at the time, 'the bottom's dropped out of the God market'. Interest in religion nowadays is low, certainly in England, and he had made a dreadful mistake.

The point of these two anecdotes is to underline what I have already said when discussing letters themselves: don't become too besotted with your product or service. There is always the nasty possibility that people might not need it at all. This is more common than you might imagine. And there is also the chance that although some people might want it, there may not be enough of them.

DIRECT AND INDIRECT COMPETITION

Your challenge is to answer the unspoken question in every customer's mind. Why should I choose *you*? That is something you are (I hope) already conscious of. It is what free enterprise is all about: your customers' right to choose; and your right to beat your competitor by offering something better.

I am astonished how few people make the not-exactly-huge leap to realizing that this is central to writing a good sales letter; *offering something better*. This, in turn, begs the question, better than what? And this leads, obviously, to: What else is available? In looking at the competition, you have to consider two types: direct and indirect competitors.

When, in the last chapter, I reviewed the alternatives available to me as a writer, you could quickly see that the PowerBook I chose was competing with not just other forms of personal computer, nor even any other writing method, but with any means of communicating my thoughts in written form, including two ways of dictating.

If you are selling fruit and vegetables, your competitor is not just somebody else in your own town selling fruit and vegetables. Your prospects may decide to spend the same money in a supermarket. Once in the supermarket, they may decide to spend the money on fish and pasta instead.

If you are selling wine, your competitor is not just somebody else selling wine, nor even someone selling beer and spirits, which your prospects might prefer. You are trying to get money from someone who is spending, not on something essential, but for fun.

It is a little far-fetched but not entirely untrue to say you are competing with *anybody* offering a pleasurable way of spending money, including the local cinema, video store or bookshop, somebody selling expensive chocolates or flowers, or even frivolous underwear or a new tie.

Professional marketers, who are never slow in coming up with fancy phrases have one which is appropriate here: the 'competitive frame'. So let's examine who might be in *your* competitive frame. A good way to start is by looking at the market in which you are operating.

AT WHAT STAGE IS THE MARKET?

All markets go through three stages. It doesn't really matter what sort of business you are in: these stages and variants of them will apply. Knowing what stage your market is at helps you determine what you must focus on in your letter.

- *The first stage*: your product or service is entirely new.
  You have to explain what you are selling in such detail and make it so appealing that somebody who has never seen or experienced what you are talking about will not only understand what it is, but want it.

  Imagine, for instance, being the first person to offer a credit or charge card. I am choosing that example because the business is one I know very well that has gone through all 3 market stages in the last 40 years.

  When the first charge card, Diners, came out, a friend tried to explain it to me. I though the idea was made so clearly he wouldn't have made a good salesman – or written a good sales letter for Diners.

  When a product or service is new, your competition is obviously not other people in the same business, because there aren't any. It is businesses you hope to supersede.

In the case of Diners, my friend was unable to tell me why a card is better than a cheque, hire purchase payments or cash. As long as most of your prospects don't even know what you offer, then you have to explain it and sell its advantages.

- *The second stage*: other people have jumped on to the bandwagon and competition is emerging.

   During this stage you must not only explain to your prospects what the product is and compare it with previous alternatives, but also persuade them it is better than the competition.

   This is hard to do, because you're attempting two things simultaneously.

- *The third stage*: ferocious competition; everybody knows what is being offered, and wants the best quality and value they can get. You have to work very hard to sell against a multiplicity of alternatives. On the other hand, you don't have to explain the *nature* of what you're selling in much detail; you have to concentrate on its competitive strengths.

I have, of course, oversimplified these stages and the many possibilities that exist within them. To illustrate what I mean, let me take the case of three letters for the American Express Card. You have already seen one of them in the Introduction.

The American Express Card is not like a credit card. They allow you to build up a debt each month, on which you only have to pay a certain minimum, with an agreed credit limit. You have to pay interest – at a very hefty rate – on the outstanding sum.

A new kind of card – The American Express Card

With American Express, you pay off all the outstanding amount a few days after the end of the month. There is no interest rate and no preset credit limit. That is determined by your payment pattern.

   The 'Quite Frankly' letter went out in the first stage of the market as far as American Express were concerned. Their competitors were the credit card, cash and cheques.

   Eventually American Express had the idea of introducing a superior card for their more affluent customers, the Gold Card.

   The Gold Card was launched with the promise that, apart from giving you added prestige and additional services, it had one huge competitive advantage – a £10,000 line of credit at a very attractive rate of interest. The letter we used to introduce the new card was not

The Gold Card*

American Express Europe Limited
Card Services
PO Box 68
Amex House, Edward Street
Brighton, England BN2 1YL

Dear Mr. Smith,

<u>Enjoy even greater financial security with an immediate £10,000 overdraft when you carry The Gold Card</u>

You know the value of the American Express Card. And you know just how often it is worth in your everyday life. Now I am inviting you to enjoy even greater financial security by applying for The Gold Card.

Yes it's a big step.

Indeed, many regard The Gold Card as the world's ultimate symbol of financial achievement. As you would expect, it is offered only to those individuals of impeccable financial standing. But the services it offers you are unparalleled.

As you are one of our most valued Cardmembers, I urge you to apply for The Gold Card today. You'll find it every bit as practical as the American Express Card. Yet you benefit from all these additional features.

<u>Now £10,000 immediate unsecured overdraft*</u>

Once your application is approved, you receive The Gold Card and you have immediate access to an unsecured overdraft of £10,000 at a preferential interest rate. This is the minimum to which you are automatically entitled - you can apply for more if you need it. It is yours to draw on as and when you wish, without the need to notify your bank manager.

> Imagine the convenience. Now you can act instantly on investment opportunities. Spread the cost of major purchases. Meet unexpected expenses with confidence. Whether you use your overdraft as a fund for emergencies or as an everyday convenience, the reassurance it gives you is immeasurable.

What's more, there is no need to change your existing banking arrangements or transfer funds. American Express Bank Ltd. will

Please read on ...

This is the first page of the letter that introduced the Gold Card.

The Gold Card*

American Express Europe Limited
Card Services
PO Box 68
Amex House, Edward Street
Brighton, England BN2 1YL

Dear Mr Boggs.

You may recall that I invited you a while ago to apply for Gold Cardmembership

As you are aware, there are now other "gold cards" - indeed you may possibly have been offered one, so you may well ask. "Why the <u>American Express</u> Gold Card?" It's a good question.

The Gold Card is designed to give certain Cardmembers a complete range of privileges, exclusive privileges which will make your life easier and more pleasant Indeed, we have recently introduced several new benefits, which is why I am writing to you now

>So The Gold Card is not simply a way of showing your
>status - though it does command a certain
>recognition. Nor is it just a convenient way to
>settle your bills. And it certainly isn't just the
>entrée to a £10,000 unsecured overdraft; other cards
>have copied this feature.

In fact what The Gold Card offers is based upon your needs and your life style. If you are like most Gold Cardmembers you probably have important business responsibilities, you travel more than most, and you may well entertain frequently. The privileges of The Gold Card reflect these characteristics.

For instance you may well appreciate one new idea, the Summary of Charges. Once a year, we itemise all your charges, month by month. They are broken down into categories such as Restaurant, Retail, Airline and Car Hire. This makes it easier for you to review and budget your finances, and is particularly useful, obviously, in assessing your business expenses.

The more you travel, the more important it is to do so in

Please read on ...

Here we are in the second stage of the Gold Card Market. We have to explain what makes it better.

particularly good: with a promise like that, it didn't have to be. A high percentage of recipients responded. (The first page of the letter is shown on page 38).

This letter went out when the idea of having a Gold Card was new. Once again, as far as Gold Cards were concerned this was the first stage of the market. But very soon the banks introduced their own Gold Cards offering the same £10,000 line of credit.

All of a sudden, the Gold Card market had entered a new stage – stage two. The old letter was no longer working as well – because it wasn't relevant.

The new letter which you see on page 39 was sent to people who had not replied to the first letter. For all I knew, though, they might have responded to an offer from their bank. They would certainly have received one because they were ideal prospects. As you see, the new letter sold the advantages of the Amex card, including its line of credit, but also made a competitive comparison. It did 93 per cent better than the previous letter.

There are three things worth drawing to your attention in this letter. First, I presented the line of credit in an almost throwaway fashion. No use beating the drum about something the reader could get elsewhere. Yet I knew it was an important lure. It is often good to flatter the reader by implying they don't want something you know they do and this is particularly true with money.

Second, I did not attack the competition aggressively. This rarely pays. Polite dismissal usually does much better. Lastly, I did not assume the readers knew all the advantages of the Gold Card and reminded them: never assume your reader knows as much as you do – or even recalls what you offer.

No limit on Amex

The third letter (see pages 42–44), also for American Express, was quite clearly written for a market in stage three. In this case we were selling the basic 'green' Amex Card. Everybody knew pretty well what the Card was. No need to go into great detail about the basics, though I did cover them.

What I had to do was dramatize the reader's ability to spend a little more to get something better. In this ferociously competitive market this letter did very well.

COMPARE WHAT YOU OFFER CAREFULLY

An essential discipline, once you are sure that, whatever the stage of the market, what you sell meets a real need, is to analyse your competition systematically.

What else could people buy that does the same job? You should list all the other products or services they could turn to – and compare them point by point with yours. Do it on a side-by-side checklist.

You next have to ask in what respect your product or service might have *unique* advantages for your prospect. Is it the first of its kind? Is it better in one particular respect? Is it cheaper? Is it faster? Is it easier? Is it the latest? Is it the best made? Is it the oldest established? Is it the one experts prefer? And so on.

Let's move aside from the exotic world of credit cards and assume you have a bookshop in a small town. The same thinking will probably apply if you have any modest retail business. If you are the only bookshop in that town, you will obviously tout the advantages to your reader of being able to buy books without going on a long trip to the nearest city.

If there is another bookshop in town, then you have to sell your advantages against that bookshop, which will usually, incidentally, involve you in trying to improve what you offer – which is no bad thing.

ASK WHAT THE CUSTOMER LIKES

In the small country town near where I live there is only one specialized bookshop. However, it does compete with the big newsagents WH Smith, who sell many things besides books.

My local bookshop could take my name when I come in, then send me a questionnaire asking me what sort of books I like and offer to get me any book I want or to keep me in touch with books in the fields I'm interested in.

Also they could let me know when they are holding a sale. In fact, the shop is pretty good and does offer these services – but has never thought of communicating this to a wider audience or in a systematic way to customers who come in.

They could argue that they sell books and nothing else, so they can offer a better service than WH Smith. When you ask in their shop about a book you want, you won't be confronted by a gum-chewing

American Express Europe Limited
Portland House
Stag Place
London SW1E 5BZ

Dear Mr. Goldstein,

Have you ever paid a little more for a better seat at the theatre, and thus enjoyed a far more memorable evening? Or paid a few pounds extra for a First Class ticket on a long train ride so that you could get a little bit more work done - or even enjoy some much needed rest?

In fact, don't you agree that sometimes a little money can go a very long way to make life easier or more enjoyable?

The American Express Card isn't free. Unlike other cards, we charge an annual fee. But you may not realise just how much extra you get in exchange for a very modest sum. Let me give you some examples.

- Suppose you have just paid a lot of money for some Hi-fi equipment. You drop it in the street 3 minutes later and damage it. Wouldn't you like to receive a full refund? Because that's just <u>one</u> of the many benefits American Express Cardmembership gives you.

- Or suppose you're in a foreign country and you have urgent medical or legal problems. Wouldn't it be reassuring to be referred instantly to an English speaking lawyer or doctor? Well, our Global Assist Service gives you that help anywhere in the world, no matter what time of the day or night, absolutely free.

- Or suppose a year from now you'd like to take advantage of a financial opportunity - but you need £5,000 quickly. Well, through our Personal Reserve Programme it's quite possible that you could get that money with minimal formalities - and at preferential interest rates.

You see, few people realise the sheer range of benefits

Please read on ...

- 1 -

Telephone: 01-834 5555, Cable: Amexcard Brighton, Telex: 939093, Prestel: 269

American Express Europe Limited is incorporated with limited liability in the State of Delaware U S A

Here we are in the third stage of the market for the American Express 'green' card. Why should you choose this card rather than any other?

Cardmembership brings you. That's why we say in our advertising:
"Membership Has Its Privileges." And you notice I have yet to mention
some of the things you might normally associate with American Express.
But here are some of the real differences between the American Express
Card and other cards.

- You don't pay interest on the American Express Card because
  you settle in full each month. That helps if you ever worry
  about spending more than you can afford. Because we don't
  set a spending limit in advance: you spend what you have
  shown you can afford.

- In finance you need records. That's why you don't just get a
  printout every month from us: you get a set of receipts. You
  can check what you bought and where.

- In any one of our 1,400 Travel offices around the world and
  the U.K. you can have your personal cheques cashed, and
  change currency or travellers cheques, receive mail and get
  advice.

- If your card's lost or stolen, we can replace it usually
  within a day anywhere in the world. (With some other cards,
  you will find it takes up to 2 weeks.)

- Buy a holiday from American Express, and your travellers
  cheques are commission free. (That's a saving of £10, for
  instance, on a £1,000 worth of cheques.)

- Suppose you lose your travellers cheques. Don't worry: last
  year 196,000 Members successfully claimed refunds. These
  refunds are available through our worldwide network of
  automated teller machines.

- We insure you automatically against inconveniences like
  losing your luggage - or even having it delayed. After 4
  hours we give you up to £300 to cover the cost of new
  clothes, toiletries, meals or refreshments.

You've probably noticed that many of these benefits relate to
travel. The reason quite simply is that we try to match our
Cardmembers' needs as closely as possible. And Cardmembers generally
tend to travel and entertain more than most. We constantly seek out
and arrange special benefits to meet your likely needs.

For instance, right now Cardmembers can have a scheduled PanAm
flight to anywhere in the United States for the companion of their
choice - entirely free - when they buy their own ticket on the Card.

In the summer, we send out a travel guide to help Cardmembers
plan, book and enjoy their holidays. The guide includes the obvious
things you'd expect - like advice on air fare savers - but some less
obvious, such as a special selection of books to read, luggage
available on extended payment, interest free. Even a 'phone answering
machine for while you're away.

Upon your arrival, you can save at least £10 on Hertz car rental.
And don't worry about arriving late: when your hotel is booked through

Please read on ...

- 2 -

American Express, the reservation is held open no matter how late you arrive.

What about your next holiday? Well, if you've bought this one through the Card, then you receive a £60 saving on each holiday you buy next time.

On a smaller scale - but nevertheless much appreciated by many Members - are the little touches we arrange. For instance, we have often arranged with fine restaurants for our Cardmembers to be greeted with a complimentary bottle of champagne or wine.

We even think about your dry cleaning. Go into Sketchleys, and as a Cardmember you will receive 'Golden' service for the same price as ordinary service.

Do you find Christmas shopping a chore? Last year 65,000 of our Members benefited from our Catalogue of Catalogues. We can send you any or all of 25 catalogues ranging from Harrods to Austin Reed to Mappin and Webb to make shopping easier. It's all part of our belief in serving you better.

It's funny to think that <u>so much</u> is offered in return for an annual fee, that frankly, is less than the difference between a First Class and a Standard Ticket from London to Manchester. And about <u>half</u> the cost of a good meal for two.

We may have asked you to consider American Express Cardmembership previously. Now I have explained in more detail what it really offers, I hope it makes more sense to you than ever before.

Quite simply, we seek to give better value to the kind of people who appreciate it. People who realise that you can usually pay a little more (sometimes no more at all) yet get a great deal more in return.

If this thinking chimes in with yours, please return the enclosed application now. As you will see in a moment, this is a particularly good time to do so.

Yours sincerely,

John de Trafford
<u>Senior Director</u>

P.S.   If you apply now, as a small gesture, I am happy to offer you - with our compliments - a second American Express Card for any person over 18 in your family whom you designate, at no charge for a year.

<u>In addition</u>, you may also appreciate a second Card for yourself to keep your business and personal expenses separate. This is also available at no charge for a year.

assistant who has never read a book since leaving school, but by someone who loves books. And despite this specialist knowledge and service, the price of a book is exactly the same as in WH Smith.

Thus, you see, the basis of a selling argument – and a good letter – is formed.

THE FIRST ESSENTIAL OF A GOOD LETTER

I hope you can follow my drift and apply it to your own situation. If you have planned and run your business properly you should be able to analyse almost without thinking what makes it better, which in turn gives you the first essential when planning a good letter.

In fact, a proper competitive analysis can often enable you to construct a letter that works even when you have *no* significant advantages over your competitors. That is because few, if any, of them will have gone to the trouble that you have, and most will fail to deploy the arguments you do. If you give every reason to buy and your competitor doesn't – you'll do better. Later in the book I'll give you an example of what I mean.

But first, let's look a little more deeply into how you determine what makes your product or service different and, you hope, better – a process that is not unlike an interrogation.

4

A Salesman in an Envelope

'Scientific creativity is imagination in a straitjacket.'
Richard Feynman

David Ogilvy was asked what made a good advertising writer. He mentioned several qualities. 'Obsessive curiosity and skill in the art of nitpicking' came first.

Only by studying *every* aspect of what you sell and what you compete against can you do a decent job. To do so you may well have to acquire a great deal of information which turns out not to be relevant – just to ensure you don't miss the details which *are*.

On pages 47–49 you will see a letter which shows you what I mean. It is not particularly brilliant and, to be honest, took less than two hours to write, and was printed and sent out overnight (it looks it!). But it took me several days to acquire the information I needed to write it.

It contains just about all the ingredients of an effective letter. It was sent to a list of people who had enquired about a range of kitchen and bedroom furniture, received a brochure, letter and order form, but not bought.

First, read the letter so you can understand what it is all about. Then take a closer look at the body of the copy, which starts at the bottom of

REG. OFFICE:
PO. BOX 5, COMMERCE WAY,
LANCING, WEST SUSSEX, BN15 8TF
Tel: 090 63 (LANCING) 60451/7

solarbo FITMENTS LIMITED

the pine people

One Month Only

<u>Save Even More On Post Budget VAT Offer.</u>

Dear Enquirer,

Your Opportunity to Save £5... £20...
<u>£50... Even £120 During This Special</u>
Summer Sale

If you're buying anything for your home, I'm sure the first Conservative budget with the huge VAT increase must have come as a horrible shock to you!

With the rise from 8% to 15% a simple household item, like one of our stainless sink tops has gone up from £80.67 to £85.90. And a set of Spacemaker Mirror faced units has gone up from £350.08 to £372.77, whilst a completely equipped fitted kitchen for a large house will have gone up £120.

<u>But don't start worrying yet because</u>
<u>if you are prepared to pay in full</u>
<u>when you order, then we'll pay the</u>
<u>extra VAT – as long as you order by</u>
<u>August 10th.</u>

Why are we happy to pay this money for you ? Because July is normally our slackest month. So in this way we can boost our Sales & maintain our raw material turnover <u>and</u> keep our staff working full out. For these reasons, we don't mind taking less profit than usual.

And, as you know, we <u>normally</u> take less profit than most because we sell the same quality of item as other Companies for a lower price.

This is because we sell to you direct from the factory and this saves money for you <u>and</u> gives you a better quality of furniture in many ways.

Check these four important savings :

1. You don't pay any middlemans
profits. No retail or wholesale
mark-ups take money out of your

Learn as many facts about the product as possible – you never know what may be relevant.

pocket, and you don't pay for the
additional VAT that is charged at
each stage of the selling chain.

2. You don't pay design fees and
planning charges, you arrange your
bedroom or kitchen to suit yourself –
with free assistance from our Planning
department if you need it.

3. You don't pay installation
charges. Even without any
experience you can install our
furniture quickly & easily
following our carefully thoughtout
step-by-step instructions.

4. You don't have to pay the extra
it would cost you if we didn't
select & import all our timber
ourselves (if you come to our factory
shop, round the back of the factory
you will see some of the huge stacks
of timber that we import – & treat
in our own kilns).

But you get additional benefits. For because we do virtually
everything ourselves, we can afford to take <u>less</u> money from you & put <u>more</u>
into building your furniture.

For example, did you know there are
<u>five</u> grades of pine — & we <u>only</u> use
the top grade ? Believe me, not all
furniture is made of this top grade by
any means because only 10% of all pine
meets this standard.

And did you know that most modern
furniture is made on assembly lines –
without ever being touched by the hand
of a craftsman ? At Solarbo you can
<u>still</u> see individual orders handled by
individual craftsmen as they go through
the various processes in the good old
fashioned way.

Fine tolerances ensure that good furniture
fits together perfectly – doesn't wobble
or have gaps – is really solidly built.
Our Craftsmen work to the most exacting of
tolerances in fractions of a millimetre.

As you will appreciate this special offer is being made to <u>all</u>
our enquirers so I'll hope you will forgive my not having addressed you
personally by name. For the same reason, I don't have an exact record of
which of our many products you are interested in. So I have enclosed copies
of some of our advertisements to refresh your memory.

However, no advertisement tells the full story. Therefore if you

would like to take advantage of this offer please check which items
interest you in the Certificate below & we'll send you full brochures
& order forms on request, or use the order form you already have to
order now – don't forget to include the Certificate with your order.

I can assure you of two things. Firstly, nobody today can offer
you finer value for your money than we can. Secondly, there has never been
a better moment to buy. If you could see how the costs of raw materials are
rising, you wouldn't hesitate for a moment. Next year prices will be really
substantial.

Therefore, I urge you to act now. Twelve months from today you'll
be patting yourself on the back at your shrewd timing.

Yours sincerely,

Paul Dunkley

P.S. In view of the current postal delays you can phone us
+ we will reserve production time for you and give you
a special reference number to put on your order
when you send it to us – but please be sure o
post your order to us no later than 10th August

✂ -

Certificate of Entitlement

Until August 10th we are holding our prices down to you by absorbing the recent V.A.T.
increase and keeping to the pre-budget rate of 8% .... instead of the new 15% rate.
But, you must pay cash in full when you order.

This certificate entitles you to take advantage of our post-budget offer on Pine Kitchen
Units, Spacemaker Wardrobes, and Pine Bedroom Units and must accompany your order.

OFFER CLOSES 10th AUGUST 1979

the first page, where I start reminding the readers why the products are good value and what makes them superior. I needed plenty of ammunition to convince people they ought to buy when they hadn't done so previously.

DETECTIVE WORK

This information was acquired as a result of a lot of detective work at my client's factory. Very few of the facts I uncovered were proffered without my asking. Yet, as you can see, it is the piling on of relevant detail which convinces the reader that the products are worth buying.

You may wonder why I bothered to repeat all these facts that one might assume the reader was already aware of, having previously sent off for information about the products. There are two reasons.

First, few people retain information, certainly not in any detail, unless it is of pressing interest – and I couldn't assume that to be the case with a purchase they had not made.

Second, your letter should be aimed at your best prospects first. The people I thought most likely to respond were those who had *almost* done so. Perhaps some detail that had not been sufficiently stressed in the first letter they received might tip the scales.

One subject I pursued at great length with my client was critical: what makes your products better?

LEARN ABOUT EVERYTHING

This led me to asking how they were built; what they were built of; and how their construction differed from that of competitive products. I also spent quite a while going around the factory watching the furniture being made. This was a noble sacrifice, because I *hate* factories.

Only by doing this could I learn about the different grades of pine, where they bought theirs, how they went about buying it, the fact that the managing director himself travelled to the forests to select it, what they did to prepare it – and so on.

A second important question, of course, was what made their products good *value*. And, as you can see, I went into that at some length by pursuing all the implications flowing from the fact that they sold direct to their customers. Many direct marketers forget that selling direct makes their prospects believe they offer good value.

Such hard work pays – in a big way. To give you some idea, let me tell you that every one of these letters generated £5 worth of sales. (And that was back in the 1970s when a pound was worth several times more than it is now.)

What is more, as I said, they went not to a list of people who had just enquired and were therefore definitely interested. Those people were what marketers call in their particular jargon 'lapsed enquirers'. People my client had, until that point, not thought worth writing to at all. Indeed, my client's records were so poor, as you can deduce from the letter, that we did not know which products these people had originally enquired about.

In fact such a list is one of the best you can mail. No enquirer should be considered 'lapsed' until you have made every attempt possible to make them buy. That's such an important subject that I shall cover it in greater detail at the end of this chapter.

DO WHAT A SALESMAN DOES

But what did I do in preparing and writing this letter? I simply followed what good salesmen would do. That is always the right way. The most powerful form of selling is unquestionably the face-to-face kind. Unfortunately, it's also the most expensive – which is why you need sales letters.

Your letter is going to have to be as persuasive as any salesman. Maybe more so, because salesmen have the huge advantage of seeing the customer face-to-face. The ability to exert the force of personality. The ability to see their prospects' reactions and adapt accordingly.

So, you obviously need all the knowledge salesmen have – and more, if possible. Thus, salesmen soon learn what motivates prospects, from their own experience and that of their colleagues. Really excellent salesmen take the trouble not merely to study the product or service, but to find out how it has been sold in the past; what tricks worked and what didn't.

Salesmen can quickly spot an easy prospect, because they have studied what types of people have been easiest to sell to in the past. They learn what objections people come up with and the best ways to overcome them, and they are constantly looking out for new sales arguments and angles to play up.

Salesman know where their products' strengths lie – and where competitive products score, so they are ready with the right arguments to rebut their claims. Indeed, they will often come up with them before objections come out.

And because their products are their living, they keep their eyes open for anything in the press or on television which favours their products. (Or, for that matter, which doesn't – so that they are ready to deal with any bad publicity that may come up.)

One of the first things salesmen learn is that the word of a satisfied customer is much more credible than theirs. So they keep files of names and addresses of satisfied customers, perhaps with letters from them. In fact when, some years ago, I helped run a sales force, one of our first objectives when introducing a new product was to create a core of satisfied customers prepared not merely to say nice things but show the work we had done for them. Nothing was more convincing.

In short, as you will have realized, a salesman, to be really successful, has to be *professional*. The salesman is well briefed about anything, no matter how small, that could give that vital edge. Yet, as we have already discovered, few sales letters are prepared with the attention to detail a good salesman would pay. Most are dashed off in a trice or even quicker.

POOR BRIEF, POOR LETTER

When letters fail it's often because those who write them are not properly briefed. Perhaps they omit some important fact which is taken for granted, but which is unknown to the prospect. Or they have not had the sense to obtain all the relevant facts.

The result is letters that don't work. Some, being more persistent, go back and try again; others give up altogether. No wonder many people conclude that sales letters don't work for their businesses, when the truth is that letters based on inadequate information don't sell for *any* business.

If a letter fails, don't give up. Just go back and see whether it was based on full knowledge of both the prospect and the product or service. Nine times out of ten that's one of the big problems.

That is why most of the previous chapter, this one and the next are largely concerned with how you ensure you have all the right information to hand. You'll find at the end of this chapter a list of all the things you should consider to construct a good 'brief' – the word used to describe the information you need before you write.

I've already discussed analysing your benefits and your competition. Now let's touch on some other things you ought to look out for.

A good phrase to bear in mind when amassing all this information and studying it is: 'Compared to what?' You are looking for the difference – large or small – which will bring you success.

THE FIRST PART OF THE CREATIVE PROCESS

Sometimes, this process of trying to answer *why* what you are selling is better than the alternative will reveal that the emperor has no clothes. That your product isn't all that good, as in the cases I mentioned at the beginning of Chapter 3. And this will set you on the salutary path of trying to improve it. Because, as we all know, a better product is worth more than mountains of persuasion.

One important point: analysing the product or service and its relationship with your reader is not just a necessary planning activity. It is the *first part of the creative process*. You are beginning to write the letter in your head, as it were. You are starting to think yourself through the various aspects of what you are offering and how you will go about offering it. You should already be beginning to play around with the various ideas that might work.

Right from the moment you first begin to look at what you are selling, you must be constantly looking out for opportunities. A good letter is not a matter of good luck. It comes from your trying to expand the borders of what is possible. One thought should be coming to your mind constantly: 'How would my reader react if I said...?'

If other letters have been sent in the past, you must study all of them and find out how well they did. Be careful: many companies keep poor records and you will often find woolly statements such as 'This one did very well', or 'This was a disaster'.

On a remarkable number of occasions I have found people were talking sheer piffle. Either they didn't know and were ashamed to admit it – indeed would rather give the wrong answer than none at all. Or, amazingly, they had never properly evaluated the difference between success and failure.

Very often they were relying upon memory, or somebody's feeling that 'it was a good letter' or 'the salesforce liked it'. Never be satisfied with such statements. Dig until you get the truth. Don't be afraid to ask, politely, how success and failure are defined. You will often find people define them quite illogically.

Try to find out in more detail exactly what happened when particular letters went out. If they succeeded, how well did they succeed, and is there any clue as to why? And if they failed, ask the same sort of thing.

FIND OUT WHAT REALLY HAPPENED

You may often find that what seemed a disaster could well have been a success but for some small circumstance people have forgotten – like a price rise at the same time, or a competitor bringing out a better product.

Timing can be *the* critical factor. In the late 1960s I nearly went broke because I sent out a mailing just before Christmas, when people tend to be so lost in a fog of merriment and present-buying that they read very little.*

Pay particular attention to letters that *almost* did well; or letters with interesting ideas you think should have done well.

A while ago I had to review 142 different direct mail programmes from the biggest British mail order catalogue company and give a prize to whichever I thought best. The one I selected featured what you might call a Spanish omelette: a confection of ideas from previous mailings which had not quite succeeded, yet which when put together created a sales blockbuster.

WATCH WHAT COMPETITORS ARE DOING

Not only should you be looking at how your letters have done. See if you can find out what other companies, especially your competitors, are up to. Without such knowledge you are like a general going into battle who doesn't know how many troops the enemy has, nor how they are disposed, nor what is current military practice.

Build a file of material. Reply to mailings and advertisements so that you receive subsequent mailings. Use slight variations of your name and address when you respond; that way, when you receive a new mailing from another company, you will know where they got your name from.

---

* In the northern hemisphere the best time to mail in the first half of the year is January; results worsen the closer you get to summer. In the second half of the year, September is best and results tail off towards Christmas. The weekend is a good time for your letter to reach a consumer; Tuesday is a good time for it to reach a business person.

A good idea is to take what appears to be a successful letter from your competitor and try, quite shamelessly, to copy and improve it.

Discovering everything you can about how the product or service you are selling is made or delivered is essential. And a history of how the product or service has developed can be important; how it was first conceived and by whom; how it has been altered to meet the needs of the market; how the sales have fluctuated with each change.

This sort of thing can often provide you with valuable insights. Sometimes you may uncover human stories which will intrigue your readers. For instance, nearly 30 years ago I was involved in selling a product for motor cars which had been invented by a Second World War test pilot. This fact gave the product – and our sales material – greater veracity and even helped formulate its name.

Clearly, you should know all the technical details of your product or service. You might be quite surprised if you looked through a file of sales letters to realize that in many cases the writer has not taken the trouble to include what for him or her may be boring detail, but which to the recipient is utterly essential. Here are some examples. What's it made of? How big is it? How heavy? Who do I call if something goes wrong or if I have any questions?

FOUR QUESTIONS TO BE ANSWERED

Any research is useful, either into the product itself or into the nature of the customer. What kind of person seems particularly keen on it? What kind doesn't?

Such knowledge provides the ammunition you need to build conviction and interest when you communicate. But above all it is designed to answer four questions your prospect is asking.

1. Why should I do what you want me to do?
2. What is so special about this product or service?
3. Why is it going to do something for me that *nothing* else can?
4. Or, alternatively, do something *better* than anything else can?

Your ability to answer these questions will not come about as a result of haphazard and gentle enquiry. You have to be *disciplined* and *determined*.

HAVE YOU FORGOTTEN ANYTHING?

Start by reviewing the facts you have assembled, making sure you have omitted nothing that could be relevant. You almost certainly will have.

You must then go back to the source of information and find out more. This is an obvious step which is often omitted. One common reason, apart from ignorance or sloth, is that if you are a relatively junior person in your organization, or if you work for outside agency which professes to be expert, it's hard to admit that you didn't understand something or that you forgot an obvious point.

Don't worry. If your letter works nobody will care how many seemingly stupid questions you asked. And if it fails, nobody will thank you for not having worried them with trivial questions.

Perhaps you would like to try the approach I have used for many years to cover up my inadequacies. I tell the truth, which is that it takes me a long time to understand anything at all complicated and I may need to have things explained to me more than once. However, I add reassuringly, once I do understand it, I will have no trouble explaining it so someone else.

Apart from having the merit of being honest, this is the best argument I can give for getting a *complete* brief, no matter how long it takes.

DON'T BE PUT OFF BY NEGATIVE PEOPLE

Of course, just as it is possible for you to expand the borders of what is possible by using your imagination, there will always be people who want to prevent you.

Sometimes you will find yourself dealing with bureaucrats or lawyers whose narrow approach dampens enthusiasm rather than kindling it. The sort who say 'We've never tried that before' as a form of criticism. The sort who know that you can rarely be blamed for doing nothing.

They will give you three million reasons why you can't do something. Your task is to find three million reasons why you can. To boldly go where no man (or woman) has gone before, so to speak. And most of your best ideas will come from thinking about what is going on in the minds of your readers. To illustrate this, here's a story about how the obvious conclusions about people's motivations are often a worry.

PICK UP EASY MONEY MOST BUSINESSES IGNORE

A great deal of money can be made – but rarely is – from people who have written or phoned you to express interest – but not bought. You may remember I said I would cover this in more detail at the end of this chapter.

Years ago I had a client who was in one sense a pleasure to deal with and in another a pain. Our relationship placed me in a permanent quandary.

He was very likeable – one of those fairly rare people it's a pleasure to do business with. However, he never had any money, because he was in a business to which the English climate is hardly suited – selling swimming pools. At regular intervals he would call me for advice – which he could never really pay for. So he used to take me to lunch. I may not be a gourmet, but I am bit of a guzzler, so this arrangement, if not perfect, was adequate.

On one such occasion he was in despair about his inability to get sales and, worse still from my point of view, his inability to invest any money in advertising. I asked him how many people he had on his files who had not bought. 'About a thousand,' he told me.

I suggested he write to them again. He had two arguments against this.

First, they had already been written to, phoned and in some cases actually visited – but they hadn't bought. Clearly they weren't interested. 'Time wasters,' he said.

Second, his wife, the guardian of the family purse, thought such a mailing would be an extravagant waste. 'Think of the postage,' she wailed. She was the sort of person who thinks on a grand scale.

EXTRA REVENUE – FOR PETTY CASH

Nevertheless, I persuaded him to do his mailing and he sold three swimming pools. To say that this was a good investment is the understatement of the century. The letters cost under £200 to print and send out in those days. The revenue was perhaps as much as £8000.

In my view, often the single greatest source of potential profit in a business – profit which can sometimes be freed for the investment of petty cash – comes from people who have not been followed up with enough zeal.

Here, as in the case of Solarbo (see pages 47–49), the letters went to people who had previously inquired and not bought. This had led my client to presume it was pointless writing to them again – a very common mistake. But, as we shall see, perhaps the most important single factor in writing a good letter is your prospects. What could be going through their minds?

In this case, it was easy to think people had not bought because they didn't *want* to buy – they weren't interested. However, when you think about it properly, this need not have been the case at all. You never know why people don't buy, unless you phone them up and ask (not a bad idea, by the way). And even then they might not tell the truth. But consider the possibilities.

They might have forgotten they were interested in the first place – after all, you spend all your time thinking how to sell your product, but your prospects have other matters on their minds. Why should they even think about it? This might have been just one thing they were considering buying. They might have had the money but have decided that they wanted to spend it on something else.

Maybe they were thinking of buying at some time in the future. They might not have had the money at the time they enquired. Maybe a sudden emergency took away the cash that they planned to use. Maybe one of your competitors has managed to sell to them before you – which is the assumption many make; but it is only one possibility.

WHY ENQUIRIES ARE USUALLY GENUINE

There could be many reasons why people enquire, then don't buy; but you have to *think* about the people you are writing to before you decide what they might be and thus arrive at a sensible plan.

One thing seemed obvious to me in the case we are discussing though; if they weren't interested, however slightly, they wouldn't have enquired to start with. So there was a fair chance many were still in the market.

One reason for not buying which is advanced surprisingly often by otherwise intelligent people is the one I almost always dismiss first – they enquired frivolously. Who on earth has nothing better to do with their time than answer ads?

The only people who enquire despite no real interest are children, out of curiosity, or people who are lured by an exceedingly attractive incentive or gift. The former category, I can assure you, is small indeed and only applicable to certain products of juvenile interest. The latter category is also not as large as you might imagine: particularly if the offer you are making relates to your product.

I shall come to the matter of gifts in more detail later, but even one which attracts a lot of freeloaders generally more than pays off. It simply attracts more attention and response overall. A letter replying to enquiries is far more important to you than one aimed at likely or possible prospects. However, 'cold' prospects usually get more attention from marketers than responses to enquiries. Madness!

A REMINDER GETS GOOD RESULTS

The conclusion, then, is that you may be sitting on a file of names and addresses that is almost bound to contain some people who are still interested and haven't bought or haven't acted.

The letter reproduced on page 60, from British Telecom, is a good example of the right way to approach this situation. It is a polite reminder. That is what a reminder letter ought to do: remind you of the original offer.

The letter also avoids one of the biggest mistakes made in reminder letters; accusing the reader of being an idiot for not accepting the original offer. In fact, except in very rare cases (and I can't think of any offhand), your letters should aim not to make the reader feel bad, but to feel good. And certainly never to insult, but to flatter.

You might like to know, incidentally, what sort of results you can expect from reminder letters. The answer is about half the number of replies you got from your first letter – as long as you don't leave the reminder for too long: two weeks to a month after the first letter is about right.

If you have not written to people for a long time – say six months – then you will need to completely 'resell' them on your proposition, as was the case with the Solarbo letter.

The answer to the important question of how often you send out reminders to people is: 'As long as it pays.' Remember, you have *paid* for those enquiries. You want to get the best possible return on your investment. So, as long as your gross profit exceeds the cost of sending out the mail and all the associated expenses, you should keep on mailing.

Sometimes you should keep on mailing even if you're not making money, but just covering your costs, because you are gaining new customers who can later be sold something additional.

June 1993

<u>**You still have a chance
to get 10% off your calls**</u>

Dear Mr Bird,

Some time ago, I wrote to tell you how you can get 10% off the cost of every direct dialled call you make with Option 15.

Since my last letter, I have not heard from you. So I thought I would write and remind you about the benefits you can enjoy when you enrol for Option 15.

Firstly, as someone whose call bill regularly comes to over £40 a quarter, you'll save money. For an enrolment fee of just £4 each quarter, you'll get 10% off your call bill. That means £100 of direct dialled calls at the basic unit rate will cost you only £94, £200 will cost only £184 and so on.

Once you enrol, every discount you get with Option 15 is clearly shown on your bill. And you'll start saving money the minute you join.

You can also enrol for Option 15, quickly and simply, over the phone. Just call 0800 800 862 to start saving right away. Or, if you prefer, you can complete and return the attached enrolment form to me using the reply-paid envelope.

I very much hope that you will decide to take advantage of Option 15 and enjoy 10% off the basic unit rate of every direct dialled call you make.

Yours sincerely,

Ian Ash
Director of Marketing
Personal Communications

P.S. You'll find a list of the questions we are asked the most about Option 15 on the reverse of this letter. But if you have a query that these do not answer, please call our free Helpline on 0800 800 862.

All prices quoted above are inclusive of VAT at 17.5%.

BT, FREEPOST (SL 1883), MAIDENHEAD SL6 7YB.
€ British Telecommunications plc Registered Office 81 Newgate Street, LONDON EC1A 7AJ Registered in England no 1800000 PHME 13879

A perfect example of a polite reminder.

A WORKING AID FOR YOU

As promised earlier, I have placed a checklist at the end of this chapter to ensure you know everything you should before you start work on your letter.

By using it you can be sure you ask yourself all the right questions when selling your own product or service; or, if you are writing on behalf of someone else, you ask them those questions.

Please don't just read it and nod sagely. *Work* with it. It will be valuable not merely when planning your letter but also when writing it and when reviewing what you have written to make sure no argument is missing.

You could photostat it and keep it by you. I am sure it would pay you to do so. I used to keep in the drawer of my desk a list of 100 successful headlines, which I referred to when I was seeking ideas as an advertising writer. I still have it. You never know.

In the next chapter, we shall look more closely into what I believe is the most important part of preparation: your knowledge of your customer.

To emphasize this here's something from Lee Iacocca, the man who saved Chrysler from going broke. 'If you want to succeed in this business, you'd better get on with people,' he once said. 'Because that's all we've got around here.'

32 things to ask when you are planning your letter

1. Background. The business context. What's happening in the market. This will indicate what problems and opportunities you have.
2. What is the objective? And *why*? This will help you determine that your objective makes sense.
3. How much money can you afford? This is important when you decide what else you should put in the envelope apart from your letter, how long it should be and whether you should try some device to gain attention.
4. When is it needed? Good work takes time. Allow as much as you can. Plan ahead whenever possible. Even if you don't know precisely when the letter will be needed, or exactly what will be required, if you know about it in advance you can start thinking, however vaguely, about the possibilities. As we shall see, such 'vague' thoughts are the first step in writing a successful letter.

5. What is it? What does it do? A complete physical description. Remember, what you sell may be very familiar to you, but quite hard to understand or even strange to your reader. This is particularly so if you are selling something technical.

6. What is the personality of the company: friendly, helpful, super-efficient, high quality, good value, bargain basement? Try to define this as compared with your competitors.

7. What makes it different? What's better (or worse) about it?

8. Who are your competitors? How do they promote themselves? Can you see their material?

9. Who are you trying to persuade – explained in human terms? How would you describe the *perfect* prospect?

10. How do they reach their decision to buy or enquire? Over how long a period? Who influences them? How many people are involved in the decision? What role do they each play?

11. How often and how recently have you written to these people before? How did they react?

12. What need does it fulfil?
    – Here are nine human needs. All products and services satisfy one and usually several of them; if yours doesn't, you're in trouble: make money, save money, save time and effort, help the family, feel secure, impress others, gain pleasure, self-improvement, belong to a group.

13. What are the benefits? And what is the most important benefit or combination of benefits that makes it so special?

14. What offers and incentives are you able to make? What about free trial, for instance?

15. What list or lists will you use? Have you used them in the past? What worked and what didn't? Is there any particular group of people who reply more than others – or who don't? That may give you an insight into what makes the product successful.

16. Are you trying a new approach? Can you think of any new ideas that make sense?

17. Make sure you examine, use or experience the product or service.

18. Take a look around the factory – or other facilities, like shops or a telephone answering service. Ask questions and write down anything interesting, unusual or special that competitors don't have or do.

19. What about examples of previous letters – those that did well, and those that didn't?

20. Look for proofs and testimonials – celebrity endorsements, media comments, scientific reports.

21. Is there something special about the company, the owner, the origins of the product or service your reader should know? Something that will add interest or authority?

22. Any physical restrictions on the mailing? For example, a certain size of envelope, or certain colours?

23. What are the terms of the guarantee? Can you change them? Is there a money-back guarantee?

24. What about complaints? They will often tell you what *not* to say or what objections have to be overcome.

25. What information will be given to enquirers? It's no use having a persuasive letter if your follow-up is not good.

26. How can people reply? Is the reply envelope prepaid by you? It should be, unless you want fewer replies (only appropriate if you are getting too many low quality enquiries).

27. How about telephone orders? What percentage of your customers order by phone? Is there an 0800 or 0345 number? What about fax or e-mail? In business-to-business, 50 per cent or more of the responses may come in that way.

28. How do people pay? (Cash with order, COD (cash on delivery), send an official order, credit and charge cards? Order to their bank? Continuous credit card debit?)

29. When are staff available to answer the phone? Seven days a week, 24 hours a day is ideal. If not, is there an answerphone message?

30. Clear style guidelines: what sort of language and manner of writing are appropriate?

31. Sacred cows – things you must or must not do. NB Don't let your lawyers screw up your sales messages. Make them expand opportunity, not constrict it.

32. Background reading and people worth talking to – salespeople or research people, for example.

5

The Customer's Point of View

'I would like to be able to stand on both sides of the counter at once.'

Julius Rosenwald, architect of Sears Roebuck

Julius Rosenwald built Sears Roebuck into a business which far outstripped all competition. At one point over 40 per cent of Americans shopped with them.

If you are a retailer, you have a great advantage. Although it is impossible to enter the minds of your customers, you can study how they buy as much as you please. The best retailers are pleased to do so a great deal. A good example comes from the Irish supermarket owner, Feargal Quinn, who spends as much time as he can watching what happens in his stores.

While doing this one day, he noticed that many of his customers were bothered by being pestered for sweets at the checkouts by their children. This was not entirely by accident; most supermarkets deliberately put sweets at the checkouts for impulse purchasers.

He decided to stop putting them there. He reasoned that he might lose immediate sweet sales, but he would gain a lot more in goodwill, and thus eventual sales, from shoppers who would prefer his stores because of less nagging from their kids. Other supermarkets have since copied him.

You cannot succeed in business without understanding things not only from your point of view, but also from your customer's, and you will have realized from what I have already written that the same applies emphatically to letters.

In fact, I believe understanding the customer is even more important than understanding the product, because you can always change the latter to suit the former – but not the other way round. And discovering what interests your customer – and what doesn't – is the key to eliminating the scourge of the direct mail business: junk.

WHAT IS JUNK MAIL?

You will remember that in Chapter 1 when I discussed why most direct mail is bad, one of the two reasons I gave was that it is too often written from the wrong point of view – that of the writer.

Junk mail is like the pub bore. Somebody you find tedious because they talk about things that interest them and not you. They don't have the sensitivity to tailor their conversation to fit you.

Junk mail is anything coming through your door (in fact, much of what people call 'mail' is unaddressed door-to-door material) that lacks this sensitivity. It is boring.

It could be boring because it's about something of no relevance to you. It could be boring because it is full of boastful puffery about somebody's product, which they find of riveting fascination, but which you have not the slightest desire to read about.

It could be boring because you receive it at the wrong time. Or the writer has not bothered to explain what is so special about what is being offered. Or you just can't believe what is being said.

Thus, you are unlikely to react well to somebody selling insurance who starts with a joke. People rarely find death and disaster the subjects of hilarity. Nor money, for that matter. It's serious and should usually be treated in a serious way. We spend too much time trying to earn it to joke about how we are going to keep it.

To make your product or service interesting, as we have already learned, you have to interrogate them; to understand them as completely as possible. And you have to be interested in your prospects and what makes them tick. You have to be a bit of a psychologist.

Your letter must make your proposition not merely interesting, but *irresistible* to your prospect. To do that, you have to consider what you know about the two and consider the context of the communication. You have to ask a few simple questions.

QUESTIONS YOU MUST ANSWER

By a happy accident, all the important questions you need to ask begin with the letter W. First, *what* are you selling? Next, *who* are you writing to? And *why* should they do whatever you want?

We began to look at these questions in the last chapter. And as we go along you will see that equally relevant are, *when* is a good time to speak to them? *Where* did you find their names or are you planning to get them from? Not to mention, *what* is the nature of your relationship with them? *When* did you first speak to or write to them? *What* was their reaction?

This book is about writing letters, not planning direct mail campaigns. However, apart from the quality of your product or service itself, and knowing who your prospects are, of the questions listed above, often the most critical is *where* you find the people you are writing to.

Even the best letter must flop if it is sent to the wrong people. Even the worst has a chance if it is sent to the right ones.

We could go on at some length in this love affair with the twenty-first letter in the alphabet, but let's move to a specific example where these questions were critical. It was a letter for the charity, Save the Children.

My client asked me if I could think of a way we could use direct mail to persuade people to leave money in their wills to their charity. The letter I wrote is shown on pages 68–71. Read it, and then I will explain how it came about.

A daunting problem

I found this a daunting project. I had to talk to people about dying. I can't imagine many people enjoy reflecting upon their demise, but it seemed hard to avoid the subject if I were to ask them to leave money in their wills. How could I open the letter?

Then there was the problem of timing. Clearly, if you write to someone at the right time – when something is on their mind, often because it is imminent – you're far more likely to succeed. However few people actually know *when* they're going to die, so the urgency of leaving money to a good cause was not easy to establish.

And, of course, we had no information on when people choose to make their wills or for that matter how many of the people we were writing to had already done so.

So there were quite a few 'W's' to exercise my mind, not least why should anyone want to leave money? Clearly, one reason would be to help children. Could I arrive at any other motives?

One fact my client revealed gave me a clue. Apparently most people don't leave wills at all. Yet why should this be motivating? After all, once you're dead, why should you care?

But you care about your family, surely. Also, you might want to do some good for others. (If not you were never going to be a charity giver anyhow.) And surely you wouldn't want the government to get all your money and squander it on ill-judged projects.

Where would we find the right people and *when* was a good time to reach them? Clearly, writing to young people was a waste of time. So we decided to write to a list of people over the age of 55. But that was merely a particular age group. It did not resolve the problems I mentioned above that we could never know how long they might live, nor at what point they might make a will nor whether they had already done so.

Your only chance to get action

Those two last points epitomize a problem one almost always faces: why should your reader do what you want NOW? When you write to someone, once you get them to start reading you almost certainly have only one chance to get them to act – until, of course, you write again.

Remember, your reader is unlikely to come back and fondly reread your letter unless it's of unusual interest. In fact, to attract more than one reading your letter must fall into one or more of the following five categories.

1. It deals with a passion or hobby of theirs, or something we *all* like to read and dream about. A well-composed letter about cars or gardening will always be pored over by those keen on these things. The subject of holidays is usually interesting to most of us.
2. It is about a complex subject or decision they have to study or think about.

Save the Children Y

REGISTERED OFFICE
THE SAVE THE CHILDREN FUND
MARY DATCHELOR HOUSE
17 GROVE LANE
CAMBERWELL
LONDON SE5 8RD
TELEPHONE 071-703 5400

****

May I send you a FREE booklet, with our
compliments, which may prove
<u>of priceless value</u> to those you love.

****

Dear Reader,

I want to ask you a question which some people don't like
to answer - or even think about.

But if you like to <u>face</u> life's problems instead of running
away from them, you may be glad I asked this question. It is
simple. Have you made a <u>Will</u>?

Surprisingly, 4 out of 5 people either haven't made one, or
the one they have made is so out of date it doesn't reflect
their true wishes.

Yet what a shame if you care about the future of those you
love... especially if you wish to leave something behind in this
world to say "Thank You" for the happiness you have enjoyed.
And even if your life has not been happy - and let's face it,
when we were young, times were often harder - you may want to
ensure others never suffer as you did.

If you do feel this way, you should find our free booklet
of priceless value. It's about something all of us have to
confront, yet which sometimes you need courage to think about:
making your Will.

The booklet is called "Making a Will - a straightforward
guide". It's written in simple, non-legal language. And it
tells you how to ensure that your Will reflects your wishes.
For instance, do you need a solicitor to make a Will - and if so
why? How many witnesses do you need - if any? How easy is it
to change your Will by adding a codicil? What are the pitfalls

Please read on...

Telegrams & Cables Savinrana London SE5   Telex No 892809 SCFLONG   Fax No 071-703 2278 (G3)
A company registered in London No 178159 and limited by guarantee   Registered Charity No 213890
Patron Her Majesty The Queen   President Her Royal Highness The Princess Royal, GCVO
Chairman Viscount Boyd   Hon Treasurer Mr W H Yates, F R I C S   Director General Nicholas Hinton, C B E

This has been printed on recycled paper

Starting with an offer helps to encourage a response.

you can fall into if you don't go about making your Will in the right way.

Astonishingly, four out of five people make no Will at all - so it would not be surprising if you yourself had not done so at the moment. Many other people leave Wills so out of date that they do not reflect their true desires.

What a tragedy if, because of this, your own family and friends were to suffer. And frankly, if this letter does ensure you provide properly for those dear to you, I will feel I have done well. But you will probably have gathered that I have another reason for offering you this booklet.

I am trying to enlist your aid for what I believe to be the greatest cause on earth - children. Helpless children, often terrified, desperate and unable to fend for themselves. Not responsible for the terrible tragedies they have to face.

Many who have received this booklet have appreciated it greatly. One lady wrote to say "Your booklet was most helpful and motivated me to make a Will." Another praised our booklet: "I am sure it will help me to make a Will that will give satisfaction and some good for the future."

These people obviously found that the booklet helped them to do something they needed to do - and took a weight off their mind.

If you love children and you have read this far, may I tell you something about Save the Children? (And let me emphasise that this is not an appeal for immediate funds - though of course, the need is always urgent and we are always grateful for any donations.)

If you, like so many others, chose to help the people of the Sudan this year, I'm sure it was the incredible pictures of the children that affected you most.

Few sights can compare with the emotive impact caused by a child's confused face, crying with fear because they

Please read on...

don't understand what's happening around them - and why it's happening to them.

　　You will be astonished and delighted to know how much good you can do for children with a relatively small sum of money. Just providing basic food, clothes and medicine - on a regular basis - means we can build a sense of security, even a future for a needy child.

　　　　You can literally give them the precious gift
　　　　of life itself. For <u>as little as £250</u> a child
　　　　you have never met will every day be grateful
　　　　for what you have done. I cannot imagine a finer
　　　　legacy you could possibly leave, can you?

And I have good news for you. Because when you read our booklet, you will see that it is actually quite possible to <u>reduce the tax liability</u> on what you leave when you make a gift to charity. (An interesting subject for you to consider when you get the booklet.)

　　If you have read my letter this far, you may already be wondering whether you might make some provision for Save the Children. This is not the occasion to "sell" our organisation to you. But there is one important point I would like to make: the money you give does an incredible amount of good, principally because of every £1 donated only 2.2p is spent on administration and 8.4p on publicity and fundraising activities. The remaining 89.4p is for the children.

　　　　　Equally important is the way this money is used.
　　　　　We find out just what is needed, <u>first hand</u>,
　　　　　from the people who are best qualified to tell
　　　　　us - our trained field workers. They know
　　　　　exactly what the priorities are on a project
　　　　　and what is needed.

I'm sure you're concerned that any money you give reaches those most in need. I think you'll be glad to know that we carefully assess the true situation in this way all over the world - including the UK. We have learned, in our 69 years of experience, how essential this is.

　　In fact, the publicity about our overseas work often overshadows the vitally important work we do in this country. Did you know that back in the 30's we introduced

　　　　　　　　　　Please read on...

school milk and school dinners to this country? Today, in these times of depression when more and more children desperately need our help, many families turn to our local Save the Children Family Centres. (There's probably one near you.)

Let me end by making one simple point. In our lifetime, we are often too busy dealing with day to day problems, and we very often simply don't have the money necessary to do good. Yet after we have gone we <u>do</u> have this opportunity. A legacy - any legacy - can achieve so much.

And how wonderful to think about the good your money can do. Is this not the best conceivable way to make your memory live on in the hearts of others?

If you have ever considered leaving a legacy to a charity such as ours, or if you simply haven't got round to making a Will and feel you ought to, then please send for our little booklet.

Yours sincerely,

Maureen Brian

Maureen Brian
<u>Legacies Officer</u>

P.S.   As I said, the booklet we send is offered entirely without obligation on your part. If you do sympathise with our objectives, then I would be very grateful to receive a modest donation from you to help cover our costs. When I send the booklet, I will also send you some information about our work.

P.P.S. If, by chance, you already support the activities of Save the Children, may we thank you - and if you feel our booklet would help in providing for your own family and those near to you, by all means please send for it.

3. It's important to them. Years ago my agency sent out a letter to insurance brokers which actually got over 100 per cent response. It was about changes in the law which affected them and was so important that they passed it on to colleagues. I'm sure it was read and reread.
4. It reaches them at exactly the moment they are thinking about the subject in question.
5. It's so well written they find it a pleasure to read and reread.

Well, the first three cases above are to do with whatever you are writing about. You can't change that. The fifth is the reason you are reading this book. The fourth is the real teaser. Generally, only a small number of those you write to, by a fortunate chance, are thinking of acting just when you write to them. In this case, we couldn't force our readers to decide this was a good time to make a will.

That's one reason why you may have to write regularly to people, hoping eventually you hit them at the right moment. (Though, as we shall discuss when looking at how to begin your letter, you can sometimes persuade people that *this* is the right time. Having said all that, as you can see from the letter I wrote, the age of the reader was important in this case.)

What we wanted these people to do was very simple. We just wanted them to *reply*. The main purpose was not to get money. Indeed, I thought concentrating too much on this might get some people to give small sums immediately, but would deter others – whom we hoped would give large sums later – from replying at all.

We just wanted to get those names so we could communicate with them over time, in the hope they would eventually leave money. It is, in any case, rarely a good idea to ask people to do two things at once – they often end up doing neither.

Offers increase replies

One thing I had determined in advance with my client. We ought to make some sort of offer. If we chose the wrong kind of gift or incentive, this would be a little tricky. After all, I was about to imply my readers might not be round for long enough to enjoy the benefits thereof.

I am not talking about offers in particular in this chapter, but as I have already hinted it is a cardinal principle in direct mail that if you make an offer to somebody they are far more likely to reply.

Everybody likes to get something for nothing. More on this in Chapter 7.

The offer we chose was essential to the message, as you can see. We determined we would offer a booklet on the subject of making your will. So, as part of my planning for this particular operation, I became an instant expert and wrote a splendid booklet on the subject called 'A Will to Leave'.

I then spent some time reflecting upon the sort of people I was going to write to.

What did I know about people of that age? I thought that, though they might not *like* talking or reflecting upon death, older people do start to think about this gloomy subject. One of my points of reference was, in fact, my mother.

The only problem I had with the letter was with one of two envelope messages we tested, which read: *Do you believe in life after death?* This was 25 per cent more effective than the other, but upset some recipients.

Sometimes it distressed relatives of the person we mailed, for the good reason that some letters went to people who were dead. This was unavoidable, since no matter how recently a list has been checked, some people on it are bound to have died. So, successful though it was, it was rightly withdrawn.

Somewhat to my surprise, the letter also got a record amount in donations, despite the fact that, for the reasons I have already given you, I deliberately underplayed this aspect of the message.

One measure of a good letter is the length of time it remains a 'control' – ie the letter which does better than any alternatives it is tested against. This letter ran for a number of years with little change, and was still running the last time I checked.

TEN WAYS TO LEARN ABOUT PROSPECTS

The success of that letter, clearly, lay in understanding the prospect. After all, this particular charity did not have anything very different or special to offer to the reader. There are many other children's charities and they all do a good job as far as I am aware.

One important lesson you can gain from this example is that you should, before writing anything, try and think if you know anybody like the people you are writing to. When you are looking at what you have written, or considering any alternatives you have in mind, you ask yourself how that person would react.

Some writers find it a good idea to write a letter literally as though they are writing to one individual and to imagine that person's reaction to what they write.

This is valuable, because it makes you concentrate on something often neglected: the fact that you are writing to one person at a time. Although the letter may go out to a 1000, 10,000 or even 100,000 people, each will read it as an individual. So your letter must be written that way.

1. Personal knowledge

If your business is relatively small, you probably do know some of your customers personally and if you think enough about them, you can isolate common characteristics they tend to share. So you can address these characteristics and the interests that go with them.

2. Do you know someone similar?

Failing that personal knowledge, try and think of somebody who fits the category in question or is similar to the people you're writing to. Somebody you know well personally, if possible.

If you cannot think of an individual who fits into the category, here are other simple things you can do.

3. Who talks to the customers?

If there is any selling or personal contact in the business, go and meet the people who talk to the customers. The sales assistants in the shops. The people who take complaints on the phone. They will tell you a lot about the objections you may have to overcome in your letter.

Discuss with them what sort of people these are. A person who has to answer queries on the telephone can often tell you things about what you sell that the chairman of the company doesn't know. Certainly that person is likely to know a lot more about what is going through the customer's minds. What attracts them; what repels them.

4. Read the correspondence

One excellent way of discovering something about the people you're writing to is extremely obvious yet hardly ever undertaken. And that is quite simply to go through the correspondence files and read the letters they write to you. That is often extremely revealing.

Many years ago I learned when reading the letters from customers who bought a certain brand of pain reliever that some of them were dissolving it in warm water and using it to soak their tired feet. Not necessarily a very efficacious remedy, but it told me a lot about the people I was talking to.

This little snippet could have led – though it didn't – to a quite different approach to the way they sold the product. An approach based on information about pain and different ways to use it. This, in turn, could have led on to producing a range of different products under this same brand name to do various pain-relieving jobs.

5. Look at the names on the list

In earlier years, experienced mail order operators found that simply reading a list of names and addresses can give you clues about who you are writing to. If a large percentage of names and addresses are in poor areas, you will obviously adopt a different tone of voice to the one you might employ if they live in leafy suburbia.

Nowadays a number of companies specialize in analysing lists, using census and other data, so as to predict the likely characteristics of people on a list, such as their age, wealth, interests and the kind of property they live in.

You can even draw conclusions from somebody's first name. Such names are subject to fashions which vary according to age and social status. Thus, Stacy, Tracey or Terry are likely to be of a different age and background to Peregrine, Hubert or Hermione.

If yours is a small local business, such a service would hardly pay – better look at a list and use your local knowledge to draw conclusions. But if you do a lot of mailing on a national or even regional basis, it is certainly worth looking into.

6. Look at company names and titles

In much the same way, if your letter is on behalf of a business going to business people, looking at their company names and their titles will often tell you what sort of people they are.

7. Who replied – and who didn't?

Analysing the names and addresses of those who have replied to a mailing and comparing them with those who haven't is immensely valuable.

Such analyses make your letters better aimed. By eliminating those unlikely to reply, you can significantly increase the probable percentage of response, thus turning what might have been a money loser into a moneymaker.

Among larger, sophisticated mailers, this process is elaborated to become regression analysis. The characteristics of respondents and non-respondents are evaluated so as to exclude those less likely to reply from a list. In this way, what would have been an unprofitable mailing to the whole list becomes profitable when sent only to those names most likely to reply.

For one client years ago, one of my colleagues discovered from reviewing the results of a mailing that those most likely to reply had names with more than the usual number of initials; they lived in houses rather than flats; and they lived in houses with names rather than houses with numbers. They also were more likely than average to own personal computers.

They were more likely to be professional people and to have ethnic as opposed to English names. And they were more wealthy than average. Much of this information was both surprising and useful, since we were selling a money-saving service, which you might have thought would be more appealing to poorer people.

8. Conduct formal research

If you are a big company, you may well have plenty of information from research. Often, group discussions with your potential readers will tell you a lot. Look for the revealing quote, the unguarded remark. But, in my experience, although research is helpful it is rarely as useful as the sort of personal stuff mentioned above.

9. Listen in on phone calls

I was very impressed a few years ago during a visit to one of my clients – an enormously successful company – when one of their top executives, who was being paid a weighty six-figure sum, revealed that he had made a point of listening regularly to incoming telephone calls. It helped him keep in touch with the daily realities of the business – and what mattered to his customers.

10. Talk to service people

Another neglected source of information – often your only one if you don't have salesmen – is your service engineers. They certainly bear the brunt of most complaints, can see what's going wrong, and pick up very quickly what matters and what doesn't.

Many executives, as they rise in majesty and their own estimation up the corporate hierarchy become too grand to bother with such things. But simple research conducted in person is much underrated. Just going into shops and asking – without revealing who you represent – whether they sell your product, whether it does well, what the customers think of it, can be enormously revealing.

If you don't have regular personal contact with your customers, I can only say that you should. The minute you lose that close understanding of the people who pay your wages, you start to lose your grip on your business – and, eventually, you go broke.

One huge advantage of a regular programme of sales letters is that, as long as you ask them to, people will give you their views; you learn from them what you need to know to do better. They give you not just sales, but the recipe for business success.

LETTERS THAT SHOULD SELL – BUT DON'T

I talked at the beginning of this chapter about 'junk mail' being letters written by people who don't put themselves in the customers' shoes. An astonishing amount of goodwill is squandered by people because of this – and nowhere more than in what are seen as 'routine' letters. Letters that should sell – but rarely do.

All businesses have to send out letters responding to requests for information, warning of price rises, answering queries and so forth. They don't call for great creative flair and are given no attention by the big bozos at the top, being left to junior people, with no indication that they are important.

Perhaps this is because they have failed to consider how such letters can build your reputation and your sales – or destroy them. If not carefully approached, they can cost you a lot of money and certainly a great deal of goodwill, because what doesn't matter to you often matters to your customers a lot.

A well-written letter of this kind is like a smiling, helpful shop assistant. Nothing can do more for your sales. An ill-written one is like a charmless, surly oaf who puts customers off. Most fall into the latter category. They are either written in the language we associate with the civil service, dull and uninformative – or down-right illiterate.

Often, too, they are badly presented; with labels stuck slightly askew on a cheap envelope, badly typed, sometimes with no signature, an illegible one or a 'p.p.' with an illegible scrawl above the name of some pompous person too lazy to sign their own mail. It's a bit like having a grubby, ill-dressed shop assistant who ignores you.

No attempt to sell properly

One common instance is where someone has replied to an advertisement which has offered information. In an astonishingly high percentage of cases the information requested arrives after a long delay or not at all – and I shall quote figures on this later.

When it does, there is often no letter explaining why the product is good; just a leaflet or brochure on its own. This is like having a store with no salesperson present – no real attempt is made to 'sell' whatever has been asked about.

If there is a letter it is a perfunctory one simply saying: 'Here is the information you have asked for.' This is folly. Small, irritating things like this do your company no good, yet it does not cost a great deal to set them right.

When people write to you about something you've advertised, it is not because they have nothing better to do. It is because they are interested, as I pointed out in the last chapter. You may well have spent good money on advertising to get them interested. What a shame to waste it!

The way you treat them will determine whether they become a customer or become indifferent – even hostile. Ignoring them makes them conclude you are either incompetent, rude or both. It may be that some of you reading this have more customers than you know what to do with. But in most cases customers are hard to come by and hard to keep.

MAKING THE BEST (OR WORST) OF A BAD SITUATION

When you have to announce bad news to your customers you are not likely to make anybody happy; but at least you can avoid infuriating them. A good example of how not to write such letters is the crude (unsigned) example overleaf.

A prime specimen of the bureaucratic style, it deals with a common task: announcing a price rise. Apart from one approach used in that letter – the needlessly obscure, which confuses and irritates – another wrong way to handle the problem is used by many people. They wriggle and do anything to avoid getting to the point that the prices are going up.

None of us likes to give people bad news. So avoiding the issue is perfectly natural. Some go about the job by starting with a list of improvements, then quietly slipping in the price rise, hoping nobody will notice it.

The results can never be good. Either readers don't notice the price rise, as you had secretly hoped, and are furious when it comes out in their bills. Or, just as bad, they see through your little deception and take exception to it.

The correct way to write such letters is simple.

1. Be honest and straightforward – and get to the point.
2. Where appropriate, apologize, and explain why the changes are necessary.
3. If you can, announce improvements in your product or service.
4. Give the name of someone people can call or write to with questions or complaints.

Another infuriating example of this sort of thing appears on page 81, where a bank is restructuring its prices. Once again, it is unsigned, though at least there is a name at the bottom.

However, I defy you, as a reader, to be able to conclude what the total effect of all the changes is. No doubt that is what the writer had in mind – but is it good communication? I think not. It is just a waste of paper – and of the time of the reader, who had enormous difficulty finding out the facts.

Scottish\Amicable

Craigforth (P.O. Box No. 25), Stirling, FK9 4UE
telephone 0786—448844

June 1993

293NU133 00318

REVIEW OF PENSION CHARGES

Over recent years the cost of administering pensions business has risen steadily and as a result many Life Offices have reviewed their product terms. Many of the increased costs have been due to legislative and regulatory factors, outwith the control of Life Offices. Despite this, the charges under our pension contracts have remained unaltered since July 1990.

We have now carried out a full review of our charges to reflect these higher overheads and as a result the following changes are being made:-

1) From 1st October 1993, the Regular Management Charge on Investment Linked Funds will increase to 0.875% p.a.

2) With immediate effect, the Member Charge will increase to £12. This charge which is taken annually is a single charge taken for each personal pension policyholder.

The Regular Management Charge is accounted for within unit prices and the Member Charge is met from the units under the policy and therefore no action is required on your part.

Incorporated by Act of Parliament The principal office of Scottish Amicable Life Assurance Society is in Scotland at 150 St Vincent Street, Glasgow G2 5NQ Registration No Z12
Member of the Life Assurance and Unit Trust Regulatory Organisation, the Association of British Insurers and the Insurance Ombudsman Bureau
Scottish Amicable Life Assurance Society, Scottish Amicable Pensions Investments Limited and Scottish Amicable Unit Trust Managers Limited form a marketing group

Is this any way to talk to a customer who has invested tens of thousands with you?

BARCLAYS BANK PLC
114, FENCHURCH STREET
P.O. BOX NO. 69, 114 FENCHURCH ST., LONDON, EC3P 3HY
TELEPHONE 071 481 3434

ACCOUNT NAME: THE CAFE SOCIETY

As part of our commitment to customer service, we promise to advise you, at least one month in advance, of any changes in our prices which affect your account.

Our new prices come into effect on 16th May 1994, and a leaflet giving details is enclosed.

You will see that there is a reduction in the price for each entry, a change which will increasingly benefit your business as it grows. Whilst there is an increase in the maintenance fee, we are pleased to advise you that some other charges have been withdrawn completely, for example we will no longer charge for letters issued.

As a service to our customers, we will continue to provide you with a detailed breakdown of your quarterly commission and any accrued overdraft interest charges approximately 10 days before your account is debited. However, to help you spread the cost more evenly throughout the year, you may wish to consider the monthly charging option. If you would like to take advantage of this, please complete the form within the leaflet.

I would also draw your attention to the fact that Barclays credits customers with the value of cheques paid in, as soon as we receive it.

If you have any queries regarding your account or the new prices, please do not hesitate to contact your relationship manager or a member of staff at your branch. For convenience, the address and telephone number are shown above.

Yours sincerely

David Lavarack
Head of Small Business Services

051

Member of IMRO
Registered in London, England. Reg. No: 1026167. Reg. Office: 54 Lombard Street, London EC3P 3AH

How not to communicate. Interestingly, when the recipient phoned the signatory on the number given, nobody knew who or where he was.

GET THE EASY BIT OUT OF THE WAY

Now, you may say (and I hope you do) that everything I have written so far about planning, preparation and trying to see things as your customers do is common sense.

That may be so. But as I pointed out at the very start of this book, most sales letters are constructed thoughtlessly, by people who see the job as simple, to be accomplished with the minimum of delay, the maximum of dispatch and hardly any preparation. And many do not realize that just about every letter we send out may affect our sales.

While revising this chapter, I heard a story about Noël Coward, who insisted all the actors in his plays arrive at the first rehearsal having learned their lines perfectly. This was not normal practice. One actor asked why. Coward explained that learning lines is easy, while acting is hard. If you get the easy job out of the way, you can concentrate on the difficult one.

It is the same with writing a letter. Amassing information about what you are selling and to whom is not hard. It takes time and can be a chore – like memorizing lines, no doubt. But it is essential, as we have seen. And once you have everything you need clear in your mind, you can concentrate on producing the best possible letter.

6

The Right Stuff

'I never tried to be original in my life.'

W A Mozart

You might call the best letters 'organized speech'. When read aloud they sound like a friend talking to you. This is so disarming you lower your guard and can be more easily persuaded.

Of course, this is the art that conceals art. Such a letter has been painstakingly planned and organized, its arguments marshalled with great care. This must be so, for the 'dialogue' between reader and writer is, of course, not a conversation, though it has similarities. It is really a sort of monologue.

Unless you are a soulless clod, when face-to-face with somebody you naturally adapt what you say to fit them. Simply by looking at them – how they are dressed, how old they are, their sex, even their expression – you can judge a good way to start the conversation.

As that conversation proceeds, you adapt what you say and how you say it to keep their interest. If they look at their watches, you get to the point more quickly. If they start shaking their watches, you shut up. This facility to react appropriately is, as I pointed out earlier, one of the important elements in personal selling which you lack when writing to people.

You can't react to somebody you can't see. When you write a sales letter it is as though you are trying to persuade someone hidden behind a curtain who never replies when you speak, but will give their decision later.

You are talking with no way of knowing how the other person is responding – until your letter either succeeds in getting a reply or fails. It calls to mind the Zen riddle: What is the sound of one hand clapping?

That is why, though it would be a frightful bore if all our conversations were conducted that way, it is good sense to make sure our letters are created to some sort of formula. A formula calculated to gain people's interest and retain that interest until you finally persuade them to do what you want. A formula that ensures every requisite part of your argument is properly deployed.

A RECIPE THAT WORKS

There is a very old recipe or formula called AIDA which you will probably recognize if you have done much personal selling. This states that first you must attract the prospect's *Attention*, then you must gain his or her *Interest*. Then you must engender *Desire* for what you are offering, before you persuade your prospect to *Act*.

Here is the earliest version of that formula I have come across, taken from a book written over 70 years ago – and I am sure it was not new then.

The *opening*, which should attract the reader's attention and induce him to read.

The *description and explanation* should hold his interest by causing him to picture the proposition in his mind.

The *argument* should create the desire for the article offered for sale.

Persuasion should bring the reader around to your way of thinking by seeing how the article is adapted to his needs. This is followed by:

Inducement which gives him an extra reason for buying, and in conclusion you have –

The *climax*, which makes it easy for the reader to order, and assures that action by causing him to act at once.

As you can see, the four ingredients in the AIDA formula are all covered in that extract, with two more added. One is the element of *persuasion* or *conviction*, which is clearly essential, since people have to believe you before they act. That is why the old formula is often adapted to AIDPA or AIDCA.

The other is in many ways the most important of all – the *inducement* or *offer*. All six, in my experience, are essential if your letter is to do as well as it can. I am not saying that you cannot succeed without one of them – I have seen many letters which were lacking in one or another, yet worked. But for the greatest possible success, every ingredient must be present in one form or another.

Many people feel that the best brief formula, apart from the one I have just described is one created by Bob Stone, the doyen of American Direct Marketers, to whom I have already referred, and whose encyclopedic *Successful Direct Marketing Methods* I recommend as a work of reference – though not for light reading.

Bob Stone suggests these seven steps to success.

1. Promise a benefit in your headline or first paragraph – *your most important benefit.*
2. Immediately enlarge upon your most important benefit.
3. Tell the reader *specifically* what he is going to get.
4. Back up your statements with *proof* and *endorsements*.
5. Tell the reader what he might lose if he doesn't act.
6. Rephrase your prominent benefits in your closing offer.
7. Incite action – *now.*

Now, the thought of writing to a formula may not appeal to you. It seems almost demeaning, somehow. After all, surely writing *anything* – even something as commercial and basic as a sales letter – must call for some imagination, for the odd flight of fancy. How can we fetter this process by applying such a straitjacket?

Many feel this way – especially those who write direct mail for a living and would like to feel they were engaged in some form of high art. Surely it can only lead to dull, predictable stuff, unlikely to break through the carapace of indifference set up by the prospect, these people say.

FORMULAE THAT PRODUCE ART

For my part, I counsel you not to be too worried about formulae. If you really want to compare direct mail to great art, it's worth remembering that Mozart wrote 41 pretty durable symphonies, all to much the same formula. If you prefer Bach to Mozart, his example is even more apposite, since he composed with mathematical precision.

If you look at less lofty forms of communication, you will soon see that, no matter how original they may at first appear, once you break them down they tend to fit into one formula or another – and what's more, people *like* it that way.

Look at just about any cinema hit or TV series. You know right from frame one that Clint Eastwood is not going to get killed. You know that whatever terrifying situation he faces, the hero will beat the odds. You know the villain will come to a fearful end. And you don't *resent* this; you look forward eagerly to the predictable moment when good triumphs over evil.

And this has not changed. Fifty years ago, you could be equally sure that Clark Gable would come out of any fracas intact and with the girl. And for that matter, when Odysseus went voyaging after the battle of Troy, since he was the hero, Homer took care to arrange things so that he survived to see Penelope again.

Even apparently new ideas are usually variations on old themes. Years ago, Heineken lager introduced television commercials in the UK with the unusual line that 'Heineken refreshes the parts other beers cannot reach', illustrated by far-fetched situations like Nero being unable to give the order to kill a Christian until he'd had his strength refreshed by a Heineken.

New way to use an old formula

When this idea came out everyone thought, quite rightly, that it was a most original way of selling a beer – which it did, very effectively. But it was merely a variation on a very old idea: the before and after sequence. It was the ingenuity with which a new way had been found to use an old formula that made the difference.

The moral is: don't forget the formulae or the rules. Indeed, keep them firmly in mind, but try to exploit them in a different way. This is much more likely to reap rewards than just going off in search of any crazy idea that occurs to you.

You may like to remember a remark on this subject made by Leo Burnett, the founder of a big international advertising agency group. 'If you absolutely insist on being different just for the sake of being different, you can always come down to breakfast with a sock in your mouth.'

As you become more used to writing letters, you will find you incorporate all the elements of whatever formula you choose without thinking consciously. I shouldn't think that I have looked at the AIDCA formula for years when writing. However, until you become experienced these mnemonic sets of letters provide excellent guidance.

In fact I doubt whether these formulae were originally written as guidelines to write a letter, but were rationalizations. By that I mean they were produced by people who studied successful direct mail and then decided *afterwards* which elements proved important.

USE YOUR IMAGINATION

Don't follow a formula rigidly. In the AIDCA recipe, you will see that the ingredients are listed in a logical order. However, it does not follow that they always need to be placed in that order.

For instance, one common ploy is to gain attention by indicating on the envelope that whatever is on offer inside is only going to be available for a limited time. A simple example is something you may well have noticed in some of the direct mail you have received: a stamp saying 'Dated documents inside. Please reply by 30 July.'

This is actually an urge to *action* – in theory the last element in the formula – being used at the beginning. It is also an *incentive* to reply, implying that you may miss something important if you don't open that envelope immediately.

There are even cases where telling people *not* to act is an incentive to start reading. One French mailer put a note on the envelope saying 'Do not open before Xmas'. A Belgian restaurant selling tables for a Valentine's Day Dinner put: 'Ladies, please don't open. You'll only spoil the surprise.' Both messages worked extremely well.

One weapon that may work for you should not come as a surprise after the way I have referred to the similarity between a letter and a personal encounter. On the envelope shown overleaf, from a mailing I wrote for the Royal Viking Line (see Chapter 7), the letters RSVP showed through a window. Simply a polite call to action in language familiar to our prospects. A variation of this has been used by The British Horseracing Board, which you can see on pages 89–93.

THREE THINGS THAT MAKE MOST DIFFERENCE

If we assume you have paid suitable attention to the research and thinking I have covered in the previous chapters, thereafter three things will make the most difference to the success of your letter.

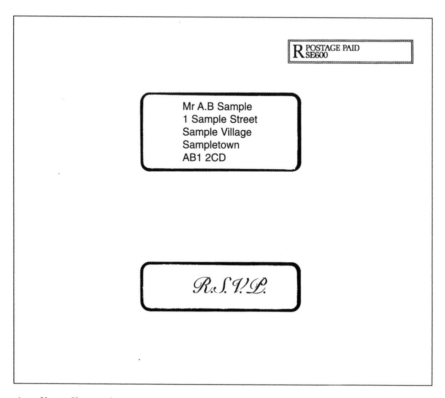

A polite call to action.

These are: first, the proposition itself; second, how well you gain attention; and third, how compelling your call to action is. The three work together, for as we shall see the offer both encourages the reader to pay attention *and* gives a reason to act.

On those very rare occasions when you are selling something *all* your prospects are familiar with and you have a very good offer, these three elements *on their own* can do the trick. The others are implicit.

Such a brief approach is only appropriate when addressing people who know your product, are already interested and already believe it is good. Such people have probably thought about getting it and just need to be nudged into acting immediately. Such people, to return to our formula, are interested, do have the desire to buy and are already convinced what you offer is good.

Suppose you are selling a magazine all your prospects have seen countless times. You can, as *Time* once did, send out a simple perforated double postcard – one half for the message, the other half for the reply – which said more or less: 'Dear So and So, You're a busy person

THE BRITISH HORSERACING BOARD

42 PORTMAN SQUARE • LONDON W1H OEN

TELEPHONE 0171-396 0011 • FAX 0171-935 3626 • DIRECT LINE 0171-343

5th August 1996

Mr A B Sample
1 Sample Street
Sample Village
SAMPLETOWN
AB1 2CD

A rare, last-minute opportunity.

Dear Mr Sample,

A limited number of places available at our 2 day seminar:
"The Thrill of Racehorse Ownership" - at Newmarket beginning on the 30th September.

I am writing because some time ago you expressed an interest in racehorse ownership. If that is still the case, this seminar, for which just a few places have become available, is a unique opportunity.

"Unique" is, as you know, a word too often used for very ordinary occasions open to anyone with the money. These seminars, however, are entirely restricted to those who wish to own (or have recently bought) a racehorse, and numbers are strictly limited.

Moreover, they are the only event of their kind, being arranged by the British Horseracing Board (BHB) on a non-profit basis to give you an impartial, informed view of what it means to be a racehorse owner. **Attending one is, I believe, an essential step in the process of becoming a successful owner.**

Although they are not expensive, it would be hard, probably impossible, for any private person or organisation, no matter how well-connected, to arrange such seminars at any price. Hardly surprisingly, they enjoy a high reputation, and those who attend are hugely enthusiastic - as a selection of typical comments indicates.

"It has convinced me that I should now take the next step and dip a small toe in the water...".

"It was really fantastic".

"Many thanks to all concerned in putting on such a professional and enjoyable seminar".

"Being a total novice to the racing world, I didn't feel vulnerable or under pressure in having to.../

THE BRITISH HORSERACING BOARD LIMITED • REGISTERED OFFICE 42 PORTMAN SQUARE, LONDON W1H OEN
REGISTERED NUMBER 2813358 ENGLAND

This invitation approach got four times as many delegates as previous efforts plus a 14.4% response from people saying 'later, please'.

.../ answer questions or complete test papers. The seminar was relaxing and enjoyable as well as being very informative".

"The seminar was excellent value for money. I have already recommended it to a number of people".

The seminars give you a privileged insight - a look behind the scenes - which non-owners never experience, besides giving you the opportunity to meet and question some of the people who make the racing world such a special, even glamorous, milieu.

To put it simply, instead of being, like the average "punter", on the outside looking in at this small, exclusive world, you experience what it is like to be an owner. Numbers are very small, to give maximum benefit.

- You go to a leading trainer's yard, attend morning exercise on the Gallops, and find out all you need to know.

- You visit the National Stud - view stallions, mares and foals.

- You dine in the Jockey Club rooms: an experience few people get a chance to enjoy in their entire lives.

- You visit Tattersalls and attend the sales.

- You spend an afternoon at Newmarket Races - also free.

And throughout you spend your time talking to and listening to experienced, knowledgeable owners, Trainers and bloodstock agents. Not just **watching** what happens, but **seeing** it through expert eyes.

The reason the BHB inaugurated these seminars is simple. We decided no advertisement, brochure or letter - no matter how wordy or detailed - can tell you how it feels to own a racehorse: we want to give potential owners the closest possible approximation to the thrill - and the prestige - of the real thing.

Since the seminars are conducted to encourage the ownership of racehorses - which is an important part of BHB's remit - they are not run to make a profit. The cost is only £150 per person for two days, including a lunch, dinner and breakfast, but not your hotel - about half the cost of a "commercial" seminar. A free copy of The Turf Directory, worth £47 is included in the price.

During the two days you get the answers to all your questions. How much does it cost to keep a horse in training? What should you watch for when buying? What privileges do you .../

.../ enjoy as an owner? What are the real chances of winning? And, of course, the "mystique" of racing involves a certain etiquette. What is the correct way to deal with your trainer or jockey? What is the done thing if your horse wins?

One indication of the quality of these seminars is that at the end of the first one we scheduled an hour for questions. However delegates on that occasion and subsequently were so satisfied that the most we have ever needed has been 15 minutes. Over 50% of previous attendees have gone on to become owners.

> If you become an owner within a year of the seminar, the £150 fee is refunded to you. You also receive free membership of the Thoroughbred Breeders Association, normally £60, two years' membership of the Racehorse Owners' Association for the price of one, saving you £50, and a year's subscription to "Pacemaker", worth £60.

This is a rare, last-minute opportunity. Attendance at these seminars is by private invitation only to genuine prospective owners; places are not easily come by.

Since time is short, numbers are limited and many places are already taken, I advise an **immediate** reply. Please remember that this invitation is in your name, for you and your guests and is not transferable.

Yours sincerely,

NJF Robinson
Chairman, BHB Ownership Marketing Group.

P.S. I would appreciate it if you could complete and return the enclosed invitation **whether you wish to attend or not**, since it gives us an idea of your future plans. (I have enclosed a pre-paid envelope for your use.) Thank you.

PLEASE RETURN WHETHER YOU CAN ATTEND OR NOT

PLEASE INDICATE YOUR RESPONSE WITH A TICK, AND RETURN IMMEDIATELY.

☐ **YES:** I ACCEPT YOUR INVITATION, AND ENCLOSE MY CHEQUE FOR £176.25 PER PERSON (£150.00 + £26.25VAT), MADE OUT TO THE BRITISH HORSERACING BOARD.

N.B. WHEN WE RECEIVE YOUR BOOKING WE SHALL ISSUE A VAT INVOICE AS CONFIRMATION, PLUS DETAILS OF THE HOTEL. THE HOTEL COST IS NOT INCLUDED IN THE SEMINAR FEE.

☐ **NO, THANK YOU:** I AM NO LONGER INTERESTED IN OWNING A RACEHORSE. PLEASE DO NOT WRITE TO ME AGAIN.

☐ **SOME OTHER DATE:** I REMAIN INTERESTED IN OWNERSHIP, BUT CANNOT ATTEND THIS PARTICULAR SEMINAR. PLEASE LET ME KNOW OF FUTURE PLANNED SEMINARS.

so I won't waste your time. If you reply in the next 30 days, we will give you a year's subscription to *Time* magazine at half price. Just return the other half of this postcard.'

This approach, clearly, is designed to appeal to somebody predisposed towards *Time* magazine; who is already persuaded it is a good magazine. So we don't worry about the people who aren't. We simply make a strong offer to those who think it is, but haven't got around to buying. They need a nudge – which is given by making the product so attractive in terms of price that they can't say no.

A MORE COMPLETE ARGUMENT USUALLY NEEDED

But what if your prospects were not all that familiar with the magazine, but quite favourably disposed to it? The postcard would be quite inadequate, would it not?

For them a very different approach would be needed. It would be a letter which went to the trouble of telling people *all* about the publication and proving to them that it was just what they needed in their busy lives. It would need every element in the formula for success to work properly.

And what about those people who were familiar with your product, but weren't ready to take the plunge and buy? Those who needed more than a reminder? They too need a complete argument. Indeed, even in the case of *Time*, the brief approach described only worked against some prospects and the magazine kept to a more complete story for most of their mailings.

American Express tried a brief approach to prospects, saying, in effect, 'You know the American Express card; we'd like you as a Cardmember; so we've made it easy for you to apply.' This only worked in the US and Hong Kong, where it seems people knew all about the card and wanted it, as well as being flattered by the message. Elsewhere – even in Canada, which many (though not Canadians) feel is almost the same as the US – it flopped.

The truth is that there will be very few occasions indeed when an incomplete argument will do the best job. You need an astonishingly high reputation among your prospects to get away with it. Moreover, those who are keen to buy already can easily read the brief description of the proposition in the order form and act immediately without studying the complete argument.

Indeed, you can use one technique borrowed from salespeople, the 'trial close' to cover off these people; you explain the proposition at the beginning of the letter and tell them to buy or reply immediately.

A good example comes from *Successful Creativity in Direct Marketing* written by John Watson, the ideal book if you wish to learn from one of the best practitioners in the world:

```
Dear Reader

You'll receive a free copy of XXXXX if you reply within 14 days
to this invitation — as your introduction to this brand new
widget service ...
```

However, never forget that of the elements within a letter those three – the offer or incentive, the gaining of attention and the call to action – are the most important and the ones you should work unsparingly to get right.

Now let's move on to consider each element in our formula in more detail.

7

Fine Writing – or Persuasive Offer?

'Imagine you have a business. You've built it up through hard work and effort. It's worth $1.0 million to you.

Suddenly the sales start going down. Your livelihood is in jeopardy. Your wife and your family's livelihood are in jeopardy. What do you want from me? Fine writing? Or would you like to see the goddam sales curve stop going down and start going up?'

Rosser Reeves

'Fine words butter no parsnips' is an old English expression. It is worth bearing in mind when you are writing a sales letter. For, no matter how silver tongued you may be, your eloquence is unlikely to be as persuasive as *giving* somebody something to do what you want – an incentive.

The reason for this is simple. It lies in human nature. People like to get something for nothing – often even when they don't need it. Thus, when my job involved me spending half my time in hotels and on aeroplanes, I *never* failed to collect airline toilet bags, and soap and shampoo from hotel rooms. I must have the largest collection of stale cosmetics in Somerset.

Exactly how strong an element the offer is, I discovered quite a few year ago, through a test conducted for a client. Tests are important in direct mail. If you want to be professional, you have to pay careful attention to how many replies you get. Indeed, one of the joys of this medium is that you don't have to guess what works. By counting those replies you know – to the penny.

As a result, direct marketing professionals become quite engrossed by statistics on what works, what doesn't – and to what degree. I am no exception. Although I loathed maths at school, when I got into the mail order business, I started to develop new enthusiasm for it.

At the time of this test, I was helping to introduce a new kind of discount shopping service in the UK. A series of carefully constructed tests of various letters was designed to find out the answers to a number of things, including the right list to use, the right price to charge, the right time to mail, the right offer to make and the most persuasive approach.

WHAT IS MOST IMPORTANT?

As you would expect from what you have already read in this book, by far the most important element was who you were mailing – how well your efforts were aimed or targeted. The best of 12 lists we tried did 6 times better than the worst.

Timing – as you have also learned – was important. If you mailed at the best time of the year, you did twice as well as if you mailed at the worst time of the year. (You saw earlier how I discovered this the hard way.)

But perhaps the most interesting result came when we tried to ascertain the right price.

We had considered charging three different annual fees: £12.50 a year, £15.00 a year and £20.00 a year. We discovered that £20.00 a year was the most successful price if it was linked with an *offer* whereby people could try the service for three months before being committed to it.

This offer, based on something I first tried in the late 1960s for a publishing business I then owned, was *three times* as successful as the lowest price without the offer.

There were tests of various other factors. These were: how we asked people to reply – phone, reply card or a choice – the colour of the envelope – white or yellow – and whether asking people to signify 'yes' by placing a little sticker on the order form would work better than having them sign (it did).

WHY OFFERS AND INCENTIVES WORK

You will find the power of the incentive is such that even the most sophisticated and imaginative of letter writers pay great attention to it. Even my friend Bill Jayme – the one who charged up to $40,000 a letter and often employed the most unusual approaches – always featured it very heavily, both on the envelope and at the start of his letter to help involve the reader.

Let's face it, nobody wakes up in the morning thinking the one thing they would really like to do that day is read a sales letter and order something. Usually they are far more concerned with other matters, whether domestic or business.

Very often when you send out a letter you're writing to people who don't know you. In some cases they may never have even heard of you. You therefore need something to prod them out of their lethargy. An offer appeals to their greed, which overcomes whatever caution they might have about responding, or buying, if you are trying for an immediate sale.

It is much easier to ignore a letter than to ignore a human being sitting in front of you. For that matter, it is much easier to ignore a letter than to ignore a product in front of you in a shop, when you have taken the trouble to go into that shop.

That is why your prospect is far less likely to buy or act when you are conducting the transaction through the post.

WHY SOME MARKETERS DON'T LIKE OFFERS

I am not going so far as to say incentives are always necessary, but they certainly work for most businesses. Yet for one reason or another many marketers don't like these. Some feel it cheapens their image. Others, I believe, through sheer meanness, don't like giving things away. And others don't like them because they can't believe that a giveaway will pay for itself.

I well recall how long and hard my partners and I battled some years ago – fruitlessly – with IBM when they first decided to sell typewriters through the post. They refused to allow customers to try their machines free for seven days.

They thought it quite beneath their dignity to make an offer. This is a common feeling among self-important merchants, though I think it downright odd, because in the everyday course of business they frequently allow their salespeople to discount products to get an immediate sale.

Go into any department store and you see salespeople giving away something if you buy somebody's cologne. And what about the advertisements offering you 0 per cent interest if you buy such and such a brand of car?

All these people realize how important it is to get a sale now. Those with sales forces know it costs money to get a salesperson in front of someone, so it makes sense to offer an incentive for a sale there and then. It saves the extra cost of revisiting that customer. People with shops know it costs money to keep them open. They have to grab every sale they can immediately and use every possible trick to do so because people who say they'll go and think about it never return.

In letters the principle is identical: if you give somebody a special inducement, perhaps they will act now, rather than later or, worse still, not at all. We are just talking about postage and printing costs rather than rent, rates and salespeople's costs.

One other reason why people baulk at making offers is that they are captivated by their product – the same reason why so many letters are written from the wrong angle. They simply fail to understand why anybody should not want to buy what they sell. As I've already observed, enthusiasm for one's product or service is desirable, indeed laudable; but it should not blind you to the truth.

As a matter of interest, eventually IBM were willing to allow customers to send back the typewriter after they'd bought it, if they were not satisfied after purchase. This, combined with the IBM name, made the mailing successful. But they could have made a much stronger offer and done even better.

GIVE MORE PROFIT THAN THEY COST

In the matter of offers, I can only quote one of the wisest men I know, Victor Ross, former chairman of *Reader's Digest* in Europe. I once heard him say during a speech that he had *never* known a relevant offer fail to pay for itself. By that he meant that it produced more extra profit than it cost.

This remark is worth framing and sticking up in your office to contemplate at fairly regular intervals. Every professional I know in this field would agree with him. Although you will get a small, usually very small, percentage of people who will take advantage of you, they are usually far outnumbered by those impelled to act who otherwise would not have done so.

That is why I stated earlier that after assessing what your product or service offers – which is obviously paramount – and thinking about the person you are writing to, the next thing to turn your thoughts to is what offer you can make to them.

I must make clear the difference between an *offer* or incentive and a *benefit* of your product or service – which we defined earlier. A benefit is what your customer may derive from the product or service. An offer is anything you are prepared to give to prospects if they will do something in exchange. And the number of offers you can make is almost limitless.

Some quite surprising offers can work. Here's one that got me to act some years ago when I was on holiday in the West Indies.

I was approached in a supermarket by a young woman who told that if I had an hour and a half to spare, I could get $100 discount towards a restaurant meal or anything in that store, or towards any one of a number of excursions, as well as a free T shirt. All I had to do was to visit a property development.

To be honest, I am always put off by the thought of anybody selling me something. My wife, on the other hand, loves investigating possible purchases, even if she has no intention of buying. This is probably why she is often better informed than me and very good at finding the best deal on just about anything you can name.

At any rate, off we went and had a one and a half hour presentation. Had I the money to spare, or possibly one or two more drinks, I might have (who knows?) actually bought what they were selling.

What is even more surprising about this is that if there is one thing Drayton Bird does not need it is another T shirt. For a number of years I have collected them and have become quite discriminating. I will normally only get something I find intriguing or amusing.

Despite this, my desire to get something for nothing was sufficient to cajole me to go and look at something I had no intention of buying. What's more, as I say, I might even have bought had I had sufficient ready funds.

THE TWO KINDS OF OFFER THAT WORK BEST

Some products or services interest almost everyone, so an offer of almost universal interest will usually work best for them. Thus, Victor Ross told me that the most successful offer he had ever seen for the *Reader's Digest* was that of rose bushes. By this he meant, I suppose, little baby bushes ready to plant.

Gardening is one of the two most popular hobbies in Britain, and most *Reader's Digest* readers have either a garden, or at least a few plants. Other very successful offers have been clocks and watches, luggage and calculators. Everyone needs to tell the time and count, and all of us, just about, travel.

If your product or service is not of universal interest, your offer must be relevant to the particular group you are addressing, to the product or service, and to the occasion. The catch in this case is that it is not always quite as easy as it might seem to discern what is relevant, though it is usually easy to see what isn't.

For instance, a free visit to Disneyworld would hardly be appropriate if you were selling a Rolls-Royce. A trip on the Orient Express might be, though. And a free visit to Disneyland might well be appropriate if you are trying to get people to test drive a cheap car. Indeed, it could be extremely appropriate because you could link it to the offer. You could say 'Test drive this car for a day, and you can visit Disneyland with your family'.

In fact that is not an imaginary example, for something similar was used by Peugeot. Readers were invited to visit a safari park which featured lions, very appropriately, because their advertising was based on the lion symbol on their cars, and the strength this implied. Thus it was relevant not merely to the type of product, but also the brand. This makes the advertising of the brand more effective.

AN OFFER THAT DOESN'T COST MUCH

One type of offer you should always consider is something printed, because paper is cheap, and most people value information. For instance, a client a few years ago, selling a series of cooking lessons, offered a chart which showed the use of various herbs and spices.

Another I suggested to a client offering loans to doctors was a booklet on financial planning for the medical profession. It worked very well. Not because it was all that original, but because it was appropriate. A variation of that for another client offering investment advice was a free first consultation. You might say that is even better than paper: just hot air.

One good way to start thinking up an offer is to reflect upon your prospect and determine something which is likely to attract only that type of person. For example, anybody interested in herbs and spices is bound to be interested in cooking. Equally, a pair of garden secateurs proved a very effective offer for somebody selling fertilizer, would you believe, through the post.

Some offers are designed to get people to reply. Others to get them to buy. You can go beyond a single offer and make two, three or even four. You can suggest that if prospects reply within a certain period of time you will give something extra. And that if they buy more than a certain quantity, you will give something on top for that.

All these things have been tested and found to work; and there are many more. Supposing you have a shop which is empty at certain times or on certain days, it can pay you to attract people in during those periods.

Or it could be worth it to encourage people to buy in a certain way, ie on the telephone as opposed to writing in. There are three reasons why. First, people who are keen enough to telephone are usually excellent customers; second, getting people to act when something is fresh in their minds is wise; third, you can sell them something else or learn more about what they want while they're on the phone.

PRIZE DRAWS AND CONTESTS

I do not plan to go into all the mysteries of prize draws, contests and sweepstakes here. However, I can assure you that they work – so well, often, as to overcome some dreadful letters, as in the case of a pretty banal one I received while preparing this book, inviting me to inspect some property in the West Country.

I seem to be a common target of those trying to sell property. The letter was like a thousand others. It did not neglect such well-worn adjectives as 'prestigious', a word which ought to be banned, particularly if, as in this case, the property was in a part of England whence any prestige has pretty well departed.

However, they said I had won a prize. All I had to do was to trot along to the property and be conducted around it in order to receive the prize.

Since this is a well-worn stratagem associated with the giving away of large numbers of virtually worthless gifts, my suspicions were immediately aroused. However, in this case the gifts were most appealing. There was a small car, a week's stay in the Bahamas, £300 cash, a portable television set and a video recorder to be won.

Because I have better things to do with my time, I did not respond. But the offer was brought to my attention again two weeks later when I received a quasi-official communication warning me that an award was awaiting my collection and that unless I claimed this award by 6 July 'issuance to another claimant will have to take place'.

I was asked to ring and number and ask for Marilyn.

Now this was not a well-aimed letter. First of all, I lived in quite a pleasant country house – more pleasant, I suspect, than the properties being sold. Why should I want to buy one?

Second, I live less than 80 miles away from the properties being sold. Why on earth should I want to buy a holiday home so close to my own? A little intelligence would have suggested that the targeting was poor, quite apart from the inept attempt at officialese. Not to mention the hilarious mention of Marilyn – which reminded me of a multitude of jokes in bad taste.

Nevertheless, reflecting upon the prizes being offered, had I nothing else to do on the Saturday this arrived, out of sheer curiosity I might have spent three or four hours going to see the property. And I might well have been swayed to go on another day by the very compelling PS 'Visit us between Monday to Friday and you will receive an extra bonus award valued at £150'.

I am quite sure a great many other people who are appropriate targets for this particular development will have done so. All because of the power of the offer.

AN OFFER HELPS YOU BEGIN THE LETTER

A chief benefit of the offer is that it makes it much easier for you to begin the letter. It is very easy to get people interested if you can start by saying: I am writing because I have something free for you. It can even help get the envelope open.

We were once selling something which sounds rather revolting but was in fact an excellent product for caterers: dried minced beef. The offer was nothing special: just a free sample. On the back of the envelope we wrote: 'Yours free, 2lb of dried minced beef worth £2.50 – just for reading this letter.'

I have placed at the end of this chapter a list, by no means exhaustive, of offers you can make. In fact, the limits to what you can offer are defined only by your imagination. And I earnestly counsel you to use that imagination to its fullest – certainly spend a lot more time thinking about offers than you do about the minutiae of the letter itself – how it is worded and so on.

To give you an indication why, let me give you another instance of how powerful the thought of getting something for nothing – even something of relatively little value – is to most people.

First, let us return to the letter mentioned in Chapter 6 with the RSVP envelope. It is illustrated on pages 105–7, and was designed to persuade people to take a Royal Viking Line World Cruise.

The offer in this case was one which, when proposed by my client, I thought was probably the least generous I have ever heard of and arguably crazy.

We were asking our readers to spend their own money making their way to Southampton so as to spend two or three hours on board a Royal Viking Line ship, with afternoon tea and a few free drinks, just to see what it was like. Obviously in many cases the offer was worth less than it cost to accept it.

The letter went to wealthy, sophisticated people. The list of prospects we had built up through advertisements, we discovered, contained an unusual proportion of people who actually had titles – Sir this and Lady that. About 6 per cent. You may think such people are above being seduced by incentives.

I had so little confidence in the offer that I did not even tell people exactly what it was in the letter. None the less, we got an encouragingly high response. Even in the follow-up letter to those who replied which did introduce it, I did not say exactly what it was until towards the end.

The response was so great we had to arrange not one but three afternoons. And some people took the trouble to drive down from Scotland to take advantage of it.

So don't be worried that rich, sophisticated people don't fall for offers. They do.

WHEN DON'T YOU NEED OFFERS?

Since I have said so much in praise of the offer, should you blindly assume *every* letter has to have an offer? Not necessarily. Sometimes you simply can't come up with one that's relevant. Sometimes it may not even seem appropriate to make an offer.

ROYAL VIKING LINE

NUFFIELD HOUSE, 41/46 PICCADILLY, LONDON W1V 9AJ
Telephone: 01-734 0773   Telex: 267823 ROYVIK

Dear Reader,

I am sure that you, like me, are often assailed by people making "limited" offers of "unique" experiences: which is why I had quite a problem when I sat down to compose this letter to you.

You see, I do have a unique experience to propose...one which indeed will be limited to very few people. In fact only seven hundred will be able to join us on our 1985 World Cruise. Fewer still will stay for the entire cruise.

I'm writing to you myself, because although - as I hope our previous letters have shown - we're proud of everything we do at Royal Viking Line, the World Cruise really is rather special. So special, we do not even operate it every year.

> As you can imagine, a cruise lasting 99 magical days,
> visiting many of the most desirable and exotic spots
> on earth ... in a style which most people have either
> long forgotten or will never experience ... is not
> inexpensive.

The lowest price for the entire cruise is £13,500. This alone limits the numbers - as does the time you need to take. Such an investment requires careful thought (and if you are interested, I will send you a modest "special offer" which may help you make your decision.)

Yet I hope, in the brief space allowed here, to give you some idea why some of our most valued clients not only think the investment worth while: they come back, time and again, to enjoy these cruises.

Even if you think you may not be able to join us for the entire cruise, or perhaps you may have to come on a later cruise, let me tempt you a moment with some of the rare pleasures you will enjoy.

In just 99 days you'll touch 30 of the most enticing points on the globe, each as different as the last. Hardly will you have recovered from the fascination of one country, than you'll be overwhelmed by another.

> Your days overflow with new experiences, exotic
> contrasts. As you slowly circle the globe, you
> encounter unfamiliar creeds ... you're challenged
> by strange beliefs ... explore relics of ancient
> civilisations. You see a prodigious variety of

Please read on ...

An offer helps you begin the letter.

art and architecture ... spanning six continents,
centuries of history, many different races and
cultures.

Accept the hospitality of proud Maoris: be enchanted by graceful
Thai dancers. Bargain with traders in Egyptian bazaars. Watch the
exotic fish of the Pacific, the beautiful birds of Asia and the great
elephants of India. Travel in Chinese junks, Australian helicopters,
Spanish mules ... and after each experience retire to the haven of
the Royal Viking Sky, to relax and gently absorb the events of the day.

Throughout the entire cruise you'll enjoy the unique "World
Class" style which has won the coveted Five Star Plus accolade for our
<u>entire</u> fleet.

I know that many of our special touches have already been
mentioned to you: the extra spaciousness, the high ratio of staff to
passengers, our splendid window-walled dining rooms, with their immaculate
service through one leisurely sitting at meals.

So when I started writing to you, I wondered: what else can I add?
The truth is, our service is built up from thousands of details. For
instance, our ships are cleaned throughout - not only your stateroom,
but the carpets outside - not just once, or twice, as in a 5 star hotel,
but three times.

It is practical details like that which assure a more comfortable
life. But they hardly set you dreaming of pleasures to come! So I
thought perhaps I should emphasise one <u>intangible</u> point.

To us, the World Cruise is the <u>summit of our achievement</u>.
The buzz of anticipation you experience when any of our
ships leaves port has a new note of intensity on the
World Cruise. Everything has a heightened excitement
throughout those marvellous 99 days aboard.

From the Concorde flight to join the ship in Fort
Lauderdale, Florida ... to the Grand Ball at the Grosvenor
House in London at its close ... on this cruise, our skills
are brought to their highest pitch. I can't find a better
way of putting it.

But in the end, it all comes down to one decision: should you make
the investment? (I say "investment", because at this level, it is not
a mere purchase).

To answer that, may I ask you a question?

Of all the holidays you have ever enjoyed, which was the most
memorable?

Although we have never met, I will hazard a guess. It was probably
the <u>first</u>. The first time you tasted the thrill of new experiences; of
strange, unfamiliar places. It is this which draws one to travel, isn't
it?

And that is why I think you should consider investing in a World

Please read on ...

Cruise with us. It is unique. With the same money, quite frankly, you could buy a new motor car. Another "thing". But not another experience.

And what I am proposing to you is a new experience. A kaleidoscope of new cities, new cultures, new faces. Wonderful opportunities to build new friendships with like-minded companions (friendships that often last for years ... maybe for the rest of your life.)

In short, our Grand World Cruise offers you a unique experience: one which will become a golden memory.

The decision to take the cruise is obviously one you'll want to mull over, which is why I've written you this preliminary letter. If you return the enclosed invitation, I will arrange for our 34-page full-colour World Cruise brochure to be sent to you.

If you – like me – have reached the point in life where other experiences begin to pall – when you insist on nothing less than the best – I commend this cruise to you.

Just return the reply paid card now for full details of all the destinations and options available. I hope you'll be able to join the "fortunate seven hundred" on this splendid adventure!

Yours sincerely,

Peter Robbins
Sales & Marketing Director

P.S. With your brochure I'll send news of an appealing "special offer" that may help you make up your mind, if you have a day to spare.

If you have a product that is brand new and revolutionary, it is quite possible to sell it without any offer because you are in the first stage of the market, discussed in Chapter 3.

Even then under these circumstances an offer should accelerate the speed with which you gain sales. And even in later, more competitive stages of the market, if the letter is carefully thought through and well written you can succeed without any offer.

Often, too, a company may not like making offers. Remember one of the American Express letters I discussed in Chapter 6? The one encouraging people who had not responded previously to become American Express Gold Cardmembers? There was no particularly appealing offer available; indeed, American Express were never very keen on offers. They felt it devalued their brand.

Since all competitors were offering what had been, until then, our big benefit, in the form of an unsecured overdraft, I thought my approach had better simply draw attention to the competitive advantages of the Amex card. As I said, it worked surprisingly well.

In Chapter 10, where we discuss openings, a letter for a competitor of American Express, Visa, also succeeds without an offer.

IT PAYS TO SAY 'THANK YOU'

Your letters should say what you would say if you were there with the customer. For example, if a customer had bought something, you would say 'Thank you', and perhaps offer them a little gift… rather like a restaurant offering you complimentary liqueurs.

Ask yourself how often people you have done business with bother to write and say thank you. This practice was until recently quite rare in direct mail, but is gradually becoming more popular. This is not, I fear, because of an explosion of the social graces in commerce. It is because tests have shown it pays.

For instance, a few years ago research was conducted to find out what difference it made if you telephoned a customer after they had bought something, simply to express your thanks. The answer: sales went up dramatically over the six months following that call.

The authors of a simple, but very helpful book called *Write Language** (Camel Publishing, Sydney) tell how well this worked for two small businesses.

---

* Written by Alan Pease and Paul Dunn.

A take-away chicken store in Brisbane, Australia, advertised an offer of flowers to his customers at Christmas with the heading: 'Fancy getting a flower from a chicken store'. He got rid of 3000 in three days, and enjoyed record sales in the new year – usually a slack period.

The letter couldn't have been simpler. It just explained they had sent the flowers as a way of saying thank you for being a customer.

Another Australian business – a motor dealership – sent out a letter with a 50 dollar note attached to customers who had traded in their old cars. The letter explained that 'Your trade-in vehicle sold much quicker than expected so we saved ourselves a little money'. Which dealer do you suppose those customers went to first when they next looked for a car?

Sometimes an offer is, in effect, an 'advance' thank you. One example is where an IT firm sent us a bunch of flowers at our offices to get us to accept a second offer of a free service visit.

THE 'NEGATIVE' INCENTIVE

Another company I mention in these pages, The Franklin Mint, does not believe in making offers, because it conflicts with their proposition. They want to persuade you that it will be a privilege just to obtain one of their limited edition ornaments.

They do, however, often throw in splendid cases and display cabinets to their buyers. And once you have agreed to start collecting a particular set of statuettes or medallions over a period of months, you receive a very attractive offer if you'll agree to buy the whole lot immediately.

In any case, the very concept of a limited edition is, in way, the 'stick' to the 'carrot' of an offer; it's almost like a negative offer which works on the basis not that you will get something extra by replying, but that you will lose something by not doing so.

In my experience, limitations, such as statements that the reader must reply within a certain period, or that there are only so many of a particular item left, invariably work – often to a surprising degree.

To sum up this chapter: concentrate on the offer. It will do you a lot more good than fine writing; it will make it easier to start your letter – which is the most difficult part of your job – and it may even overcome bad writing.

Study the list that follows this chapter. During the time you are marshalling your thoughts before actually writing, half an hour spent looking through it should stimulate your thinking.

HOW A GOOD OFFER MAY SAVE A STINKER OF A LETTER

I would hate you to think that I spend every evening and most of my weekends musing rapturously over good letters or cursing sulphurously over bad ones. However, there are a few examples that have given me pleasure over the years – as many of them bad as good.

One favourite was sent to my neighbour a few years ago. A successful lawyer, he probably received quite a lot of direct mail, but this piece, with a cheque pinned to the top, made out to him but not signed, certainly got his attention – so much so that he showed it to me.

Take a look at it on pages 111–12 and see what you think. Then read my comments.

If this letter succeeds, it will have been despite the gallant endeavours of the writer, since both style and construction are a priceless exercise in conceited fatuity. The opening is devoted to what can most politely be described as self-regarding prattle.

It is about the writer, not the reader. The writer assumes everybody is, firstly, interested in the success or otherwise of his marketing programme. And, secondly, that they will be amused by the whimsical way he explains it. It is thoroughly bad. As you go through this book you will see a number of other reasons why this is so.

But the offer is splendid. It simply says that he will happily pay you £25 if after seeing him you think it has all been a waste of your time. This offer, personalized and displayed in a way impossible to miss was sufficient to attract the attention of anyone interested in themselves and money – ie most of the population. Certainly nothing else in the letter could have done.

Such an offer depends upon two things for its success. First, the product has to be good and well presented. Second, the value of the business gained has to be sufficient to offset the possibility of a very small percentage of those who see the presentation being disappointed.

Here are some other points to consider about this letter.

1. Nine times out of ten, it pays you to feature your offer either at the beginning or very near the beginning of the letter. The unanswered question in the prospect's mind on receiving this letter is unquestionably: 'What is this cheque doing here?'
2. Make sure you always answer, pretty quickly, any question you have aroused. Otherwise the reader will feel cheated and quickly

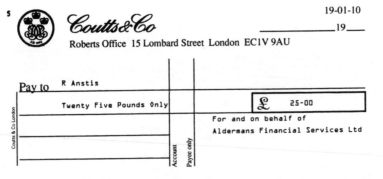

19-01-10
_____19___

Coutts&Co
Roberts Office 15 Lombard Street London EC1V 9AU

5

Pay to   R Anstis

Twenty Five Pounds Only

£   25-00

For and on behalf of
Aldermans Financial Services Ltd

Coutts & Co London

Account   Payee only

⑈⑈009071⑈⑈ 19⑈9999⑈0540411⑈ 10

Dear Mr. Anstis

The Parable of the Better Mousetrap

Some while ago, my colleagues and I identified a yawning gap in the
personal pensions market and set about filling it by devising a
"Better Mousetrap". Just over six years ago, the result of our
efforts was presented to an incredulous populace and, surprise,
surprise! not a single person beat a path to our door! Undeterred, we
went forth to demonstrate the benefits of our new approach and were
gratified to find that our ideas struck a sympathetic chord with a
high proportion of those who we were able to see.

The process has continued over the years and has now reached the
point where we have several hundred clients, many of whom have
substantially increased their investments placed through ourselves;
we have even had the odd person or two stray to our door! However, we
have lately found it vastly more difficult (and expensive) to put
forward our case, because the market has been flooded with competing
"Mousetraps", all purporting to be "Better", so that our message has
been submerged in the general clamour. We have found this
particularly frustrating because

(a)   the competing products are, in the vast majority of cases,
      merely facelifts and contain few really significant
      improvements;
(b)   the results achieved by our approach have bettered by a
      substantial margin our earlier targets and
(c)   we have introduced a further complementary approach with even
      higher growth targets, whilst sticking to our principle of <u>very
      high security</u>.

We are therefore driven to the conclusion that the only way forward
is to adopt a more direct approach which implies the presentation of
our case from the very beginning on an individual, face-to-face,
basis; it is only in this way that one can hope to deal with the host
of half-truths and over-simplifications which surround this subject.
But I am well aware that time is the professional person's single
most valuable commodity and that you would probably be unwilling to
grant me a meeting merely on the basis of what I have been able to
cover in this letter and so, to make the case for a meeting virtually
irresistible, I propose the following:-

Cont...

How an offer saved a bad letter.

(a)   I am enclosing a reprint of part of an article I have
      contributed to the Law Society's "Gazette", in the hope that
      you may find it contains the germs of an idea or two which you
      might wish to explore further.

(b)   Should you fail to agree within 20 minutes that your present
      arrangements could be diversified to your greater advantage, I
      will sign the enclosed cheque by way of compensation for your
      time and depart.

I should very much welcome the opportunity of a "meeting of minds"
and so I shall shortly call you by telephone in order to find out
when the brief exploratory meeting I propose would be most
appropriate.

                                        Yours sincerely

                                        R W R Round
                                        <u>For P E P C</u>

RWRRijbl

P.S. Partners in over 120 law firms have already taken advantage of
our services - why not you?

turn off. Here the writer perversely refuses to mention the cheque until right at the end of the letter. So, at a stroke, he manages to do two things wrong. But he is not satisfied with this promising start.

3. Because then we have a first paragraph so long that getting through it feels like walking through treacle. Particularly because it consists of a facetious recital of the writer's marketing efforts, which may be of consuming interest to him and his immediate family, but cannot be of any interest whatsoever to the reader, and certainly have no relevance to the purpose of the letter, which is simply to get an appointment.

4. The poor reader's interests, which should be paramount, do not begin to emerge until near the bottom of the first page, when, just as he is about to sink apathetically into a coma, he sees the word 'you'. 'Ah, there *is* something here for me' he cries. But we are underestimating our writer's incompetence. Because we then have to keep going until we get to the point at the end of the letter.

5. What provides the perfect grace note to this letter is the fact that the end – the PS – is fine. Indeed, it is touching to see how the whole effort gets better as it goes along. I have long wanted to know whether it worked or not, because the offer is so well-conceived.

So, how should this letter have been written?

Well, given such a good offer, it is very easy to write a good letter. It could have opened:

```
Dear So and So

As you can see, I have made out a cheque for £25 to you and
stapled it to the top of this letter. My purpose is simple. I
want to draw your attention to a remarkable new pension scheme
we have developed specially for the legal profession.

You may think the claims I shall make for this scheme extrava-
gant — which I will quite understand. That is why I am prepared
to sign the cheque and hand it over to you without quibble if,
after listening to me explain what we have to offer, you think
I've wasted your time.

It's as simple as that. There are no strings attached; there's
no obligation to commit yourself to anything; just spare me
half an hour of your time.
```

> I think you'll find it's one of the most valuable half-hours
> you ever spend. I have good reason to believe this, because
> over 425 firms like yours have already signed up with us. Here
> are some of the reasons why: ...

Incidentally, someone who read the first edition of this book adapted
this idea for their direct marketing agency. They offered a sum of
money unconditionally and phoned up with a second offer – a free
trial of their skills. It worked.

SOME OFFERS THAT HAVE WORKED

- Free trial.
- Easy terms.
- Pay no interest – or less interest.
- Free gift whether you keep product or not.
- Sweepstakes entry.
- No deposit.
- Temporary price offer.
- Buy now – pay in a few months (eg pay for your Christmas gifts in January).
- Sale.
- Two for one: saying 'Buy one and get one free' usually works best.
- Six books for £1.
- End of stock close-out.
- Mystery gift.
- More than one gift.
- Discount or gift for quantity.
- Discount or gift for buying in a certain period.
- Double your money-back guarantee.
- We'll buy back from you after a certain period.

8

Desperate Beginnings

A man was beating a mule over the head with a plank. 'What
are you trying to get him to do?' someone asked. 'Nothing,'
he replied. 'I'm just trying to attract his attention.'

As you probably know, *Gulliver's Travels* was not an adventure story,
but a satire. In one part the Laputans fought a war over whether one
should cut off the rounded end of one's boiled egg or the more
pointed. This was Jonathan Swift's comment on the stupid reasons
why people kill each other; it remains relevant today.

The humble envelope has caused no wars, but surprisingly heated
discussions arise on whether it should bear a message. In much the
same way, the use of 'gimmicks' – devices to attract attention – seems
to polarize opinion. Some like them. Some hate them. In both cases,
the question is not whether these things are automatically right or
wrong; it is more complicated than that.

Those new to direct mail often imagine an envelope message puts
people off because it lets them know in advance that you want to sell
them something. However, you may recall that in the second paragraph of the introduction I mentioned a survey of the mailings which
have proved most enduringly successful in the US. Eighty-nine per
cent bear a message on the envelope.

My view has always been that you may conceal your intentions by putting nothing on the envelope, but the moment people are inside they will see what you are up to. You are merely postponing the fateful moment when people decide whether they are interested or not.

So what you do with that envelope can be critical. Indeed, most experts believe that, after the offer, the treatment of the envelope (and that does include, as I shall explain, doing nothing) will make the most difference. To you, the envelope may be nothing more than a necessary expense, because you have to send your letter out in something. Actually it gives you an opportunity.

The reason why is obvious. Just as you have to get through the shell to eat the egg, so you have to open the envelope to read the letter. You cannot ignore it; and something that is impossible to ignore can obviously play a big part in attracting the right sort of attention.

Moreover, since unless you gain attention you aren't likely to get readership, gimmicks are popular – and sometimes, but not always, very effective. So let's deal with these two matters of weighty controversy in turn.

WHICH PILE WILL YOUR LETTER BE IN?

In 1985, David Ogilvy sent me a direct mail course. I wondered whether this was a not so subtle way of telling me I should try harder or just to get rid of excess paper on his desk. Since he was an indefatigable self-improver, I imagine he had scanned it himself.

The course was written by an American called Gary Halbert (you will see one of his letters on page 126). He pointed out that each day's post is either consciously or subconsciously divided by the recipient into two piles. The 'A' pile and the 'B' pile.

The 'A' pile is those letters the recipient finds sufficiently interesting to open immediately and the 'B' pile, those set aside to be looked at later… or in some unlucky cases, never. You have to make sure your letter is on the 'A' pile. Gary Halbert has some interesting views on this, to which I shall come later.

Before going any further, let me remind you that as I pointed out earlier, and contrary to what you may think, a high percentage of direct mail is opened and read to some degree. In the case of consumers, the figures are, in Britain, around 49 per cent.

There is good reason to believe that figures understate the truth. That's because to most people *anything* that comes through the letterbox is classed as direct mail, whereas much (as I have suggested already) is unaddressed door-to-door material, usually pretty tatty and far more likely to be discarded without being read.

In the case of mail sent to business people, readership may even be higher, which surprises most people, including me. In research conducted for Rank Xerox, 73 per cent of European business people claimed to read *all* the mail they receive. (I admire their stamina.) Only 3 per cent claimed to read none. (I marvel at their stupidity.)

In America, around 50 per cent of business people said they actually *open* their own mail. These surveys are about eight years old, but I doubt habits have changed that much. Equally, though, I wonder whether some of the respondents were not professing a diligence they did not really possess.

Be that as it may, the purpose of the envelope is not merely to contain the letter, nor to get itself opened. It is to get your prospect in the right frame of mind even before starting on the contents.

MESSAGE OR NOT?

To my mind, those who say you should always have a message on the envelope are as foolish as those who say you never should.

The issue is, can you think of anything you could put on the envelope which is likely to make people put it on the 'A' pile rather than the 'B' pile? Which is likely to make them open the envelope more eagerly?

And, of course, one service the envelope message can render is to give some idea of the subject. If readers are interested, they're more likely to open; if they're not, they won't be irritated by opening the envelope only to find it's of no relevance. So a good envelope message can help eliminate junk.

The envelope can either be off-putting, pleasantly unobtrusive, eye catching or downright seductive. Even if there are no words on it, that envelope conveys some sort of message, obvious or subtle. So give plenty of thought to it.

How do you determine whether to use a particular message or not? First, ask yourself whether what you have in mind could do any harm. If the answer is no, ask if it could do any good. If the answer is yet, run it. So let's look at the effect of particular types of envelope.

TEN POINTERS ON ENVELOPES

1. You don't necessarily need a larger envelope than normal

I have rarely seen a larger envelope increase the response. To the contrary; and my experience is common. At one of my regular seminars for the UK Institute of Direct Marketing, a delegate writing to businesses told me she had repeatedly tested such envelopes against ordinary sizes. They always *reduced* results.

The reason for this seems obvious to me. Such an envelope gives away the fact that the contents are commercial. As I have noted above, this is not necessarily a bad thing; but it is if the envelope treatment is neither relevant to the content nor sufficiently involving to encourage interest.

2. However, an envelope of unusual size or shape can work

For example, an exceedingly small envelope. I have seen this used effectively for 'a small reminder'. Or a huge envelope. A mailing produced by my agency in London used this when launching a giant television screen. Or an envelope which is longer than usual, which was used to great effect for a legal insurance policy, because it was the shape of a legal document.

So a *different* size is not all that interesting in itself, but an *unusual* size may be. Make sure, though, that whatever you send will fit in people's letter boxes, and does not contravene Post Office regulations. One famous advertising agency lost a huge international client largely through ignoring the first of these points.

3. Colour can make a big difference

As far as I am aware, the least effective colour is brown, because it is cheap, and makes you look the same. Exceptions include where you want to appear cheap – ie you run a bargain basement or a charity. Charity donors hate to think you might be wasting their money.

Another exception is where you wish to suggest a quasi-official message. The *Reader's Digest* are rather good at this. Some people don't approve and think it a low trick. However, I think anything which is not really offensive but just an innocuous play to gain attention should not objected to. After all, any device which makes your direct mail work better makes you more efficient, which in turn keeps your costs down.

So, with the above exceptions, a white envelope will do better than a brown envelope. And in my experience, unless the colours are ghastly or inappropriate – as in bright pink for male sporting goods – brightly coloured envelopes tend to do better than white envelopes.

In one case I found that simply changing the envelope from white to yellow increased response 20 per cent.

4. What about the way your envelope – and letter – feel?

Paper manufacturers, for their own selfish reasons, have commissioned studies to find out what happens when you change the texture of the paper to make it more interesting. And the answer is, yes, you've guessed it – response goes up. One fundraiser experienced a 17 per cent increase in replies; in one case in Germany, response went up by over 90 per cent.

In the past I have used envelopes with what looked like watermarks to add prestige. It seemed to work.

5. Little necessities that make a big difference

Some things you must do, whether you like it or not – like putting the name and address on the envelope. They are much more important than you think.

People spend more time looking at their names and addresses than anything else in a mailing (that's because many do little more than open the envelope, glance briefly at the contents and decide they're not interested enough to read any more). So the way in which the person's name and address appear is important. For example, you should always keep your prospect's address information up to date by having a prominent space for correction in your mailing: eg 'Have we got your name and address right? Please correct here if not.'

If it is quite clear from the application of a slightly askew sticky label that somebody has sent you an impersonal message, you are less inclined to pay attention to it than if it is neatly typed. A window envelope or a closed-face, with the name and address carefully typed on, just like a personal letter, both look good, though the former may make readers feel they are getting a bill.

The Royal Mail allows you to use any one of a number of designs of the postal 'indicia' – an attractive and appealing one will attract more attention, and produce a more favourable reaction than one which is not. A proper stamp will do even better – though when mailing in large volumes this is not often practical, and generally too costly to pay.

6. The simplest message is your company's name

If people already do business with you and are happy, your company's name should encourage them to open the envelope. If you are a bank or somebody from whom they are used to receiving information they simply cannot ignore, this should also encourage them to open the envelope.

However, when I receive messages from my bank which are not important to me, but merely attempt to sell me something I'm not interested in, or do so badly, what a waste of time. Worse: I am irritated. One example is shown from my bank in Chapter 11. (This bears on an issue that is not the subject of this book but very important: having a database which contains sufficient information about your customers and prospects for you to be able to write to them about the right things at the right times.)

7. When not to reveal the name

One occasion on which you might consider not putting your company's name on the envelope is where you have written to people several times before and they have not responded.

Quite clearly there is a very high chance they are not interested in what you are offering. You therefore have to find some different argument with which to beguile them. It might be wise not to reveal who you are to start with. You may even choose to camouflage your identity to some degree inside the envelope. I shall say a little more on these lines later, when talking about letterheads.

8. Don't reveal the full story

This is primarily a book about how to write letters, so I will not go too deeply into the gentle art of writing a good envelope message, save to say that whatever that message is, it should not give the complete game away. Because if people know the entire story before they open the envelope, why should they bother?

A wonderful example of doing it right was a mailing a few years ago designed to sell cookery books. It gave the beginning of a recipe on the envelope. People obviously had to open the envelope to get the rest of it.

9. Remember, an envelope has two sides

Use both if you can. You can't guarantee which will be seen first.

10. Other messages

If the message is to be more than your company name, then the options are countless. For instance, an Italian company put Disney cartoon figures on an envelope and lifted response to their mailings by about 50 per cent.

In Chapter 7, when talking about offers, I mentioned the mailing sent out by my agency a few years ago to introduce a new catering product which said on the reverse flap of the envelope that there was a free gift 'just for reading this letter'. It was very successful.

I also mentioned the company that offered a pair of garden secateurs. When they illustrated these and guaranteed their quality on the envelope their response went up by 27 per cent. Had they given them a value, they would have done even better.

The *Reader's Digest* a few years ago sent out mailings announcing a future offer which looked just like the sort of envelopes people used to receive their wages in. You can be sure they got opened in a hurry.

In short, there are endless little wheezes you can employ to encourage people to open the envelope. Putting bulky objects inside – things that arouse curiosity – always commands attention. Cheap little pens to use when replying work for charities. Stickers which show through windows in the envelope also lift response – especially gold ones. The same applies to seals on the back.

Your own ingenuity and the relevance of what you do place the only limits on the possibilities. The envelopes shown in the following pages are good examples.

WHY GIMMICKS OFTEN WORK

As I have observed, the subject of gimmicks gets some people hot under the collar. It is felt, particularly, that they don't work if you're writing to serious business people – that they're inappropriate.

This envelope for a book club is pretty well perfect. It uses cartoons – the most attention-getting type of illustration; it features the offer; it uses both sides of the envelope – and it doesn't reveal the whole story.

Envelope messages single out your message from the mass.

Nothing could be less true. A *relevant* gimmick will quickly get your letters on to the 'A' pile. This is even more true when talking to business people. Even if it is true that they read so much of what they receive, you still need something to get their attention. If it appears valuable, that is always useful. The secretary will be less inclined to throw it away.

Pioneers in the use of the gimmick were *Reader's Digest*, who started putting coins and stamps in their mailings over 40 years ago, using a number of plausible excuses. They use them to this day.

Anything to do with money is hard for readers to ignore. Postage stamps to pay the return postage; a note pinned to the top of the letter

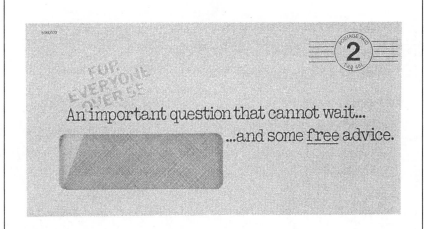

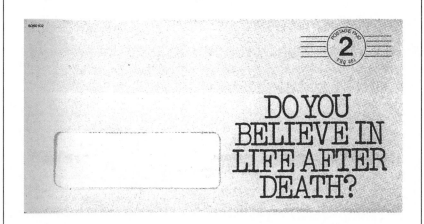

These two envelopes were tested against each other. Guess which did better.
(The answer is on page 73).

Envelope messages single out your message from the mass.

This envelope contained a mailing selling a philatelic product.
Simple, highly appropriate – and successful.

Envelope messages single out your message from the mass.

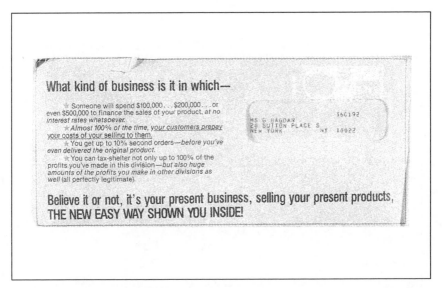

If you're entrepreneurial, you'll find it hard to ignore a message like this. It was written by Gene Schwartz who sold more books by post than anyone else.

– I gave you the example earlier of the Australian mailing that used a $50 note successfully.

The impact of cash is so great that this has even worked using worthless currencies from around the world. And of course, this sort of thing gives you an easy opening to your letter. On page 126 is the beginning to a mailing by Gary Halbert which used this approach. Despite its other shortcomings, as I said, I very much like the unsigned cheque for £25.00 on the letter from the financial adviser which I discussed earlier. We are talking about money and not only was this relevant to the subject, it also constituted the offer.

Copy of original letter

A gimmick can be very simple. For example, one trick I tried years ago was to send a second letter following the first, which consisted simply of a carbon copy with a note commenting that since the post was so unreliable, the recipient may not have read the earlier letter.

This letter used to get nearly half as many replies as the original. I am sure the same technique, suitably adapted for the times, would work today.

Make sure that whatever device you use relates to the benefit or the feature of the product, or failing that, the theme of the mailing itself.

Dear Mr. Hobday,

As you can see, I have attached a nice, crisp $1.00 bill to the top of this letter. Why have I done this? Actually, there are two reasons:

1. I have something very important to tell you and I needed some way to <u>make</u> <u>sure</u> this letter would catch your attention.

2. And secondly, since the message in this letter can quickly double or even triple your income, I thought using a dollar bill as an "eyecatcher" was especially appropriate.

Here's why I'm writing: Apparently, you've got a friend out there who respects you and... respects you a <u>lot</u>. How do I know this? That's easy. You see, your friend Peter Allen gifted you with a six-month trial subscription to my newsletter which is cleverly named... *The Gary Halbert Letter.*

What's the big deal about you getting a gift subscription to my newsletter? Well, for one thing, I never discount my newsletter (it's $195.00 per year) and I never send out sample issues. For another, my newsletter has probably helped more people become multi-millionaires than any other publication on earth. Every time you receive one of my letters, it will be like getting your hands on a secret weapon. You're going to get so much inside info on new ways to make money, it will probably make you dizzy. Here's a <u>small</u> sample of just a few of the inside secrets revealed in my newsletters:

(go to page 2)

Gary Halbert's excellent use of a dollar bill.

Some years ago a very successful mailing to financial people in Norway asking them to consider investing in a company, incorporated a little sprung plastic frog which leapt out of the envelope when it was opened.

You may find it surprising, but this little device worked when a whole series of more conventional mailings had failed. As I said before, though, the gimmick must be relevant. In this instance, the readers were being told to 'Hop to it' or they would miss a good opportunity.

Property developers have used scale models of multi-million dollar building projects to let them. Mailings to architects incorporating brochures laid out in the form of blueprints have done well for, among others, Polaroid. Mailings with pieces inside which pop up often work, too!

CAN YOU DEMONSTRATE THE PRODUCT?

On page 128 is the beginning of a letter I wrote some years ago to sell a fire-proofing treatment. The treatment retarded fire if wood or paper were soaked in it.

I had the paper treated with the product. Then I had it stacked up, and the top of each letterhead burned with a blow torch. I invited the recipient to set fire to the bottom of the letter and see what happened, thus demonstrating the product.

Notice the difference here between what the feature of the product was, and the benefit to the reader. The feature was that it simply stopped things burning. But the benefit to those I was writing to – who were people in the timber business – was, I considered, financial.

That is why the heading says 'How a little arson can improve your sales and profits'. As you see, I pointed out that nowadays, if you want to succeed in business, you have to add value. And one good way to do this at a time when fire regulations were getting a great deal stricter was simply to have their timber fire-proofed.

In this way they could charge more and so make greater profits, which was a very appealing argument, especially when backed up by knowledgeable references to the new regulations and to recent tragedies.

Despite not being personalized, the letter – which was designed to get leads for salesmen – was so successful it was then used as an insert in some publications.

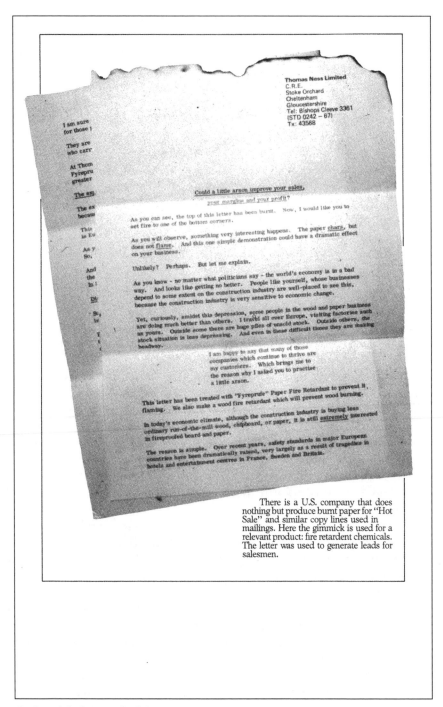

There is a U.S. company that does nothing but produce burnt paper for "Hot Sale" and similar copy lines used in mailings. Here the gimmick is used for a relevant product: fire retardent chemicals. The letter was used to generate leads for salesmen.

A gimmick that worked for me.

Any device which allows the reader to try out the product or illustrates the point you are making can be a good idea.

A company selling stain-proof carpet simply sent the piece of carpet along with the letter and asked people to subject it to various forms of maltreatment, which in itself would demonstrate the product.

Another company wanted to communicate the beneficial effects you get from using plastic cards like credit cards when you have them show through the envelope of your mailing.

Such cards are seen by readers as having some value and, being personalized, attract attention. The company's mailing to me showed such a card showing through a cut-out in the envelope.

They claimed one of these cards could increase response by as much as 50 per cent. I have no reason to disbelieve them. The mailing got my attention and I already know from a test conducted by my own agency some years ago that there was a significant increase in replies when we used one of these cards.

A FLYING LETTER

I mentioned David Ogilvy earlier in this chapter; so it seems a good idea to end with him. I saw him recount in London some years ago how Ogilvy and Mather in New York helped Cessna, the aeroplane manufacturers, sell their expensive executive jets.

The solution was three extremely gimmicky mailings. The first consisted of a carrier pigeon which was delivered to wealthy executives – millionaires and the like – with a suggestion that if they wished to try the jet out, they simply had to free the bird.

Follow-up mailings included a record to show how quiet the jet was (it was called the Whisper Jet) and a set of little plastic barrels to demonstrate how economical it was compared with competitors.

David Ogilvy stated, with a commendably straight face, that many of the pigeons sent out in the first mailing never came back because 'some of those mean bastards cooked and ate the birds.'

But be careful. One of my friends was about to try it in Thailand. His boss, a Thai, told him the prospective clients would definitely eat them. I do know that the same device had been used previously in New Zealand, and has been used since in South America; the moral being, if you see a good idea that might work for you, steal it.

9

The Right Approach

'A man may write at any time, if he will set himself doggedly to it.'

Dr Johnson

In his best book, *My Early Life*, Winston Churchill told how he coped with the Latin paper he had to take as part of the Common Entrance exam to Harrow School.

Young Winston was not academic. He spent most of the time staring miserably at the first question, getting only so far as to write the word 'Latin', followed by the number '1', and two ink splodges. I remembered this story when faced with the Latin paper at the end of my first year at university.

I hated Latin. More to the point, I had studied little during a year devoted to carousal and all-round sloth. For no good reason I recall, I translated the beginning of the paper into Spanish (I was better at that), then went home.

Everybody knows the worst moment one faces when writing is the beginning. Staring at that blank piece of paper or, nowadays, that blank screen. In fact, I spent two hours playing about with chapters I had already finished so as to put off starting this one. (Winston Churchill, by the way, had an advantage: his father was chancellor of the exchequer. He got into Harrow. My father ran a pub. I did not stay at Manchester University.)

How do you make it easier to begin? I have told you some of the secrets already. You brief yourself fully so that you know as much as possible about what you are selling and to whom. You understand the nature of the relationship between you and the reader. You think about the context of the message – when it is going out and why. You reflect upon possible reasons why your reader might want to do what you wish.

You spend time thinking up offers that might interest your prospect. These you know will help gain attention and get the reply. You consider the envelope message; you wonder whether some device might help gain attention.

Now, to the letter itself. There are two parts to writing: what you want to say; and how you want to say it. The first – the content – is more important than the second – the method. You will do better saying the right thing in the wrong way than the other way round. Also, once you have determined what to say, it's much easier to work out the words themselves.

This is a good time for you to bear in mind the 'W' questions I listed in Chapter 5: **WHAT, WHO, WHY, WHEN** and **WHERE**. You could do worse than have them pinned up in front of you when you start to write.

QUESTIONS IN THE READER'S MIND

As we have seen, the letter may well not be the beginning of your message. If you have an envelope message or a gimmick, these have already communicated something to the reader, however vague. If this is so, then the opening of the letter ought to follow logically on.

Fairly quickly, the opening should answer the implicit question in the reader's mind: why did you put that on the envelope? What's that gimmick all about? What exactly is that offer you mentioned? Other questions will come into the reader's mind when they receive your letter, which I shall deal with in a moment. First, let's look at what kinds of opening are most likely to attract attention.

Remember the letter with the cheque on it? Immediately the reader wants to know: what's this cheque doing with my name on it? That letter failed to answer the question. This is confusing. Your letter should quickly keep any 'promises' you have made previously.

An example of a perfect sequence is shown on pages 133–36. It is the letter and questionnaire written by Bill Jayme to sell a magazine called *Psychology Today*. The envelope line read:

'Do you close the bathroom door even when you're the only one home?'

GIVE THE READER SOMETHING QUICKLY

There are many, many ways to open a letter, as we shall see. But however you choose to start, either right at the beginning or very close, you should be *giving* the reader something; some reward in exchange for reading on.

This is not my opinion. It is based upon research.

In the 1930s and 1940s John Caples, whom I have already mentioned, spent years trying to find out what makes people start reading advertisements. He did this by conducting a number of carefully controlled tests, inserting advertisements alternately to discover which pulled the most replies.

He discovered the differences between advertisements that failed and those that succeeded were so great that general principles could be deduced.

The headings most likely to work promised the reader some advantage or benefit. The second best featured some news of interest to the reader. The third best appealed to curiosity; but these were far less effective than the first two types. Then there was, of course, the great mass of advertisements which – as any newspaper reader knows – aim at nothing in particular and hit their mark.

As we have learned, a sales letter is an advertisement aimed at an individual. So it is natural that those ingredients – benefit, news and curiosity – are the ones which either individually or in combination make the best openings to your letters.

Your benefit can be of several kinds. It can be just the benefit that the product offers; or it can be the offer that you are making to induce people to start reading. It could be a psychological benefit, like a story, or flattery, or something less tangible which makes the reader feel good, like the joy of giving to charity. If you can manage all of these, so much the better.

If no appeal to the reader's self-interest appears in the early part of your letter, it is almost certain to fail. An American publication called *Who's Mailing What!* gives 'Axel Awards' to the most successful letters. They are named after Axel Andersson, a Swede who went to

psychology today

Portland Place, Boulder, Colorado 80302

Dear probationer:

It happened to a friend who's a teller in a bank on New York's lower East Side.

The woman in the black babushka approached his window, her smile radiating gold teeth, and presented a savings passbook only slightly less worn than her face. She wanted to withdraw twenty dollars.

Our friend counted out two tens, but the woman pushed the bills back. "Is not my money," she said. "My money is fi' dollar size."

Experienced at meeting all kinds, our friend grasped the situation immediately. He replaced the two tens with four fives, and the woman went happily on her way. To her, a bank is a place where they put your money in a drawer. When you want it, they give it·back. Since she had always deposited fives, those tens belonged to somebody else ...

... and the point of our story is this. You never really know what's inside people's heads until you have occasion to dig around.

We publish Psychology Today, which is all about people's heads. And we'd like to send you a complimentary copy. But before we do, we'd like permission to dig around a bit in your head. To find out what sort of person you are. To get some idea of whether our magazine is a journal you'll really enjoy.

And so, on the next two pages, you'll find a short psychological quiz. On the last page, you'll get the interpretation. Got a moment now? Feel in the mood? Don't mind? Then take up the enclosed pencil ...

... and GO:

A famous letter written by Bill Jayme. Note the clever salutation. Did it make any difference? We discuss this subject later.

From the Editors of Psychology Today
A COMPATIBILITY TEST
to help determine whether you'll find·
our magazine a bore or a boon

	Yes	No
1. When stopping to talk to someone on the street, do you remove your sunglasses?	☐	☐
2. Do you prefer to do your own gift-wrapping instead of using the store's?	☐	☐
3. Have you ever changed your style of handwriting?	☐	☐
4. Do you think nothing of throwing out wilted flowers, but hesitate to discard a plant past its prime?	☐	☐
5. After giving a party, do you mentally keep track of who phones to thank you and who doesn't?	☐	☐
6. Do you often have a desire to be alone, to pursue your own interest and thoughts?	☐	☐
7. When washing windows, do you do the outside first?	☐	☐
8. Are you careful to glue stamps on envelopes right side up?	☐	☐
9. Are you pleased when someone turns up at the party wearing the same thing as you?	☐	☐
10. Have you changed your affiliation from the religion of your childhood?	☐	☐
11. Do you ask other people's children to call you by your first name?	☐	☐
12. Male or female—have you ever changed your hair color? . . .	☐	☐
13. Do you ever go to the movies alone?	☐	☐
14. After you've finished reading the paper, do you put it back together again?	☐	☐
15. Do you, when instructed, write your account number on your check when paying bills?	☐	☐
16. If or when you wear pajamas, do you tuck in the top? . . .	☐	☐
17. Do you turn your dinner plate so the meat faces you? . . .	☐	☐
18. Without looking, can you reel off your social security number?	☐	☐
19. Do you often tell jokes at parties?	☐	☐
20. Do you keep a list of people to whom you send Christmas cards?	☐	☐
21. Do you give your teeth a good scrubbing before you go to the dentist?	☐	☐
22. When the teller has already counted your money twice, do you forego counting it a third time yourself?	☐	☐
23. Do you habitually tip bartenders?	☐	☐

	Yes	No
24. Do you feel awkward talking on the telephone when you're naked?	☐	☐
25. When parking parallel, do you back in whenever possible?	☐	☐
26. Have you ever seriously considered changing your name?	☐	☐
27. When giving a party, do you have a drink before the guests arrive?	☐	☐
28. When the tableware is simply dumped down in front of you, do you place the knife, fork and spoon where they belong?	☐	☐
29. Must all closet doors and dresser drawers in your bedroom be closed before you go to sleep?	☐	☐
30. When using book matches, do you tear out each match in order?	☐	☐
31. When lunching or dining by yourself at home, do you bother to set a place?	☐	☐
32. Do you set out your clothes for the morning the night before?	☐	☐
33. Do you feel guilt when you go to the movies in the daytime?	☐	☐
34. Can you remember what you were wearing the day before last?	☐	☐
35. At the end of a meal in a restaurant, do you re-fold your napkin?	☐	☐
36. Do you usually try to arrive at appointments ahead of time?	☐	☐
37. If it's the last one on the plate, do you hesitate to take it?	☐	☐
38. When leaving a theatre, do you fold up your seat?	☐	☐
39. Are you a collector?	☐	☐
40. Is the fruit you take the one that's just about to go bad?	☐	☐
41. When filling out an application, do you try to answer all questions?	☐	☐
42. Do you close the bathroom door, even when you're the only one home?	☐	☐

```
End of quiz. Now turn
the page to see what's
been learned about you.
```

People love quizzes. They are all about their favourite subject – themselves.

Interpretation: Generally, the more questions you answered with "yes," the more you'll like Psychology Today. What we've learned is that you are somewhat adventuresome (changing hair color, religious affiliation). You're concerned about what others think (altering handwriting, doing your own gift-wrap, tipping bartenders.)

You're highly considerate of others (writing in your account number, folding up your theatre seat, arriving ahead of time, putting the newspaper back together.) You're practical (backing in, setting out tomorrow's clothes, eating the one that's about to go bad.)

In short, you're a person who's highly self-aware -- and that's good. Moreover, the fact that you allowed yourself to be tested shows that you're interested in learning more about yourself -- and that's what Psychology Today's all about, as you'll discover from leafing through the enclosed folder.

> A monthly magazine that's written for laymen as
> well as professionals in psychology. A magazine
> that's a triumph of graphics. A magazine that's
> as fascinating to read as the palm of your hand.
> And a magazine that can tell you more about yourself
> than the conversation when you've just left the room.

Our test also shows that you have a commendable sense of thrift (wanting to save the plant.) And our offer is made to order. Just place the token in the slot on the enclosed order card, place in the envelope and mail -- you'll get back

A COMPLIMENTARY COPY OF THE CURRENT ISSUE

You'll also be reserving the option to buy in at

HALF PRICE

Psychology Today is a dollar a copy -- $12 a year when bought on newsstands or by regular subscription. We'll bill you for only $6. And if you don't like the first issue, just write "Cancel" across the bill, and we're even-steven. You don't owe us a penny, and the sample issue is yours to keep.

"Oh, that you could turn your eyes towards the napes of your necks, and make but an interior survey of your good selves," said Shakespear's Menenius circa 1607. Oh Menenius, that thou wert alive now that we might send you our complimentary copy. What insights! What sapience! What <u>soul</u>!

> Cordially yours,
>
> *T George Harris*
>
> T George Harris
> Editor

TGH/dci

Germany and made a fortune through direct marketing, before retiring to the US where he now pursues his old career as something of a hobby.

He told me he had analysed all the letters that had won his award and the most effective approach was an appeal to greed, followed by flattery. A slightly depressing thought which tells us a lot about human nature. But it does not surprise me.

After all, we have already discovered that the offer is the most important element in a letter – and most offers appeal to greed, whilst flattery is a psychological benefit.

TWO VERY SUCCESSFUL OPENINGS

Here are the openings of two famous letters, one of which I have already mentioned.

'Quite frankly, the American Express Card is not for everyone.'

This is, of course, flattery, with the implied benefit that as an American Express Cardmember you are going to be superior to fellow mortals. This is followed up by other, more tangible benefits.

The other (shown on page 139) opens the text of a letter by Robert Collier, which immediately suggests one benefit – then follows up with others, taking you right the way to the inevitable conclusion. Collier, whose book I referred to in the Introduction, may well have been the best writer of letters to sell who ever lived.

You have to have a very good reason not to feature the offer or benefit – and preferably both – at the beginning or very near the beginning of a letter. There are two instances when you might not do so.

1. Because there isn't one

Remember the opening to the letter I wrote to sell the fire-proofing treatment? The heading combined the element of curiosity with the benefit by linking arson with more profits. But my client had, unfortunately, no offer to make.

2. The offer is weak

Look again at the letter I wrote for the Royal Viking Line on pages 105–07. They sold the most expensive cruises in the world. They thought strong offers would not fit their position – and they were probably right.

Moreover I didn't think their offer – for prospects to visit the ship at their own expense – would be very alluring to my wealthy prospects, so I aroused curiosity by promising something, but not saying what it was. I do not mention the offer until the middle of the first page, and nowhere do I reveal exactly what it is.

So I used the offer to encourage people to keep reading which, after all, is your prime objective. If you can't get them to read the letter, then unless the offer is so appealing that people rush thoughtlessly to fill in the order form with no persuasion at all (as in the *Time* magazine double postcard quoted earlier), you certainly are lost. In fact, I was clearly wrong about the offer, because this letter was so successful that, as I have already noted, we had to repeat the event.

MAKE IT 'NEWSY'

Virtually any letter you write can introduce an element of news, often in respect of the offer. It may not be a new offer, but if your readers haven't heard of it before, then it's news to them. Indeed, much of the information you weave into the fabric of a letter *should* be news to your readers – why should they keep on reading about something they already know?

For example, in the letter I quoted earlier asking people to leave money to Save the Children, I revealed that four out of five people don't leave a will at all. That certainly came as news to me and I suspect it was to most of those who read it. In such cases the effect on the readers is that they say 'Gosh, I didn't know that. I wonder if there's something else here that might interest me?'

One fine example came from Belgium. It combined benefit, curiosity and an unusual device. It was sent out following a telephone call to businesses with obsolescent Xerox machines.

The phone call simply said: 'Keep an eye on your post. In two days we'll have a pleasant surprise for you.' Two days later a box arrived with a letter and a stopwatch inside. The heading at the top of the letter said: 'Urgent: please reply before 1 o'clock today.' Another heading said: 'Get 1000 francs for every 5 minutes.'

The letter said: 'Here is the surprise we promised on the phone. It is a very good discount for you as a loyal customer if you buy a new machine. Just pick up the phone before 1 o'clock and order your new machine. We guarantee to deliver it by 6 o'clock; and for every 5 minutes we're late, we'll give you 1000 francs.

Over 50 per cent of readers bought new machines.

Dear Subscriber,

Would you risk $1 for the most effective collection letter we have ever seen, a letter that bought in 85% of all past-due money when every other appeal had failed?

Would you spend 16.50 cents each to get the six essential steps which a master salesman found most important in selling, or the plans which have proven most successful in job analysis, measurement of work, group bonus, and incentive systems?

If you would, then send the enclosed card for the first six issues of the new Journal of Modern Business Management. For it has taken on new life, new pep, new interest. You see, we are facing new conditions today. We've been in a rising market where circumstances made money for many people who could never have made it for themselves.

That's past. It's going to take real ability, a thorough grasp of modern management methods to reach the top or stay there in the period now in front of us. Such inequalities as one manager getting only a third as much for his labour-dollar as another will not be tolerated. The man who cannot produce will go — the manager too!

The next few years will be hard on drones. They are going to be known as the 'levelling years' for they will bring down many a man who is now in a high place, and put the real workers in power — and by workers we mean not those who merely go through the motions, but those who produce!

In such a period, every man must look to himself, and we have set the example. The new magazine is different. It is more practical. It is, in effect, a continuous course in modern business management. It gives to the forward-looking executive the plans, the methods, the letters, the incentive he needs to meet the new competition of today.

Will you risk $1 to try it for six months? It doesn't matter if you have already taken it for the last six years — YOU NEED TO READ THIS NEW MAGAZINE! You'll miss an essential factor in your success if you don't! Will you risk $! on that?

The enclosed card is your answer. Will you send it now — today?

Sincerely,

WHAT ARE THEY THINKING?

A letter is paradoxically both intimate and intrusive. Something pushed through your letter box, with your name on it, is hard to ignore. So its opening may not require mighty fanfares as with the headline of an advertisement or the start of a television commercial.

Of course, we have already seen how a relevant device can work, but you can often achieve what you want by beginning in the same way as you would a conversation with someone; politely, quietly and confidentially, slowly building their interest to a greater and greater height as you go.

You don't have to be funny, clever or dramatic. You just have to make sure what you write is appropriate and follows a logical sequence, carefully responding to your reader's likely reactions.

Returning to the matter of questions in your reader's mind, I believe one difference between what works best for sales letters as opposed to advertisements may lie in the degree of curiosity. This is more important when getting people into your letter than in the case of an advertisement. One reason is that engendering curiosity is almost invariably a sound tactic on the envelope. The other lies in the context of the two types of message.

People rarely look at advertisements and say 'Why are they advertising?' The reason is usually apparent: to sell. But when they receive a letter, certain inevitable questions come up. First of all: 'Who are you? Why are you writing to *me*?'

This may seem so obvious, even trivial, that you may wonder why I bother to mention it. However, I assure you it is far from obvious to most people and paying attention to it will have a far from trivial effect on the results you get from your letters.

I have already suggested you should liken your letter to a personal meeting. The only reason you write is because you haven't got the time or the money to go round and speak in person. You believe that if you could, you could persuade them to do what you want or, at least, influence them favourably. Indeed, if you *don't* believe so, there is no point in writing at all.

WHO AND WHY?

When you speak to someone in person, the first thing they do is look at you. They want to see *who* you are. If they don't know, you have to tell them, otherwise they won't give you the time of day. If they're not sure who you are, you'd better remind them. And whether they know you or not, they want to know *why* you are talking to them.

You have to answer those questions. As I suggested above, this may sound obvious when I put it like that. But read through some of the letters you receive. A surprising number simply launch into a selling pitch with no attempt to answer either.

You may say such niceties are unnecessary in what is clearly not a genuinely personal, but a commercial letter. And certainly many letters succeed without them. However you will do better if you incorporate them.

I know this because a few years ago, during a speech in New York to some of my clients, I touched on this subject. One took the trouble to analyse a number of letters. On average, those that incorporated a proper explanation did markedly better than those that didn't. Around 20 per cent was the difference, as I recall.

Take a very artful opening – maybe the best I have ever seen – written by the American Ed McLean: 'If the list upon which I found your name is any indication, this is not the first, nor will it be the last letter you receive inviting you to subscribe to a publication...'

The writer answers the question 'Why are you writing to me?' by answering another question people have: where did you get my name? He says, in effect, I'm writing because your name is on a list. He also knows these people have received previous letters asking them to subscribe to magazines, because millions of such letters go out every year in America. This flatters the reader slightly and advances the argument a step further.

Do you recall the opening to the letter in Chapter 3, written to persuade American Express Cardmembers to become Gold Card-members? Notice how deceptively simple the opening is: it merely acknowledges the previous relationship – someone invited them to apply before, but they haven't replied.

So why write to them again? Because the market has changed; there are now similar cards available. Knowing this, I have considered how they might feel about what I am trying to sell and, based upon what I think, I have constructed an argument. This approach clearly was valid, since the letter did so much better than its predecessor.

WHAT IS THE RELATIONSHIP?

But never mind recognition, what else goes through your mind when you meet someone? You automatically register how *well* you know them. You recall how you first met them and what contact you've had with them – what previous discussions you have had. You summon up what you know about their likes and dislikes.

That's what enables two human beings to have a friendly conversation. And it's what enables you to write a good sales letter. You are trying to visualize what kind of person this is and take into account whatever you know about the previous relationship. This enables you to start talking about the right things, in the right way.

In real life, if somebody were a complete stranger, or you barely knew them, you would not talk to them as you would to someone you knew well. It would be much easier for you to broach a subject with a friend – you would have the advantage of knowing if they were likely to be interested.

Think about the letter with the burnt top on page 128. Well, here I certainly couldn't claim any previous relationship – this was a letter out of the blue to gain appointments for salespeople. But my reason for writing was fairly clear: I was going to tell them how they could improve their businesses; and in the letter I explained why I thought this should interest them.

If you look at the list of questions about understanding your prospect I gave you in your briefing checklist, you will see that they try to replicate all the information you might have if you knew someone – to whatever degree. We have written to this person before; how did they react? How often have we written? What has been the effect of previous communications? And so forth. These questions attempt to establish the nature of the relationship.

What you want to do is get in step with your reader. It's just as it would be in real life – except you don't have much time to spare. Say the wrong thing and your reader can simply stop reading. You're not there in person to persuade them not to.

So you have to get instantly on their wavelength. You consider not only what kind of person you are talking to, but also what concerns them. Not just what they are interested in generally, but what they might be interested in at the time you are talking to them. And how they feel about you.

PERMISSION TO SPEAK

There is a lot of waffle nowadays about 'permission marketing' and 'relationship management'. The principles behind both are not new. One of my colleagues has for years used the phrase 'permission to speak' when talking about how you approach a prospect. You have to have a legitimate excuse to start writing.

Turn again to the Royal Viking Line letter on pages 105–07. Here my argument to the readers was based upon the only thing I knew about them. They were almost certainly wealthy, perhaps even jaded; such people receive more direct mail than most; therefore it was pretty certain they had received lots of offers through the post. By sympathizing with them, I enlisted their interest.

I learnt a great deal about the importance of the previous relationship with a customer some years ago when I was working for the Franklin Mint.

The Franklin Mint more or less invented the idea of the instant collectible. Their founder realized human beings love collecting – but many don't know what to collect. This simple insight led him to build one of the world's most successful direct marketing businesses.

Much of their success derives not merely from their making – often in replica – beautiful things. It also lies in the fact that they very often try to give people some occasion which gives them an excuse to buy. A variation on what I was talking about above: why are you writing to me?

When I was a consultant to them, the most successful promotion I worked on offered a special medallion to commemorate the Silver Jubilee of Queen Elizabeth II. This unique event was widely celebrated, as you would expect, in Britain. There was an endless series of events, great press coverage, people held street parties: the whole nation was *en fête*.

Many people wanted something to commemorate this occasion. The medallion was one such example. This was a lesson to me: if you can just find an *occasion* that matters to your customer, and hang your story on it, you are likely to have a success.

WHEN IS A GOOD TIME?

Many effective letter openings revolve around timing. There is a mountain of examples to show this, which reaffirms the importance of one of our famous 'W' questions – *when* are you writing.

If you write at no particular time, you cannot know whether people are inclined to reply. But if you can make your suggestion timely, you are far more likely to do well. One example I have already touched upon is the Belgian restaurant with its Valentine's day dinner. It is quite appropriate to go a restaurant with your wife on that evening; so the letter makes sense.

Christmas, Easter, wedding anniversaries, all offer opportunities which are generally missed. I recall a delegate at one of my seminars mentioning his surprise that when he and his fiancée announced their engagement in a local paper, no local merchant had the sense to write to them, though they were obvious prospects for everything from housing to insurance.

The New Year is a good time to write – especially because in January direct mail gets its highest responses. In Chinese communities, you can add effectiveness to such a mailing because it is the custom for people to give each other money. Perfect for a financial offer.

Some timely approaches

Suppose somebody has been a customer for a year. You can capitalize on this easily by writing something like:

```
'Looking through my records the other day, I noticed that you
have now been a customer of ours for exactly one year.

We really appreciate your business. So to mark this anniver-
sary, and to express our appreciation, I have a rather special
offer for you.'
```

The offer, of course, would be based on their previous purchases. Let's say you sell furniture and they have bought bedroom furniture; you could offer a discount off kitchen furniture of the same design.

There are many other possibilities. Suppose they spend £20 on average each time they buy. Offer them a free gift on any purchase worth over £30.

If they have borrowed £2000 and are repaying promptly, offer an addition loan on favourable terms.

If they like detective novels, make them a special offer on the next Elmore Leonard book. You get the idea.

This, of course, is simply a way of saying 'thank you' – which, as I mentioned in Chapter 7 is extraordinarily effective.

An insurance company wrote a letter which simply had on the envelope: 'We have reviewed your policy…'

Inside, it explained that each year on the customer's birthday the company reviewed their policy just to make sure their insurance was still adequate.

	Scottish Widows
Head Office	PO Box 902
	15 Dalkeith Road
	Edinburgh EH16 5BU
Telephone	031-655 6000
Telex	72654 Widows G
Facsimile	031-662 4053

Dear Policyholder

Policy No 6673726/1-2   D C C BIRD

We are pleased to enclose your renewal statements for the above policy.

Page 2 is a statement of the contributions currently being paid (where applicable) and the benefits being provided, including illustrations of the possible benefits payable at retirement.

You may wish to consider improving the policy benefits. To help you reach a decision Page 3 provides an illustration of the benefits available from an increase in contributions. It is recommended that you discuss these with your Financial Adviser.

If your payment is not made by Banker's Order, please send a cheque together with the slip at the foot of Page 3. The slip should also be returned completed if you intend to alter the current level of premium.

Yours faithfully

Ian Sutherland

MR IAN SUTHERLAND
OB PENSIONS CLAIMS
TEL: 031-655-6426

PAGE 1

XOINTR/290492/02

How not to do it.

PERSONAL PENSION PLUS  **SCOTTISH WIDOWS**

ILLUSTRATION OF RETIREMENT BENEFITS FOR ADDITIONAL SINGLE CONTRIBUTION OF £1000

THE FIGURES BELOW WOULD APPLY IN ADDITION TO THOSE SHOWN ON THE PREVIOUS PAGE

Guaranteed *With Profits* Cash Fund at PPA   £   950.00

Illustrated Cash Fund at PPA   £   1070.00
(Not guaranteed, see separate sheet for notes on the illustration basis)

	Assumed rate of return per annum	
	8.00%	10.00%
Producing:—		
Pension (p.a.)	£ 104.00	£ 120.00
Or		
Maximum Cash Sum	£ 252.00	£ 283.00
plus		
Pension (p.a.)	£ 79.70	£ 88.70

......

PREMIUM NOTICE

Personal Pension Plus

Plan No 6673726/1-2

Name D C C BIRD

Renewal Date NOT APPLICABLE

Branch LWE

1   I wish to pay with effect from the renewal date shown a new total contribution of £
for Retirement Benefits, including the cost of Waiver of Contributions Benefit, where applicable.
(Minimum *Increase* £240 p.a. / £20 a month)
I wish to pay an additional single contribution of £
(Minimum £750).
I am interested in adding (further) Lump Sum Death Benefit cover of £
(Scottish Widows will advise you of the additional premium and what further evidence of health is required).

2 * Please collect the contributions under the mandate you hold.
   * I enclose a cheque for the contribution due.

3   I confirm I am still a qualifying individual.

4   Other instructions.

   * Delete as necessary.

Date   _____

Signed   _____

Return to :   SCOTTISH WIDOWS
15 DALKEITH ROAD
EDINBURGH
EH16 5BU

PAGE 3

This was much appreciated by the customers and very successful.

This concept can be developed further by relating offers to stages in a customer's life. Thus, for instance, a young married couple normally do not have a great deal of spare income.

They need all they can get to support themselves and their family early in their careers, for which reason, straight life insurance cover is usually the most they can afford.

However, as they get older, their income increases and they have more money to spare. What is more, they start to think a little bit more about the future. At that time it is probably a good idea to start approaching them about insurance policies which have an element of investment involved for the future.

Obviously, as they get older still the thought of retirement and whether they are going to be sufficiently equipped to cope with it become not merely of interest, but downright critical to them. Pension plans are an appropriate subject.

A good example of how not to do it is the letter an insurance company sent me, reproduced on pages 145–46 in which they guarantee to give me back *less* than I invested. But the principle, properly applied, can work for many businesses. A splendid example is a letter from Guy's Hospital, one of a sequence which I discuss in Chapter 16.

Older people also start worrying about what will happen when they die. A good instance of the relevance of this is the Save the Children letter we have already discussed (shown on pages 68–69).

So you will see that in the opening to your letter, just as in every other respect, the more you know about the people you are writing to, the better you will do. Do you have an excuse, based upon what you know, or what you can surmise, to talk to them?

Put that together with the knowledge you have about what you're selling and you are two-thirds of the way to success.

10

Write to Somebody, not Everybody

'Your message should single out your prospect like a man being paged in a crowded hotel lobby.'

Claude Hopkins

If you try to appeal to everybody, nobody listens. People ignore messages which have nothing for them personally.

Remember, you are not trying to persuade the whole world to reply to your letter, unless you're offering something free that everybody wants – in which case you don't need this book.

In most cases, if half your prospects replied you would be doing *spectacular* business… Often, if only 4 or 5 out of every 100 replied, you would be doing very well. (In fact, the average response rate to mailings in the UK is about 4 per cent. In the US, it is higher.)

You must, therefore, go hell for leather after the right people. Don't worry about those who are not interested. Why should you? You aren't suddenly going to change the way they think. Write to some-body who is, to some degree, likely to be interested and persuade them.

Divide your audience step by step, eliminating those who aren't appropriate at every stage.

Take the example of *Time* magazine in Chapter 1, when we were discussing the brief postcard mailings they did. As you saw, these were aimed only at certain people among the possible buyers – those people who not only knew the magazine but liked it.

As I pointed out, a different approach would be right for those who are fairly familiar with it, but can't decide whether they want it. And a different approach again for those who know little or nothing about it. But it would be a waste of time to people who don't like it at all or who simply don't read magazines.

Just as it is a waste of time and money to mail those unlikely to be interested, so it is a waste of words to talk to them even if, by chance, they do end up among those you mail. If your letter is well aimed, there shouldn't be too many of such people anyhow.

PICTURE YOUR READERS

So you are going to single out your prospects. Picture them in your mind. Imagine what they would be like if you met them personally.

What would be their hopes, their fears, their loves, their hates? What do you think they read, look at, think about, watch? Where do they go on holiday? What sort of friends do they have? How do they dress, behave and speak – using what sort of language? How much money have they? Are they keen on the opera or TV quiz shows?

And what are you going to start writing about? I hope you know that already. Something that links *you* and what you are proposing to *them*, and what you know about them – or think you do.

In this chapter we shall look into more ways of opening your letter, starting with two more examples where a particular event was very special to the reader, making a good opening possible.

The first is a letter I wrote, shown on pages 150–51, with the admirable aim of acquiring customers at birth. It was to reach mothers who had just had babies. In hospital they are given bags of samples of baby products and this letter was to be placed inside one of these bags.

This was an odd case, since the letters were not personalized. When my client explained what he had in mind I thought that writing an opening which was not at best tactless, and at worst in downright bad taste, would be very hard.

However, having been responsible in a minor way for three babies, it wasn't so difficult to put myself, in a surrogate way, in the place of

Oxford Life Assurance Company Limited
37/39 Great Marlborough Street, London W1V 1HA
Telephone 01-434-1465

Dear Parent,

  The arrival of a new baby is such an emotional time it can be difficult to think about the more practical needs of a family ... but I think you'll agree that nothing matters more than your baby's future protection.

  Of course most parents recognise that it makes good sense to provide adequate insurance cover for the whole family, but many of the schemes available can be confusing and are simply too expensive.

  That's why I think this is the right time to tell you about a plan which has been designed especially for young families to provide as much as £26,620 protection for less than £1 per week for young parents.

  May I give you a few reasons why I believe you ought to think about this special plan now.

- It's guaranteed to provide the best value for money currently available and if you can find and be accepted into a similar scheme offering better benefits at a lower cost within two months of joining we will refund your money in full.

- There is no red tape needed to join, just a simple application form which takes two minutes to complete.

  The figure I quoted is actually for a man aged up to 30 or a woman aged up to 34, but the value is just as good whatever your age. You're probably wondering how such low cost is possible ...

  The reason is simple. The plan is offered direct to you - no sales commissions, no insurance brokers to pay. And as I said, this plan has been specially set

Acquiring customers at birth.

up for young families (it includes a special inflation-fighting clause, so you stay properly protected over the years).

So you have nothing to lose by returning the attached enquiry card. There's no postage to pay and we will send full details to your home address so you can read about the plan at your leisure.

Of course you're not committed to go any further and you could be missing an opportunity to provide financial protection for your family at a very low cost.

I look forward to receiving your enquiry card.

Sincerely,

Ann Chivers

Ann Chivers
Administrator
Young Family Plans.

P.S. Please remember that this plan is only offered direct to you. No salesman will call, so you and your family will be the only judges of the plan's value. I look forward to receiving your enquiry card.

────────────── ◀DETACH HERE▶ ──────────────

The Young Families High Value Protection Plan

Information Card

Simply return this card, you will be sent full details about this Plan so that you can read more at your leisure. Under no circumstances will any sales representative or other person acting for Oxford Life call at your house nor are you obliged to continue further unless you wish.

Please write your name and home address below

Name _____

Address _____

_____

Now post this card in the pre-paid envelope provided

my prospects. The letter which I have reproduced on the previous pages does not look very pretty, but it worked extremely well, for many years.

Notice that I wrote to *both* parents. The letter may have been given to the mother; but such a decision would clearly be joint.

EMOTION MEANS OPPORTUNITY

Any situation filled with emotion can offer you an opportunity. Apparently, after marriage, death and divorce, moving home is the most traumatic experience we face. On page 153 is a letter I wrote some years ago to people who had just gone through that trauma.

They probably needed friends and money more than usual, which was as well, because I was trying to persuade them to become agents for a mail order company. The scheme, with which most people are familiar, was very simple. Agents got commission on everything they sold.

There wasn't any real competitive advantage; this was exactly what a number of other catalogues offered – including some put out by the same company with the same goods. Yet knowledge of the people I was writing to and their situation – *where* I was going to find them and *when* I was writing made the letter very successful.

Where was the mailing going? To a list of people who had recently moved home. I realized good mail order agents are usually gregarious.

So the letter I wrote suggested they could not only make more money, but make friends in their new neighbourhood. This is a normal desire in anyone moving into a new home – but particularly if they are naturally friendly.

The type of people I was writing to were ordinary folk, with no intellectual pretensions. (I had read some of the correspondence to the company.) So my style was carefully adapted to suit them. This is something I shall discuss when we come to the secrets of good writing.

That letter worked because it related the special benefits of the catalogue to the right sort of people. And that is all your letter has to do: put the benefits and the people together.

The Galleries
Millen Street
Preston PR5 4QR

How to make more money as you shop —
and make new friends around <u>Chalk Lane</u>

Dear <u>Miss Berger</u>

Hello. How are you enjoying life at <u>Number 18</u>? Let me tell you about an idea that could make (or save) you money as you shop ... help relatives and your family with their gift problems ... and even make friends for you amongst your new neighbours.

Frankly I am not familiar with <u>Barnet but at Ace Gifts and Cards</u> we have thousands of friends all over Britain and no matter where they live, their families and neighbours love our bright colourful catalogue.

You see, our super Christmas cards (from only 6p each) and clever gifts prove simply irresistible. You only have to show people your catalogue and they are keen to buy. And everything they buy saves you a big 23% commission plus a small delivery charge of 35p per order. <u>You also save 33% on the things you buy for yourself.</u>

Best of all you need send no money.

The opening of a letter which uses 'fun' personalization. Each underlined word or phrase was actually highlighted in yellow.

A UNIQUE GROUP

Sometimes, people are uniquely qualified for what you offer. Such a case stands out in my mind from my time with the Franklin Mint. I wrote to people in Italy who had collected the first three of a series of plates specially created by the Mint.

By looking at the information available we saw that there were very few people indeed in Italy who had *all* three plates. Not exactly a smash hit, if you'll excuse the pun. But this led to an opportunity. I was able to open my letter by saying:

> You are one of only 87 people in Italy who have all 3 of the plates in the Limited Edition series created by the famous artist so and so.
>
> Now, before we write to anyone else, you have the opportunity to acquire the fourth.

The flattering thought that they belonged to this unique subsection of humanity and would be among the privileged few who had *all* this collection was sufficient to galvanize virtually all of them to buy.

A FEW IDEAS TO GET YOU STARTED

From what I have already indicated the number of ways you can start a letter are almost unlimited and success is determined mainly by the context of the letter.

A respected American, Herschel Gordon Lewis, writes a monthly column in a magazine called *Direct Marketing*. One month he started listing the ways you could begin a letter, planning to give the grateful reader 50 suggestions. The subject was so vast and his imagination so fertile that he added another 50, then another 50 – and for all I know came up with even more.

It would be tiresome for you to have to go through an endless list of possibilities, so I'm going to content myself with 20 approaches that have been proved to work time and again. You will not be surprised to learn that they all revolve around the five Ws – Who, Why, What, Where, When.

You will also not be surprised to see that quite a few of the examples I give employ more than one of these approaches in the same letter. When you are reviewing letters you receive yourself, you will advance your skills by analysing the techniques used, particularly in the openings.

1. Simply announce the main benefit

A good example is the letter for the Amex Gold Card to introduce their card, featured earlier in this book. Nothing fancy, but it works.

2. Make an invitation

This is one of the most common forms of letter in private life... so not surprisingly it works commercially. Note, for instance, the RSVP approach on the Royal Viking Line letter, which incorporated an invitation card, and the British Telecom mailing.

3. Start with the offer

I've already said this, but don't forget: good offers make easy openings.

One letter offering life insurance for a limited period is on page 156. See how much it is based on the offer.

It did spectacularly well, producing a 10 per cent response where previous efforts had produced under 1 per cent. Although not all who responded kept the insurance, it was several times more effective.

The approach did well for three reasons: first, people like something for nothing – and this sounded like a lot; second, most people are under-insured, so it sounded sensible; third, most people are lazy. It was almost as easy to say 'Yes' as to say 'No'.

4. Give news

For instance, a decision by the bureaucrats of the European Commission implied that no business would be allowed to write to people without their prior permission. Another stated that nobody could ask for money for goods before delivering them.

To anyone in the direct marketing business, these decisions are of great interest, to say the least. A trade lobbying body could start a letter with something like: 'Did you realize that European Bureaucrats you never even voted for plan to close your business down? Now's your chance to do something about it'.

5. Address the reader as one of a group

The simplest examples are: 'As an old age pensioner; as an accountant; as a doctor etc.' It is dull but effective, requiring no imagination; a way of showing that 'I have taken the trouble to find out who you are' – weak flattery, I suppose.

The impact can be substantial. I have seen it double and triple response.

American Express Bank Ltd
American Express Financial Services
4 Shenton Way
Shing Kwan House
Singapore 0106
Tel: 226 2626

May 6, 1991

<u>The enclosed Certificate is active from today.</u>
<u>You are now covered for up to $400,000.</u>

Dear Cardmember,

The **<u>Cardmember Accident Protection Plan</u>** is now yours. It was designed exclusively for people on the go - and it covers you in the event of accidental loss of life or disability.

From today, you are covered for :

     o Up to $400,000 for accidents while you're travelling as a passenger on a public conveyance such as an airplane, train, bus, hovercraft, ferry or ship (this cover is ideal for people who travel a great deal - at home and overseas).

     o Up to $80,000 for accidents involving taxis, private vehicles and pedestrians (if your job or leisure activities keep you on the move, this plan keeps you covered as you continue with your daily activities).

     o Up to $40,000 for all other accidents (that's complete protection for you, 24 hours a day).

<u>But your protection runs out on June 5, 1991</u>
To enjoy this complimentary 30-day cover, all you have to do is to sign the Option Form attached to your enclosed Certificate, and return it to us by <u>June 5, 1991</u>. You will only be billed from June 6, 1991, for your continued coverage.

<u>For cover of up to $400,000 a day, you'll pay only $0.48 a day</u>
This value-for-money plan gives you high cover of up to $400,000 for accidents on public vehicles - at only $0.48 a day. This is <u>one of the highest</u> levels of cover you can receive for accidents involving public vehicles. You are also covered for up to $40,000 for all other accidents. And you'll be pleased to know that this Plan <u>pays in addition</u> to any other plans that you may have.

Amex Singapore slide

Nothing fancy, but it works.

To me, if the recipient is an accountant, he or she knows it all too well and it's worth finding a more interesting way of saying the same thing.

Insurance companies in particular have made a great deal of money from selecting specific groups: older people, non-smokers, careful drivers, union members. This success will not surprise you if you recall my emphasizing how aiming your letter well, at the right people, will do more than any amount of fine language.

To give you an idea of what I mean, some years ago, I wrote a highly effective letter to teachers. This is how it began:

> 'Were you aware that there is an insurance company which offers preferential terms exclusively to teachers and their families?'

Other good targets include shareholders, to whom you can offer special discounts. Few people are more inclined to buy from you than those who have already shown the most earnest commitment of all to your company: investing in it. Some far-sighted companies send out a pack of their products to new shareholders. It is an appreciated 'thank-you' and a reminder of what to buy in their own interest.

The argument here is exceptionally convincing. Apart from the fact that they are shareholders, you can point out that you want to demonstrate to them the quality in which they have invested their money. And, of course, as investors, they ought to investigate this anyhow.

6. Flatter the reader as one of a superior group

Here we go beyond merely saying you are one of a group: you are special. A classic example is 'The American Express Card is not for everyone'.

Gross flattery rarely fails. An outstanding instance is shown here. Written by one of the most able British writers, Graeme McCorkell, it is, as you see, designed to extract a fair amount of money from the prospect.

A total of 493 of these letters were mailed; those who did not reply were called on the phone, simply to ascertain their intentions, not to 'hard sell'. Well over 30 per cent of recipients accepted. I have to admit, I laughed at the disingenuous opening; but being as susceptible to flattery as anyone, I still responded. Then I was able to save my money as the Institute made me one of their first six Fellows.

**THE INSTITUTE OF
DIRECT MARKETING**

Mr Drayton Bird   9th December 1993
Drayton Bird Direct
133-137 Westbourne Grove
London
W11 2RS

Dear Drayton

As Chairman of the new Institute of Direct Marketing, it is my
pleasant duty to extend this invitation to you.

It is an invitation you may find rather flattering; yet when
our Board of Trustees vetted our proposed invitation list
flattery was the last thing in their minds.

The fact is that you have played an outstanding part in the
development of direct marketing. Indeed, I do not think I
would be contradicted if I said you are one of the <u>shapers</u> of
the business, having helped put UK direct marketing in the
forefront of European practice.

The Department of Trade and Industry has recognised direct
marketing's professionalism and has authorised the Direct
Marketing Centre to become the Institute of Direct Marketing.

Now it is time for The Institute to recognise you...and to
acknowledge your contribution.

Accordingly, I am instructed by the Board of Trustees to
invite you today to become a Founder Member of the Institute
of Direct Marketing.

Of course, The Institute has few reserves and so, alas,
Founder Membership cannot be free. But it is for a lifetime.
Ordinary Members will pay an annual fee of £70. Founders will
pay a once-only fee of £500.

After today's invitation no other lifetime membership category
is permitted by the constitution. Indeed, as soon as it is

Cont'd...

Gross flattery rarely fails. However, I think this letter would have benefitted
from a more interesting layout and a P.S.

practicable, qualification for Membership will be by a
combination of experience and examination results only.

It is therefore a signal honour to be a Founder of The
Institute and it is an honour I hope you will feel able to
accept.

Before you do so, you will want to know what obligations your
acceptance entails. Your first concern will be time. I
promise you are under no obligation to give us time. We may
ask you for advice; we may ask you to join a working party or
sit on a committee. If you agree, we shall be grateful, but we
don't think we have the right to expect your consent.

If we don't demand time, what do we demand? The Institute's
aim is to establish direct marketing as a profession and to
raise professional standards of practice. As a Founder, you
will be an Ambassador for The Institute. Your professional
conduct will reflect credit on The Institute. If we were in
the slightest doubt about that, your name would not have been
on the list.

But you will be more than just an Ambassador. Your role is
for life. You will, in effect, be something of a Godparent to
The Institute. You will keep a careful and caring eye on the
infant and you will, I hope, feel some pride as you see it
grow into a world leading body in direct marketing.

Looking back and seeing what we have all achieved, I am sure
you will agree that such a goal is not beyond us. You will
remember what a short time ago it was that direct marketers
struggled for any kind of recognition or acceptance. Now,
thanks to you and me and a few others like us, direct
marketing is growing up fast.

Here at The Institute we have already trained more than 11,000
people in direct marketing. Our services are increasingly in
demand abroad, while the DMA Diploma qualification has gained
the respect of employers at home. The importance of the
Diploma will increase as, combined with a specified experience
requirement, it will become the main route into Institute
Membership.

The formation of The Institute is a recognition that we
professionals have an obligation to keep on improving the
quality of what we do and to keep abreast of current
developments. The Institute aims to provide a full menu of
services that will help Members to do these things.

This widening of our scope will not, of course, lead us into
becoming another trade association. Membership of The

Cont'd...

-3-

Institute is open to individuals who meet our required standards. The services we will provide are those that will help individuals to develop their professional skills and to advance their careers.

In due course we hope to see many members carry the letters MIDM to which they will be entitled, into fields beyond direct marketing. In doing so they will earn respect for what has become a serious and significant business skill.

But that is for the future. For now, I need your acceptance of my invitation. If you want to know more about our plans, please call Derek Holder or me. If I'm not at The Institute, they will find me and I'll call you back.

It would be marvellous to have you as a Founder.

Yours sincerely

Graeme McCorkell
<u>Chairman</u>

7. Solve a problem

This approach may well be the most effective of all judging by the fact that Bill Jayme employs it almost exclusively.

A typical example is the New Yorker letter shown on pages 162–63.

8. Surprise, shock or startle the reader

In a letter to business people I started by saying: 'Did you know a factory inspector can come into your premises without your permission and close it down immediately if he doesn't like what he sees?'

An extraordinarily powerful example is shown on page 164 – the letter from Cesar Chavez's widow: 'This afternoon I buried my husband'.

On a more frivolous level, look at the opening to a letter from *Time-Life* on page 165.

9. Tell a story

The letter for the *Wall Street Journal* uses this technique, as does the excellent letter for Visa shown on pages 166–67, written by David Tetther, one of Britain's most talented writers.

Here the writer, by implication, sympathizes with the reader. We all know how appealing it is when somebody says to us: 'I know how you feel. The same thing happened to me.' That's precisely what this letter's doing.

Notice, too, the clever way in which the short heading tells the readers they could probably get a Visa Card while telling them why the card would be useful: it would simplify your life.

When you read this letter you feel not as though somebody is trying to sell you something but as though they are trying to help you. This is in my view, the difference between old-fashioned 'hard sell' – where something is being rammed down your throat – and the more subtle approach where you feel somebody has taken the trouble to offer you a service.

There are other noteworthy features about this letter.

First, the writer gives a reason why an offer is being made. This always adds conviction. When somebody offers you something for nothing, you may accept it, but you'll be suspicious of the giver's motives.

THE
NEW YORKER

AN INVITATION TO SUBSCRIBE. JUST 49.9¢ A COPY.

Dear Reader:

If you have days when almost everything goes wrong ...

... when the headlines are scary ... when the stock market is down ... when the bureaucrats have done it again ... when rain is predicted for the weekend ... when they've had the audacity to serve you a bread pudding that contains only two raisins ...

... there's a magazine that can cheer you.

The New Yorker.

Its colorfully drawn covers can gladden your heart. Its cartoons can put a smile back in the day. Its observations and comments can help you regain your perspective. Its stories, articles, and reviews can help restore your faith in your fellow-man.

On one occasion or another, The New Yorker may have brightened your grandparents' lives. It has surely perked up your parents'. And now that your own time to be cossetted is at hand here's some happy news, first, for your wallet.

When you return the enclosed subscription form promptly, you'll get a full year of The New Yorker for only 49.9¢ an issue. Not the $1.50 you'd pay at the newsstand. As we said, just 49.9¢.

The New Yorker was created in the nineteen-twenties as a journalistic and literary magazine. Its aim is to keep readers in touch with the main social, cultural, and political currents of our times, and thus it seeks to do so with probity, style, and wit.

Past contributors have included some of the most celebrated writers and artists of this century. Storytellers like John Cheever, Shirley Jackson, and John O'Hara. Critics like Edmund Wilson, Clifton Fadiman, and A. J. Liebling. Cartoonists like Peter Arno, Mary Petty, and James Thurber.

Journalists like Janet Flanner, John Hersey, and E. B. White. Poets as diverse as Marianne Moore and Odgen Nash. Humorists

(over, please)

Solve a problem.

such as Robert Benchley, S. J. Perelman, and Dorothy Parker, a
resolute city dweller who once dismissed all bucolic phenomena
as fresh air and trees with the statement "I am at two with nature."

Today's contributors are no less distinguished, and their range of interests
is astonishing. In one recent issue alone, you might have had the start of
a fascinating probe of the geology of the Rockies ... a communique from Mott
Street, the main drag of New York City's Chinatown, where the shrimp dumplings
make doing jury duty nearby not a civic duty but a civic delirium ...

... news of a Peruvian writer who has replaced Gabriel Garcia Marquez
as the South American novelist for gringos to catch up on ...
brief encounters with (1) the man who's behind the Montrose Pet Hotel,
a new inn so exclusive it doesn't accept people, and (2) the woman
who's behind the Critter Car, a pet-sensitive chauffeuring service ...

... a report on an important new study on ballet and Tchaikovsky,
along with the lamentable tidings that bookstores no longer seem to
stock what has been called "the greatest act of historical witness
of our century," Solzenitsyn's "The Gulag Archipelago" ...

... anecdotes from an aficionado who uncannily remembers virtually
all the whos, whats, whens, wheres, and whys of early jazz ...
a report on a new show of conceptual art that includes one room
entirely devoted to charts and graphs recording how the artist
has spent each moment of her life for the last fifteen years ...

... plus one poem ... two short stories ... reviews of a new play,
three movies, and six concerts ... all interspersed with twenty
cartoons, one of whose captions reads, "Have you seen my castanets?"

How much will you give to have a look at the drawing that this caption
accompanies? To revel in The New Yorker regularly? To keep up with The Talk
of the Town? To know better the world's movers and shakers through the
magnifying glass of the magazine's Profiles?

To keep in closer touch, through the magazine's listings, with
New York theatre, dance, night life, art, music, sports, movies,
special events? To be stimulated, edified, moved, nourished, delighted?

You say you'll offer 49.9¢ a week? $25.95 for a full year? It's a deal.
Just complete the order form, then mail it in the envelope enclosed. No
postage needed. Thank you. Welcome to The New Yorker. High time!

Cordially yours,

Frank Mustacato
Circulation Director

FM:aa

THE
NEW YORKER
25 West 43rd Street New York, New York 10036

Helen Chavez
United Farm Workers
La Paz, CA 93570

WESTERN UNION

April 30, 1993

Jay █████████
Ridgefield, CT █████
║║║║║║║║║║║║║║║║║║║║║║║║║║║║║║║║║║║

I buried my husband this afternoon.

Yesterday, thousands of us walked in funeral procession through Delano, the same little town where so many years ago it was only Cesar, only Cesar and a faithful few walking door to door with a dream.

I never stopped being amazed by Cesar. Somehow, from those first lonely days in Delano, he managed to plant his dream into many, many caring hearts. He was the kind cultivator, the compassionate sower, the gentle field worker, working in rocky soil where few believed justice could ever bear fruit.

I suppose I was the toughest one to organize. With eight children and only a beat up '53 Mercury wagon, I wondered how far a dream could take us. But with Cesar, if something was not worth giving your life to, it was not worth doing. And in the end, he gave his last ounce of life to his beloved cause.

People say Cesar is with God now, but to me Cesar has always walked with God. He led us from fields of sorrow to the edge of the Promised Land.

I know that, truly, Cesar would not have left us without knowing that one day, working together, we will reap a safe and just harvest.

The work of the Union has now been given to farm workers who first learned from Cesar that their voice could command change. This work has been passed on to our many friends who helped build our Union with unyielding generosity. And it has been entrusted to the Union's leadership who worked daily with Cesar and learned that action and commitment are the ultimate signs of love.

I ask you now, as we begin to look forward, to continue to help sow and harvest that dream that has brought us together. It is what Cesar wanted for the Union.

You can send gifts, in Cesar's memory, to the Cesar E. Chavez Non-Violent Action Fund.

Thank you,
Helen Chavez

Jay █████████
Ridgefield, CT █████████

Account Number: 80177

Enclosed is my donation of $_____
in memory of Cesar Chavez.

DETACH AND INSERT SO THAT RETURN ADDRESS & PERMIT NO. SHOW THROUGH WINDOW OF BUSINESS REPLY ENVELOPE. NO POSTAGE NEEDED, HOWEVER, YOUR STAMP SAVES THE FARM WORKERS MONEY.

FIRST CLASS PERMIT NO. 2 KEENE CA
--------POSTAGE WILL BE PAID BY ADDRESSEE-------

RETURN TO:

CESAR E. CHAVEZ NON-VIOLENT ACTION FUND
C/O UNITED FARM WORKERS
P.O. BOX 62
KEENE, CA 93531

Contributions or gifts to the United Farm Workers of America, AFL-CIO are not tax deductible under IRS regulations.

Startle the reader.

Second, the writer flatters the readers by saying they are the sort of people the bank wants to get to know.

The third thing is one I hope you will bear in mind when you are writing your own letters: it is sometimes good to disregard the 'rules'. When you read a book like this, it is so full of injunctions to do this and do that, you may begin to think you should *always* do what I say.

Not so. Every guideline in this book refers to what is *generally* true; there are occasions when you ought to ignore them – or you may have to. In this letter, for instance, you will see there is no offer. So the writer simply says that the fee is a very reasonable one.

Later, when talking about writing technique, you will see that I lay great stress on how important it is that the word 'you' is employed more often than the word 'I'. But obviously this is not so when you are telling a personal story. In the opening of this letter 'you' is used in the heading and the rest is all 'I' – essential for this approach.

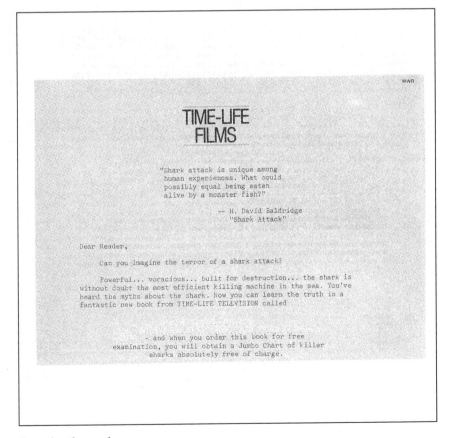

Surprise the reader.

ANNE J. O'NEILL
Director of Bank Services

<u>Would a Visa card, now, simplify your life?</u>

I remember how tough it was after college, getting any kind of reasonable credit. Lots of us went through the routine time after time: you may already have come across it yourself. We'd apply for credit or a credit card. We'd get asked for our "credit record" -- which in most cases we simply didn't have. The result -- no result. Catch 22. On the whole, people weren't willing to take the first step - even though most of us at that time could show we had good jobs to go to.

So when I joined The Philadelphia Bank (Delaware), I thought I'd try and do something about the situation. I talked about it to senior management. I've become used to positive attitudes here, and I wasn't disappointed. They told me to follow through and see if there was indeed a demand for the service.

That's exactly what I'm doing. If I can help you obtain a Visa card now, when you need it, I will feel the effort has been well worthwhile. I do have to ask you for some information. But as you will see from the accompanying application form, the Bank has allowed me to keep form-filling down to a minimum.

Why am I -- or rather, why is the Bank -- making this unusual offer to graduates and students at graduate and professional schools? Three reasons. The first is that we believe that individuals such as yourself are almost always "good risks", and we welcome doing business with you on that straightforward basis. The second is because we hope that if we serve you well now, you will want to consider using some of our other services later on. The third is that, as I said at the beginning, I

(Over, Please)

P.O. BOX 8924 / WILMINGTON, DELAWARE 19899

Tell a story.

have been through the "graduate credit" bind myself, and discovered
so had many of the management people at the Bank. We genuinely
welcome the opportunity to ease -- and perhaps speed -- the progress
of qualified people such as yourself.

As I'm sure you're aware, there is a fee for the Visa card. It
is, however, modest - just $18 a year - especially when you consider
the many benefits and conveniences of card membership. (And the
charge is not made until after you've received your card.)

I look forward to hearing from you, and I will get back to you
promptly - within two weeks of receiving your application.

Sincerely,

Anne J. O'Neill
Director of Bank Services

P.S. As I've said, I believe I have a good idea of the credit process
you may face initially. This opportunity to acquire a Visa card
could be really helpful and I recommend that you take advantage
of it now: the Bank cannot guarantee to keep the offer open
indefinitely.

10. Say you've improved your product

To a good prospect or customer it could well be interesting, allowing you to write something like the following:

> 'I am delighted to tell you that since I last wrote to you we have found a way to make our engines 29 per cent more fuel-efficient — without costing any more money.
>
> I know this is important to you, because last year in the questionnaire you sent back to me, you said economy was what mattered most to you.'

You can use this news sometimes as a way to suggest that, although your prospects may not have been interested in what you offered a year ago, this improvement means they should reconsider.

11. 'You and I'

People like people like themselves. So an opening that, as it were, puts its arm round the shoulder of the reader can be very effective.

A good example is the letter from Volvo on pages 169–71, which was sent to my home accompanying a very elegant brochure. Both the opening to the Save the Children legacy mailing and to Royal Viking Line customers began in this way. (Another good example is the letter for VISA in the US).

12. Refer to past purchases and make a helpful suggestion

> 'I'm writing to you because last year you went on holiday with us to Jamaica. In your comments, you said you enjoyed the Caribbean, but you'd enjoy somewhere quieter.
>
> So I thought you might be interested in a very attractive package to St Lucia — particularly because as a past customer, you are entitled to a 10 per cent discount — between £173 and £220 off the cost of a fortnight's holiday for two.'

Volvo Concessionaires Ltd.

Globe Park, Marlow,
Buckinghamshire, SL7 1YQ.
Telephone: (0628) 477977.
Telex: 847379 Volvo G Fax: (0628) 476173

February 1992

Dear Mr Bird,

Perhaps, like me, you still have some fond memories of your
first car.

Mine was something you could only describe as a 'run-
around'. And run it did.

In the thick of winter my car would start on the coldest
morning. It would pass other drivers hunched over their
engines, marooned at roundabouts and junctions where 'STOP'
meant precisely that. As my car made its slow steady
progress up hilly roads, other drivers stamped down the snow
to keep warm and wait for a tow.

Looking back, I now realise that the pleasure of a new car
depends as much on the way it's designed and built as the
enjoyment you get from driving it.

Perhaps you'd like to rediscover this in a car that enjoys
an enviable reputation for lasting so long it becomes part
of the family. I am talking, of course, about a Volvo. The
Volvo 440 hatchback and the 460 with its classic saloon
styling. Both share Volvo's preoccupation with secure, safe

Please read on...

The personal touch.

driving. The unique steel safety cage - with unequalled side
impact protection in all four doors - underpins the
distinctive Volvo style and design.

Unlike my car of many years ago, the 1.8 litre engine
delivers a healthy 89 bhp (84 bhp on the 1.6 litre version).
Power and acceleration are smooth and responsive through all
the gears and inspire confidence on the busiest of today's
motorways.

A visit to your local showroom will show you that Volvo pays
as much attention to interior styling as we do to outward
appearances. Both cars are deceptively spacious.

We consulted with orthopaedic experts to ensure that
everyone would remain comfortable on the longest journey.
Because a comfortable family is a safer family - especially
from the driver's point of view.

Test drive one of these cars and the arrangement of the
controls soon becomes second nature. Everything is where you
would expect to find it. Easy to see and within easy reach.
You will also find some thoughtful ideas that aren't usually
found as standard: like a courtesy light for the ignition
and map-reading lights.

Yes, it is a far cry from the days when a torch was standard
equipment for night driving and performance concentrated on
just getting from A to B without a hitch. I can only
suggest that you put what I have written in this letter to
the test. Visit your local Volvo dealer and get a feeling
for a Volvo 440 or 460. Take it for a test drive and
rediscover the pleasure of motoring. The prices start at
£9,880 for the 1.6 litre LI plus a standard delivery charge
of £295. A quite remarkable price for a car that will be

Please read on...

part of the family for many years to come.

When you visit your Volvo dealer and test drive one of these
cars, your name will be entered in our special <u>prize draw</u>
<u>where the prize is either a 440GL or 460GL.</u> If you win, the
choice is yours.

To mark the occasion we've also arranged for your photograph
to be taken by David Bailey at a private session.

Twelve other people will win the new Olympus mju camera
- an ultra-compact, fully automatic 35mm camera.

All the details are enclosed with this letter. I have also
included the name, address and telephone number of your
nearest Volvo dealer with whom you can arrange a test drive.

If you are tempted to take a drive, the dealer will give
you a 10" x 8" frame for one of your favourite photographs.

Whether you use it for a photograph of you with your first
car or a brand new Volvo makes no difference. Just as long
as it brings back fond memories in the years to come.

Yours sincerely

Pat Doble
Marketing Director

13. Ask for help; this give a pleasant feeling of power

The letter on page 173 is the simplest example I can find of this.

14. Imply an introduction

In this, you go beyond the approach mentioned in the last chapter – 'If the list upon which I found your name etc.' – and write something like: 'Your name has been passed to me as someone who is keen to preserve our environment'.

You can do this when you have rented a list of prospects.

15. Give the name of someone who has passed the name to you

This is the equivalent of a personal introduction. Only use it when you have been given a prospect's name by someone who knows them and is happy for you to say so, otherwise it will rebound on you. In this case you might write: 'Your neighbour, Mrs Jones, suggested that you might be interested in our swimming pools'.

In a somewhat jocular way, I opened such a letter for my own business as follows:

```
You may well wonder why you are receiving the enclosed booklet.
Quite simply, Antony Craddock is to blame.

I sent him a copy, as I thought he might be interested and,
quite unprompted, he gave me your name — I suspect because he
shares my belief in the wide applications of direct marketing

I hope you find it mildly stimulating.

If, even better, you know somebody with some interesting,
serious, long term direct marketing programmes who could
benefit from our help, that will delight me even more.

PS I must warn you that I plan to send out more of these commu-
nications — though not too many. If you'd rather I didn't, just
drop a note to us, and I'll have your name taken off the hit
list.
```

Incidentally, the easiest form of new business for you is by recommendation. If you don't encourage customers to pass on the names of

American Express slide

Ask for help – it makes people feel important.

friends who might make good customers, you should. I shall discuss this further.

16. Mention an anonymous referee

Here you have been given the name by someone who does not wish it to be known. In this case you can write: 'Your name has been passed to me by one of our best customers, who tells me you are interested in etc.'

17. Get an endorsement from the list renter

Where you have rented a list, you can sometimes persuade the renter to endorse your product in a covering note from their boss:

```
Many of our customers say they can't find a good widget at a
sensible price. So we went out to see if we could find one,
which is the reason for the enclosed letter from the Great
Widget company.

As far as our technical people can ascertain, this is the best
available for the money. We recommend it. See what you think.
```

This is an occasion when it pays to have two letters in one envelope. But make sure that they don't fight with one another. One has to be the hero, as it were, doing all the real selling; the other is merely introducing and endorsing your product or service.

18. The price is going up! Act now

Often, news of a price rise can be parleyed into good business, as with the Solarbo letter I discussed earlier, where the government, by raising a particular tax, had effectively increased the price of the product.

Intelligent marketers realize that the prospect of price going up is, if handled properly, a good incentive to get people who are sitting on the fence to buy.

19. Make your mind up

Write to people who have expressed interest, been mailed several times but haven't replied and put it to them straight.

```
The last thing I want to do is pester you if you're not really
interested. So do let me know whether you are or not.

I have included a little form for you to indicate 'yes' or
'no'. If I don't hear from you I shall stop writing.
```

Many people plan to buy or do something but are prevented by sheer lethargy. Such a letter can galvanize them into action.

Such a letter generally gets more negative than positive replies. But it very often gets more positive ones than an ordinary mailing with no option and has the valuable benefit of 'cleaning' your list. So you save money next time you mail.

You might call this your last chance to make money. On the contrary, it can be the beginning of something better if you go beyond simply asking for a 'Yes' or a 'No'.

Consider the possibilities. You can get people to tick a box on the reply form saying, 'I'm not sure. Can you send me more information about [a series of alternatives].' Or, 'Not now, but in 3/6/12 months.' Or, give a list of alternative products they might be interested in.

A good example of this sort of thing is the mailing from British Telecom, designed to get readers to make their minds up about the credit cards. Another, very similar, approach is employed in the American Express letter on the previous page.

20. Beware the negative approach

Every other point on this list is a positive suggestion, but this is a warning, because people are very often tempted to take a negative line. It rarely works and then only if the positive comes in very quickly.

On page 177 is a letter from *Yellow Pages*, which shows what I mean. Take a look at it and see what you think.

There are two lines on the envelope, the first – '211,000 potential customers in your area could be waiting to hear from you.' – I think is good. It conveys a promise. The second one – 'What have you got to say?' – seems to me to be straying from the point because the writer is trying to be clever. Why not simply say: here's how to reach them?

When you get inside the mailing we see that these people who want to sell to me want to know what sex I am – because they haven't taken the trouble to find out. When you consider that once somebody starts advertising in *Yellow Pages*, over the years their business is worth a lot of money, telephoning to verify exactly who you should write to seems a modest investment indeed. That is assuming that the recipient is already a customer – which in fact I am! So they haven't even done that basic piece of research.

The letter opens with a negative statement and it's very difficult to see how it could get much shorter without being in the form of the sort of brief message one sees on lavatory walls.

As you can see from the facts which *are* shoehorned into this letter, there is a great story to tell for *Yellow Pages*. Think of all the examples that could be given of companies that have succeeded through advertising; think of the stories that could have been told!

A wonderful opportunity – lost.

YOU MUST GET THE NOD

This brings me to the final subject I am going to cover in this chapter: the art of persuasion; which is in truth the art of obtaining agreement.

If your letter doesn't do as well as it could, more often than not it's because you say something your reader cannot accept. It's not believable for some reason. Either it's simply not true or it doesn't fit their experience.

However you begin – with a promise, an offer, a story, an example, a reason for writing – at some point you have to get your readers *nodding* in agreement. You don't want them hesitating, or even dismissing what you have said as incredible, or irrelevant to them.

In fact, generally, the sooner you gain that agreement, the safer you are, since at this point you have *involved* your reader. Let's imagine you want to lend money. Here's a simple opening I've thought up as an example.

```
It's an old joke, but I'm sure you will agree very true that
when you need money, nobody will lend it you. But when you
don't need it, the whole world is clamouring to help you.

That's why I am writing now to give you the opportunity to be
sure you will have money in hand when you need it, by offering
you a very special interest rate on up to £3000 worth of etc.
```

YELLOW PAGES SALES LIMITED

Directories House
50 Wellington Street,
Slough, Berkshire SL1 1YL

Tel (0753) 553311

The Managing Director
Drayton Bird Direct
M C B House
133-137 Westbourne
Grove
London
W11 2RS

2nd February 1994

Dear Sir/Madam,

IS YOUR BUSINESS MISSING AN OPPORTUNITY?

Or, to be more exact, over 211,000* opportunities? Because that's how many potential customers there are in your area. The question is, how many of them know you exist?

There's no doubt about it, everyone knows Yellow Pages! It's delivered to virtually every home and business with a telephone.

It's a national favourite - the first choice for consumers and business people alike when looking for a suitable supplier like yourself.

Is it any surprise, then, that Yellow Pages is used 150 million times** every month and by over half† the adult population?

With a massive 80%†† going on to contact a supplier with every intention of buying, it is not difficult to see why the majority of our advertisers have stayed with us for at least 4 years.†††

So if you're interested in a cost-effective way of generating new business and helping you to retain your current customers, **return the reply card TODAY.**

Yours faithfully,

Henry Wright
General Sales Manager

PS The power of advertising in a national favourite already works for over 300,000*** businesses - make sure it works for yours.

*Copyright © CACI Limited 1992 using data: Source TGI
(© BMRB 1992) OPCS (Crown copyright 1989)
Plus Yellow Pages Database © British Telecommunications plc 1992
** Average monthly usage NOP Corporate and Financial © British Telecommunications plc 1992
† Copyright Target Group Index © BMRB 1992
†† MRE © British Telecommunications plc 1990
††† MRE © British Telecommunications plc 1991
*** Yellow Pages Database © British Telecommunications plc 1992

Yellow Pages Sales Limited is part of British Telecommunications plc Registered Office 81 Newgate Street, London EC1A 7AJ
Registered in England No 1403041

● Registered trademark of British Telecommunications plc in the United Kingdom

4702F/1A/007666

Don't be negative.

Do you see how this works? Once your reader has accepted one easy proposition, you put forward a series of subsequent propositions. These, had they been at the beginning of the letter, might not have been plausible. But the reader, having accepted the earlier propositions, is more inclined to accept subsequent ones. The habit of agreement is established.

That is the process of persuasion which makes for a successful letter – leading to the final proposition you hope people will accept: Why don't you do what I have asked you to do? And people are inclined to do this because so far everything you have said has been, step by step, acceptable. A good example of the technique comes in the Robert Collier letter on page 139.

So look at the opening of your letter and make sure the 'nod factor' is there. Find some simple proposition that is hard to disagree with. It need not be right at the opening, but it must be there.

Then you can go on with the rest of your success formula: to interest your reader further, make them want what you offer, convince them it's right for them and finally get them to act.

So let's turn now to the body – the guts, as it were – of your letter.

11

The Guts of Your Letter

'Then to church; and there being a lazy preacher, I sleep out the sermon.'

Pepys' Diary, 2nd November 1662

How few words Samuel Pepys uses, yet you can almost picture him nodding off as the dull cleric droned on. Good writing never uses more words than necessary; a subject I come to soon. But perhaps an even more important lesson is that if you do not work hard, nobody will listen – or read.

As we have seen, getting people to pay attention in the first place is your greatest challenge; and getting them to take action is the next hardest. But many fail in the body of the letter, where persistence and attention to detail are critical.

These are the main reasons for the failure.

1. The letter is not structured properly. It hops from point to point, confusing the reader.
2. It does not flow in a way that will keep your reader with you.
3. The writing is too dull to interest, let alone motivate the reader. When people read your letter you want to excite them about what you are selling. This excitement can only come through writing

with vim and enthusiasm. Emotion always sways more than reason.
4. None the less, reason is important. Your letter will fail if it does not convince the reader that what you say is true, using facts, figures, impartial advice.
5. The argument is incomplete. You have omitted some significant reason why your reader should do what you want; or you have failed to overcome some possible objection to your proposal.

Let me take the first point first, for it is the easiest. Before writing your letter, write down a simple sequence that will make sense to the reader.

This is more than just the formula we have covered – attention, interest, desire, conviction, action, with an appropriate incentive. The flow should be so logical that you should be able, when you review the letter, to write beside each paragraph a phrase in summary. These phrases should themselves sum up your argument in a sequence that makes sense.

But there is an even simpler matter of structure to be concerned about. That is the way the letter moves from paragraph to paragraph; from sentence to sentence; even from phrase to phrase.

KEEP THEM READING

What should be your greatest fear when writing? That the reader might stop reading. One US mail order wizard, Joe Sugarman, states quite simply that the only job each sentence has is to make sure the reader reads the next. Since he has become a multi-millionaire writing advertisements for his own company, his view deserves respect.

When looking at the body of your letter, one good idea is to read each sentence as it comes and ask yourself: if I were the reader, what would I like to know next?

There are a number of simple ways – tricks, really – to encourage people to read on, which I have listed in Chapter 13. One I have not covered, however, is what I call the 'double take'. It is particularly strong when you are making a statement that beggars belief.

A good example comes in the following passage where you will see I make some strong claims in the first three paragraphs which I suspect the reader may find hard to believe, following them up with a sentence beginning 'Impossible?' to reassure them.

> This remarkable monitor actually 'teaches' your body to relax. You're familiar no doubt with the saying 'a healthy mind in a healthy body'. But only in recent years have doctors and psychologists learned how true this saying is.
>
> Now it is possible, by measuring the stress your body is undergoing from minute-to-minute, to train yourself to relax.
>
> And this unique device does it all for you, measuring how your system is physically reacting to surrounding pressures, and then enabling you to adjust your emotional reactions so as to relax easily.
>
> Impossible? I myself thought so until I actually placed this Monitor in the palm of my hand and used it.

Do you see what I am doing there? My reader has just said: 'I don't believe it!' So I hasten to *endorse* this disbelief – and once again there is something to nod about; in fact I can now go on to persuade the reader that what I claim is true.

ENSURING EVERY POSSIBLE REPLY

Now let's take a closer look at the guts of the letter – the part between the opening and the close which ensures your letter squeezes every last possible reply out of your prospects. If you accept that *dull* writing kills your chances of success, how do you avoid dullness?

You will recall my harping on the idea that your letter is a surrogate salesman. And you will remember that, when discussing involvement devices, I said that anything which demonstrates the product is a good idea – because it is what a salesman does.

In the body of your letter, you must try to use *words* to demonstrate your product; to paint pictures. These will whet the reader's appetite as well as adding conviction. Another fine example applied to two very dull products indeed, is below.

> A varnish manufacturer sends along a sample panel finished with his varnish and writes: 'Give this panel the most thorough test possible — stamp on it with your heel or hit it with a hammer. Then hold it to the light. You will find that although you have dented the wood, the varnish has not been cracked.'

> A paper manufacturer is even more successful when he says, 'You can prove the excellence of our goods in a second: just tear a corner off this sheet; then tear a corner off one of your present letterheads; now get a magnifying glass and examine both torn edges. You will find long fibres — linen threads — on ours, while on yours the fibres are short, woody.' The man who reads this learns something new about paper. He learns how to judge it intelligently, and learning, he learns what the writer wished him to know about his product.

That was written some 80 years ago. Another wonderful example of this is the opening page of a mailing for Omaha Steaks, shown on pages 183–84.

BE EXACT: QUANTIFY YOUR BENEFITS

Once you have established what benefits you offer and which are most important, *quantifying* them will usually make more difference to the success of your letter than anything else. This is not only more convincing; it arouses greater interest and desire. Never be vague about what you are selling; always put a number on it if you possibly can.

A good way to see why is to look at money. About 30 per cent of all sales letters in the UK are written to sell financial services – more than any other category – and most are very bad. Those familiar with all the jokes about accountants and actuaries might assume this is because financial people are dull.

However, I suspect it is more because of the paradox of money itself. It arouses great emotions; it is what we spend most of our lives working for and worrying about; people kill for it. But in itself money is not interesting. Of course we all enjoy the pleasant heft of a wad of £5 notes or bemoan the uneasy feeling that we only have £3 left in our pockets. But money only exists because you can buy things with it.

It is easy to wax lyrical about the joys of a holiday or even the advantages of central heating, but what do you say about money? The answer is: you put a number to it. If I say to you: 'I'll make you rich', the first question in your mind is, 'How rich?' What's the number?

If I promise you a pension for the rest of your life, the first thing you wonder is whether it will be enough to live on. How much will you get a year? What's the number?

Frederick J. Simon
4400 South 96th Street • P.O. Box 3300
Omaha, Nebraska 68103

▲▲

USE THE ENCLOSED CHECK IN YOUR NAME -- in the amount of $23.00 to
get more than a 43% discount on your first box of succulent Omaha
Steaks. Treat yourself to the world's most tender beef, guaranteed
to please you ... at attractive, introductory savings. So please
read this letter right now. If you love good steaks, you'll find
my story interesting -- and my offer very tempting!

FOR STEAK LOVERS ONLY

F.J.S.

▲▲

Dear Friend,

Can you recall the best steak you ever tasted in your life? One
that was tender, juicy and just full of flavor. I'll bet you can. Most
likely, it was served at an exclusive restaurant or supper club.

I'm writing to you because I believe you would enjoy a box of my
"fork-tender" Omaha Steaks ... the same steaks I sell to fine
restaurants ... shipped frozen, directly to you. Here's my story.

TOP QUALITY

Have you ever wondered why the steaks fine restaurants serve taste
so good? It's simple, really. The chefs in fine restaurants know that
all their skill in food preparation is absolutely useless -- unless they
begin with first quality cuts of meat.

Where do smart chefs get this superb beef? From suppliers like me
in the heart of America's beef country -- the Midwest -- who select and
cut steaks to their exacting specifications. We specialize in fine
quality meats for elegant restaurants and clubs. In such places,
customers pay a premium price. So the meat has to be the very best.

My company, Omaha Steaks International, has been a beef supplier to
fine restaurants since 1917. That's the year we began supplying a few
of Omaha's posh steak houses. Today, we supply USDA Prime and Top
Choice Omaha Steaks to restaurants in every part of America. In fact
it's quite possible that you've enjoyed one of our steaks at a fine
restaurant, without even knowing it.

MAGNIFICENT STEAKS — AT HOME!

But that's only half our business. Over the years, we found people
who wanted our magnificent steaks for personal use. We had to charge
them a premium price. But, to these people, quality was their greatest
concern. They simply wanted to enjoy our top quality steaks at home --
and share them with family and friends.

This gave us the idea of actually seeking out discriminating steak
lovers, especially in places where aged, corn-fed, Midwestern beef was
not available. So we sent out our first mail order catalog. And the
response was tremendous. As a result, about half of our business is now
devoted to supplying people all over America with the best steaks money
can buy ... for their dining, entertaining and gift needs.

To introduce you to Omaha Steaks ...

ALL THE WAY FROM THE HEART OF BEEF COUNTRY, U.S.A... TO YOUR DOOR!

Whet the reader's appetite.

... I have a very special offer. An introductory discount, typical of the specials we offer to our regular customers all year long.

I'll send you 6 (6 oz.) Filet Mignons, each 1-1/4" thick -- (the regular price of these fine steaks is $52.95) -- <u>for</u> only $29.95, plus $4.00 for shipping and handling. You save $23.00; that's more than 43% off the usual price.

SAVE $23.⁰⁰

As soon as I receive your order, I'll send you a confirmation by First Class mail. Then, within two or three weeks, your Omaha Steaks will be delivered right to your door. (They're boxed and wrapped for your freezer, placed in an insulated, reusable cooler, packed with over 20 pounds of dry ice ... and shipped out freight prepaid.)

With your order, I'll enclose, FREE, our full color catalog of succulent steaks and gourmet foods you may order by mail or phone.

Also -- you get the Omaha Steaks Cookbook FREE. This booklet contains recipes and instructions by food expert James Beard. So you'll be certain to cook your steaks to perfection.

NO-RISK GUARANTEE

In addition -- I want to enjoy these steaks <u>at no risk</u>. So I offer you this guarantee:

IF YOU ARE NOT PLEASED FOR ANY REASON, WE WILL REPLACE YOUR ORDER OR REFUND YOUR MONEY, WHICHEVER YOU PREFER.

So place your order now, while everything is right in front of you. The fastest way to get your steaks is to call us TOLL FREE at 1-800-228-9055 and charge to your American Express, Visa, MasterCard, Diners Club or Carte Blanche account. You may phone 7 days a week, day or night. (Nebraska residents call 0-402-391-3660, COLLECT.)

CALL TOLL FREE TO ORDER

To order by mail, just endorse the enclosed check, fill in the order form, enclose your payment -- then use the postage-free envelope I've provided. <u>Whether you phone or write, I must receive your order before the date shown on your check.</u> After that date, I'll select a new group of people to receive this rare offer -- and your chance will be past. So please respond now.

Your satisfaction is fully guaranteed.

Sincerely,

DOUBLE OFFER -- FOR EVEN MORE GOOD EATING !

Frederick J. Simon

Frederick J. Simon
Executive Vice President

P.S. To more than double your enjoyment, you may order 12 (6 oz.) Filet Mignons -- at the special price of $58.95 plus $4.00 for shipping and handling.

CALL FREE WITH YOUR CREDIT CARD ORDER ... 1-800-228-9055

If I say I'll insure your life so that your dependants won't have to worry should anything happen to you, once again you want to know what sum I am talking about; what's the number?

Don't be vague

One number can be mouthwateringly large; another can be too small even to interest you. And a vague statement with no number is almost meaningless to you.

To give you an idea of what I mean: study the letter from Acuma (see pages 186–87). As you can see, the opening is just a short list of quantified benefits, carefully selected to appeal to the types of people Acuma know are the best prospects for the financial advisory service. Readers can relate such examples to their own situations.

Finance is an easy area in which to show how to quantify. But the same principle applies to almost anything. Years ago, I learned many lessons about writing letters when I helped launch the Bullworker, a device which makes you big and strong faster than you would ever believe possible.

I quickly learned that just promising strength quickly was not as effective as being precise. How quickly? How strong? Soon I developed a line which said: 'Here's how you can build a power-packed body in under 5 minutes a day.' This worked well; but not as well as other lines I developed when I knew more about the product.

First, I discovered that each exercise took seven seconds, and you only needed to do seven. Then I found out that you only had to use two-thirds of your strength; you only had to do the exercises once a day – it wouldn't make any difference if you did them two or three times: results would not improve. And I learned you could actually double your strength in six months.

In the end I could promise a splendid physique in 'exactly 49 seconds a day, with 7 simple exercises you can perform in your own home – and I guarantee you'll *double* your strength within 6 months – or all your money back instantly, without question'. That little mouthful seemed to sell the product everywhere and did for many years.

How big? How many? How long?

There are many other things you can and should quantify in a letter, depending on what you are selling. All are important. If you are

Acuma

An American Express company

Acuma Ltd
Personal Financial Planning
Acuma House
The Glanty
Egham
Surrey
TW20 9A1

00318

Dear Mr. Bird,

Whatever your goals in life, Acuma's Free Guide to Financial Planning could help you to reach them.

Every one of its pages is packed with practical suggestions for making your money work harder.

Just some of the valuable things you'll learn in your Free Guide to Financial Planning are:

> How a middle aged couple with an annual income of £38,000 can see their two children through university <u>and</u> securely take early retirement by making a few simple adjustments to their savings and investment plans...
>
> How a young man on a salary of £17,000 can save towards his future without having to adjust his lifestyle...
>
> How you can start maximising your income without sacrificing your lifestyle...

And, if you're a high rate taxpayer, the Guide points out a number of additional tax benefits you may have overlooked.

Perhaps you're even thinking about buying a new home? We've some useful tips that could help you save on your mortgage.

And if you're planning to retire early, a quick glance at our Guide could help bring the happy day even closer.

over...

The Acuma Marketing Group Comprises:

Acuma Life Assurance Ltd
Reg in England & Wales No 1878575
Member of LAUTRO
Acuma Fund Managers Ltd
Reg in England & Wales No 2372436
Member of LAUTRO & IMRO

Acuma Portfolio Managers Ltd
Reg in England & Wales No 2403298
Members of IMRO
The Reg Office of these companies is
Acuma House, The Glanty, Egham
Surrey TW20 9AT

Acuma Ltd
Incorporated in Delaware USA with
limited liability is an
Appointed Representative of the
aforementioned companies

Acuma Life Assurance Ltd
Acuma Fund Managers Ltd
Acuma Portfolio Managers Ltd
Acuma Ltd

Q50 001 QC02   02895332-04   888033047-0

Be precise.

Helping you through the financial jungle

The Acuma Guide covers these practical situations in clear, no-nonsense English. And gives dozens of other pointers to help you through the enormous choice of financial products:

You'll learn...

* How to choose investment options that help you achieve higher returns and lower tax liability.

* The best place to keep your cash: Is it a bank, building society, deposit account or an interest-bearing current account?

* The financial options which offer you the greatest tax benefits. How to minimise inheritance tax. And which life policies entitle you to tax-free sums.

* Choosing the right time to retire. Which pension should you go with? And will it be enough to keep you comfortable and secure?

* Which insurance protection makes most sense for a growing family.

* How to pay less interest on your loans.

We'll take you through all the options and help you make decisions that are right for you.

The Guide concludes with a fascinating self-assessment that lets you calculate how much you're worth today. For many people it proves to be a real eye-opener.

Send for your free copy now

The Acuma Guide to Financial Planning comes to you with no obligation at all. It's simply a way of introducing you to Acuma's Personal Financial Planning service.

To receive your copy, simply complete and return the accompanying reply card in the postage-paid envelope we've provided or telephone <u>081-759 9462.</u>

We'll post your free Guide immediately.

Yours sincerely,

Graham Leigh.

Graham Leigh,
Vice President-Marketing, Financial Planning.

P.S. When you apply for your Free Guide, you'll see how it could help others reach their financial goals. If it works for them it could work for you.

To ensure speedy delivery of your Guide, please telephone <u>081-759 9462</u> and ask for your free copy today.

selling a book or picture, people want to know how big the book is, how many pages and illustrations there are, how large the picture is and so forth.

If you are selling a garment they want to know obvious things like the measurements; how long a pleat is in a skirt; how many colours does it come in; is it 100 per cent wool? If you are selling hi-fi, what is the output? If you sell a golf ball that's guaranteed to go further, how many yards further?

If your product has been wildly successful with the public, don't settle for 'lots of people liked it' or 'most people liked it' but that '356 people from 23 countries liked it'. If you are selling double glazing and you have a new design which is better, people want to know how much more so.

You can see that the reason for quantifying is clear and obvious. But it's amazing how many letters neglect it. The majority, I think you will find. And this is not a sin committed by amateurs alone. I am writing this book because I am supposed to be an expert. However, I was reminded of the importance of quantifying a few years ago.

The example was not a letter but an advertisement; the principle is the same, however. The headline of the advertisement said 'Wanted: account handlers who can see the wave of the future in advertising' – my agency was looking to recruit new people.

I sent the advertisement to my then boss, David Ogilvy. He made a number of comments. The first was: 'Tell them *how many* account handlers you want. Then they will see how quickly your business is growing and how many opportunities there are.'

How to quantify

In almost all cases, you can find some way to quantify, and so make your benefit both more appealing and more credible.

Generally – but not always – it pays to quantify benefits in time and money rather than percentages. The sums of £53 or £7.5 million are something I can readily comprehend, as opposed to 20 per cent, which begs the question, '20 per cent of what?' One exception is where a percentage sounds more attractive than money. For instance, '20 per cent off' may work better than 'Save 50 pence'.

Returning to money, let's take an example where the amateur writer finds it difficult to convert a percentage into something more meaningful, though with a little expertise one can be dug out.

Suppose I offer you a loan at a very favourable rate of interest. Let us say that because you are a good customer, I will give you a rate of interest which is 2 per cent lower than I would offer to ordinary customers. The amateur writer says just that: 'because you've been one of our best customers, I'll lend you money at 2 per cent less than our normal rate of 10 per cent APR.'

Professionals will use facts from the databases they hold on customers to make the whole thing more personal and more precise.

(I must apologize here and tell you the figures I am using are made up – I may be a writer, but I am no financial expert. The copy is written to make a point.)

Dear Personalized

An additional line of credit of up to £3000 is waiting for you. At favourable terms which could save you £150 ... £200 ... even £400.

You are one of our very best customers. In fact, we have now been doing business, I see from my files, for five years. Your payment record has been impeccable.

<u>Frankly, I wish we had more like you, because you obviously know how to handle money. That is why I'm writing now to offer you a new line of credit at very special interest rates, 2 per cent below what is normally available to others.</u>

There is no arrangement fee or other charge as you are already a customer.

You can get as much as £3000 immediately for any purpose you wish. All you have to do is indicate the sum you want on the accompanying application form, and sign at the bottom where I have placed an x. The money will be with you within a week.

The amount of money you will save in interest depends on the sum you wish to borrow and the repayment period you choose — which you can also indicate on the form.

If, for instance, you chose to borrow £2500 over one year, then you would save £50 in interest charges compared to an ordinary borrower. If you chose £2000 over two years you would save £200 and if you chose £3000 over three years, you would save £400.

This offer is valid to August 15th. Apply now even if you don't need the money immediately.

As you will appreciate, the funds we have available for lending vary according to other factors within our business and the

---

economy. At the moment we have considerable funds available, which is why I am able to make you this offer.

Even if you don't require a loan right now, but would like to be sure you can get the money for some project you have in mind over the next few months, fill in the application form. It will be held as your personal line of credit, to use when you need it. You pay no interest until you actually draw upon it.

I will write back to you to confirm the money is at your disposal whenever you require. We can arrange the fine details later.

Quantifying without numbers

Sometimes you quantify without a specific quantity being given. Take the American Express Card. As we've discussed before, their benefit is that there is *no* preset spending limit if you are a Cardmember.

This is clearly almost unquantifiable – yet it does set some sort of a figure. The promise is that you can spend as much as you've shown you can afford, as opposed to the precise spending limit imposed by credit cards.

This is a benefit whose exact value depends upon your financial status. What it means is that as long as you keep on paying your bills promptly at the end of every month, your credit will be good. So you do have a pretty precise idea in your mind of what that figure is.

But other aspects of the American Express Card are generally very precisely quantified in their letters. You are told how many offices American Express has around the world which you can call upon for advice or money when you are travelling. You are told how many establishments around the world – shops, restaurants and the like – honour the card. All these things reassure and convince you.

PROVE WHAT YOU SAY IS TRUE

Your readers may find what you offer appealing, may even want it. But they need more than promises. If many letters have weak openings and lackadaisical endings, even more make no attempt to convince the prospect or customer that what you say is true.

Never before have your customers been bombarded so frequently by advertisements, commercials – and direct mail. Never before have they been subjected to such a media onslaught and become so cynical – about their politicians, their newspapers, everything; and that includes the promises you make. They need a reason to believe.

This is important, particularly if you are asking people to do anything that takes effort or costs money. Even when getting a qualified enquiry, some indication that what you say is not the usual advertising waffle is needed. You need points to support your argument. It is a good idea to list them when preparing to write.

If you can come up with scientific or impartial validation – from a newspaper, perhaps, or an independent expert, so much the better. But there are alternatives available if you have assembled enough relevant information. One reason you must find out as much as you can about whatever you sell is that you will often discover something which will give your claims greater validity.

When, in a letter for Royal Viking Line, I wanted to emphasize the quality of service, I pointed out that they had a higher ratio of staff to clients than any of their competitors. I also pointed out that independent judges rated them more highly than any of their rivals.

Good, convincing stories can come, sometimes, from the company history. When I was working for Xerox, we learned that they had invented the personal computer – how they failed to make millions out of it is the subject of quite an entertaining book.

You may sometimes find that a local establishment of one kind or another has an interesting history attached to it. If, say, you are promoting an old pub near London, it could be a place where Dick Turpin was alleged to stable his horse.

Years ago when I started in the mail order business there was a cynical joke that the business was doing well when you no longer had to write your own testimonials.

Of all the many ways to convince people what you say is true, perhaps the easiest is to quote your customers. If you don't have any happy customers then either you have just set up in business or your business will not last long.

Encourage testimonials

If you conduct your business well, then automatically from time to time somebody will thank you or congratulate you. Make a point *immediately* of asking them if you can quote them, because the enthusiasm that motivates these spontaneous 'thank yous' is likely to evaporate.

Believe it or not a few years ago one client asked me if testimonials had to be genuine. I was pretty astonished by the implications about her business morals from this remark.

What if you receive few such eulogies? Then it is your job to make sure that you *get* some. Ask your customers what they think. They appreciate it. This is standard practice in restaurants to the point where it verges on embarrassing the number of times a waiter asks you if you are enjoying your meal.

But the principle is sound. In the first place if people are *not* happy you want to know it so you can improve what you sell – which in turn will lead to more satisfied customers prepared to testify on your behalf.

In my book *Commonsense Direct Marketing*, I specifically asked people if they would let me know what they thought; and I had quite a few helpful suggestions – and compliments – as a result. (I also offered to pay the cost back if any reader was not happy. Only 1 person in 20 years has done so. More on this in a moment.)

But you can actively 'manufacture' testimonials as it were, simply by systematically enclosing questionnaires that you send to your customers after you have served them, asking what they thought.

Few will sit down and rack their brains to think what they might say. But most will be perfectly happy to mark the various aspects of your service on a scale from one to five, one being poor, five being excellent. (This is always the best way because it is so much easier.) If a space is allowed, they will often write comments.

The content of a questionnaire will vary according to what you are selling. If it were a slimming product, you could have a section where you ask: 'Please tell us how much weight you lost'. On the question-naire you should always put in a box asking people whether they are happy for you to use their name, title if any, as well as the company name where relevant. If at all possible, try to get their signatures and photographs; this is very convincing.

People who run educational seminars use questionnaires a great deal. On pages 193 and 194 is a typical example issued by my friends at American Express. When I first did an executive seminar for them, I was able from the results of this questionnaire to claim proudly that 100 per cent of the delegates would recommend it to their colleagues.

As I said above, when the news is not all good a questionnaire can show you what to improve. I also conduct seminars for the UK Institute of Direct Marketing. In 1993 three delegates complained that there weren't enough opportunities to join in and ask questions. I

DIRECT MARKETING - AN EXECUTIVE OVERVIEW
TORONTO
APRIL 16, 1993

I. GENERAL EVALUATION

What was your overall reaction to the course?

```
 (1)    3     5     7     9
  |__|__|__|__|__|__|__|__|
Excellent    Good       Poor
```

What general comments do you have about the seminar?

EXCELLENT MIX OF THEORY AND PRACTICE!

What parts of the program do you think will be most helpful to you?

- _GENERAL GUIDELINES FOR DM –_
- _5 QUESTIONS TO ASK TOWSELF IN TRYING TO SOLVE A BUSINESS PROBLEM WITH DM_

Generally, how will you apply what you learned to your daily job?
- _REFERENCE THE MATERIAL FOR EACH MAJOR "PROBLEM" I HAVE (eg resoliciting cus, preventing cus from attriting, etc...)_

II. SUBJECT MATTER

How well did the seminar meet your needs?

```
 (1)    3     5     7     9
  |__|__|__|__|__|__|__|__|
Very Well   Fairly Well   Did Not Meet Needs At All
```

How well was the course organized?

```
  1  O  3     5     7     9
  |__|__|__|__|__|__|__|__|
Very Well   Fairly Well   Poorly
```

To what extent was the level of the seminar (materials, pace and process) appropriate?

```
  1     3     5     7     9
  |__|__|__|__|__|__|__|__|
Too Advanced   Just Right   Too Basic
```

Find out how to improve.

III. INSTRUCTIONAL MATERIALS

How was the quality and relevance of the:

		Excellent	Good	Poor
Handouts/Binders	✓	Excellent	____ Good	____ Poor
Slides/Overheads	✓	Excellent	____ Good	____ Poor
Samples/Examples	✓ Superb	Excellent	____ Good	____ Poor

Do you have any specific comments about the instructional materials used?
No

IV. PROGRAM INSTRUCTOR - *DRAYTON BIRD*

What was your overall reaction to the instructor?

```
        1    ◯  3        5        7        9
        |__◡__|____|____|____|____|____|____|
    Excellent          Good             Poor
```

How flexible was the instructor in responding to the needs of the group?

```
            1   ◯  3        5        7        9
            |__◡_|____|____|____|____|____|____|
      Very Flexible        Somewhat        Inflexible
```

VI. COURSE INFORMATION

Would you recommend this seminar to any of your colleagues?

Yes ✓   No _____   Maybe _____

If yes, please list their names, titles and locations:

_____

How did you find out about this seminar?

_____ Through another Direct Marketing Course I took
_____ Direct Marketing Education and Development Catalog
_____ Colleague
✓ Other (specify) Amex, MDP

Thank you for taking time to answer these questions completely. The information will prove helpful in designing future courses and programs.

Name ___Denise Dorton___ . Title: ___Mkt - Mar___

Business Area ___Cardmember Acqusition___ Country (if applicable) ___Mauritius___ rejigged the programme, leading to another 100 per cent satisfaction rate.

In short, you should be organized about getting good testimonials – as you should with everything else connected with your letters.

Famous people

I mentioned Dick Turpin earlier. Anything that adds interest and authenticity to your product helps, and nothing helps better than the names of famous customers. Again, when working on Xerox I suggested that they featured names of their famous customers such as Boeing who relied upon their machinery to help design their planes. I thought this a good idea, although they didn't. They were wrong.

The idea of using the names of well-known customers is not new. The famous London hatters, Lock in London's St James's, feature the fact that people like Winston Churchill and the Duke of Wellington had their hats made there; in a similar way one long-established London bank names celebrated customers in their advertising, such as Charles II's famous mistress Nell Gwyn.

Although the best testimonial may come from somebody famous, such a person should be qualified to comment. My old boss David Ogilvy was the perfect person to recommend my previous book or indeed this one. He was not perfect to recommend a course on how to drive a racing car.

Almost anybody is appropriate as a testimonee to something everybody uses – like a restaurant or a dry cleaning service. But there again, if you could get a famous chef to say that your restaurant was good; or get somebody working in his kitchen who is constantly being covered by stains from sauces to say your dry cleaning service was special, they would be better.

An example is worth more than scores of boasts

Of course, a testimonial is a form of example. Instead of saying 'Our customers like it', we give an instance or instances of such customers. Examples are much more credible than claims. Saying 'It doesn't cost much', is far less effective than saying 'less than the price of a beer'.

When talking above about the importance of quantifying, I referred you to the opening of the Acuma letter, which is just a list of quantified examples, each expressing a benefit. In the same way, the letter for 'Marketing Breakthroughs International' on pages 196–97 is nothing more than a list of examples.

Marketing Breakthroughs
INTERNATIONAL

● 4TH FLOOR, BRITANNIA HOUSE, 960 HIGH ROAD, LONDON N12 9RY, ENGLAND. FAX: + 44 81 446 3659 TELEX 9419208 WBP G. ●

Dear Marketer,

Date as postmark

<u>WILL YOUR NEXT PRODUCT LAUNCH BENEFIT FROM A LARGER SHIRT-POCKET?</u>

In a world of intensifying competition, success increasingly depends on the ability to "think laterally".

When Sony launched the first of its revolutionary personal hi-fi products, salesmen wanted to demonstrate its compactness by carrying it in their shirt pockets. But it was just too big. Rather than delay the product launch, Sony ordered shirts with extra large pockets...

The giant US toy maker Mattel wanted to give its through-the-year sales a lift, so it started a frequent purchaser club, complete with newsletter and advice -- not for children but to help their grandparents choose presents for them

A Japanese contractor improved the productivity of its sales order clerks by 50 per cent - not by expensive re-training but by injecting a lemon fragrance into the air conditioning

A US maker of security doors rejigged its advertisements following use of psychological research techniques which indicated that consumers felt threatened when closed-doors were depicted in ads. They were opened and sales took off

A British garden products superstore prints its promotion on paper bags rather than leaflets, encouraging customers to go straight to a "pick-and-mix" counter when they visit

Some of Germany's most successful exporters are small companies which have focussed on niche markets. A chemical company with a <u>50 per cent</u> global share in its field has just 25 employees

A Canadian publisher was worried about the declining presence of its daily newspaper on the breakfast table. So it had its logo printed on millions of fresh eggs

These examples underline that <u>many fruitful sales and marketing concepts can come</u> not from your competitors or colleagues - or even from the corporate think tank - but <u>from looking at how companies in unrelated industries and distant countries solve problems.</u>

That's why "MARKETING BREAKTHROUGHS INTERNATIONAL" has proved such a boon to forward-looking marketers since its launch in 1986. Unlike other marketing publications, "MARKETING BREAKTHROUGHS INTERNATIONAL" focusses

A letter packed with examples.

entirely on <u>usable</u> ideas, concepts and techniques, sourced from <u>all over the world</u> and presented in an <u>easy-to-digest</u> newsletter format which is entertaining and time saving.

There's no agency gossip, no punditry and no padding in "MARKETING BREAKTHROUGHS INTERNATIONAL". Just 100 per cent fresh ideas in <u>product creation, selling, distribution and promotion</u>, along with significant new <u>research findings</u> about consumers and markets, plus the latest <u>"leading edge" technology</u> to ensure that marketing and advertising strategies are handled cost-effectively.

Here are just a few examples from recent issues of the sort of information you'll get every month as a "MARKETING BREAKTHROUGHS INTERNATIONAL" subscriber.

NEW SALES/DISTRIBUTION OPPORTUNITIES
* Mail order stimulation via restaurant table cards
* New ways of boosting sales through dealers
* Sampling products at airports
* The growing choice in East European databases
* Vending machines create new ways of selling fresh produce

PRODUCT DEVELOPMENT IDEAS
* How smell impregnation can enhance business equipment
* Next year's important colour trends
* Anti-noise technology opens door to quieter products
* Hot new markets in overcrowded cities
* Why many more people are now working from home

NEW TECHNOLOGY
* TV ads in odd places; shopping trolleys, petrol pumps, waiting rooms
* Incorporating commercials within automated telephone messages
* Why not put posters on military vehicles?
* How selective binding gives readers their own exclusive publication
* High visibility from small spaces: stamps, dartboards, annual reports

With a subscription to "MARKETING BREAKTHROUGHS INTERNATIONAL", our stimulating monthly 12-page newsletter, you'll get <u>hundreds of practical, transferable ideas</u>, often well before others in your industry are even aware of them.

In a world of intensifying competition and accelerating technology isn't it time you started "thinking laterally" and put this valuable information resource to good use?

Yours sincerely,

L. Cooklin
Publisher

<u>PS:</u> The latest issue of "MARKETING BREAKTHROUGHS INTERNATIONAL" is hot from the press now. To receive it by return post, mail your subscription form today.

Again, take the American Express letter I refer to on pages 3 and 4 when talking about the stages of the market at the start of this book: it begins with a series of examples to illustrate the way it's sometimes worth paying a little more for our money.

A search for examples is always worth while; and nowhere more, incidentally, than when establishing that you have enough relevant material – a good brief. Someone may tell you what they sell is wonderful in some way. Always ask: 'Can you give me a few examples?' The same applies when looking at your own business. Examples make the subject come to life in a way claims never can.

WHAT IS MOST CONVINCING?

Perhaps the most convincing weapon in your sales armoury is a guarantee. And the best kind is a money-back guarantee. Whole businesses have been built on this. In England, Marks & Spencer became the most successful retailer on the basis of good value and quality – plus a money-back guarantee with no conditions whatsoever.

You might imagine this would persuade most businessmen of the value of such a guarantee. Not so. Relatively unsophisticated marketers often fear it may arouse suspicion, and even encourage people to ask for their money back. If your product or service is good the odds against this are high.

I can merely tell you that there is only one company I know of who have discovered offering a money-back guarantee actually reduced response. I am not going to tell you their name, but the reason for this suspicion, in my view, was that they were so reputable that people were surprised they should even think of offering such a guarantee. And this did arouse suspicion.

But unless your company enjoys such an impeccable reputation, my advice is: make the strongest possible guarantee. This is of particular importance where people are likely to doubt the claims you are making are credible – often the case with investments or self-improvement courses of one kind or another.

Thus, for instance, one of my clients guaranteed to teach you a foreign language in 30 days. That sounds remarkably easy. (As a matter of fact, I tried this course and, while it doesn't have you speaking with the fluency of a native, you certainly are speaking the language within that period.) But that course is advertised with a money-back guarantee.

As I pointed out above, people are cynical and suspicious. Apart from anything else they are often worried whether, having paid or sent their money, you will deliver what you promised. The money-back guarantee allays their concerns. This is particularly true if yours is a new product or a newly established business.

It is many years since I conducted a formal test on the money-back guarantee. I always thought if it was good enough for Marks & Spencer, it was probably good enough for my clients.

However, the last time I recall it being tested, the prominent mention of the money-back guarantee increased the number of replies by the order of 50 per cent. The number of people who ask for their money back will rarely be as high as 10 per cent – and then only if there's something weak about what you offer. Three per cent would be much more usual.

In fact *any* reassurance you can offer is generally a good idea.

HAVE YOU MISSED ANYTHING?

The things I have mentioned above cover four of the five reasons why many letters lack 'guts'. But we have not covered the fifth, and in some ways the most obvious: the letter lacks some essential argument.

Is there any reason why somebody might not reply? Is it expensive? Is it suspiciously cheap? Does it lack some feature you know many people want? These are objections you must deal with, for each one that is ignored will allow possible customers to drift away.

Just as you must deal with objections, so you must give all the reasons – even the minor ones – why people should respond. Each one of these ignored could mean the difference between a modest return and a thumping great profit.

In this area, as in most of those I have dealt with in this chapter, your greatest allies will be a good brief and many hours studying the letters in this book, and others.

ONE LETTER WITH GUTS – TWO WITHOUT

To encourage you to do so, I shall end this chapter with three examples of letters for you to think about.

The first, though it is not perfect, did a pretty good job of persuading me, despite the fact that (conceitedly) I think I already have more of the commodity being sold – marketing know-how – than most. The second and third failed dismally, though I should be a perfect prospect for both.

As you see, the heading beneath the salutation seizes your attention by talking directly to you about 'your next product launch...', then goes on to imply a benefit in the second half of the heading. As often happens with really successful lines, the benefit is a little intriguing. It not merely gains my attention but also gets my interest at the same time.

Notice, too, how the writer *assumes* I am involved in launching products. If I'm not, I probably won't be a prospect anyhow – so in this way he cuts the cackle and gets to the point. As it happens, I'm not at the moment; but many of my clients are.

Further interest is built in the series of examples below the opening which in itself makes a simple bridge from the heading to the body of the copy. These examples also convey conviction about the product and about the thought at the top – that you need to think laterally.

This is essentially how you move the reader from paying attention to becoming interested; you enlarge upon your first statement – in the process beginning to make your reader *want* what you offer.

Here, as you see, the writer goes on to convince you by pointing out that you need to look at companies elsewhere to solve your problem. Then the letter relates the product to the price once again, while enthusing the reader by pointing out that these ideas are usable, they come from all over the world and are easy to take in.

The writer overcomes the objection that there may be padding or waffle. And then he gives lots more examples which further convince that there is something here for you. He ends, of course, by telling you it is time to respond and saying the latest issue is hot off the press, thus instilling a sense of urgency.

How would you improve this?

I think this is a very good letter, but let's look at it together and see if it couldn't be improved in any way. Pause for a while and ask yourself if there is anything you would do?

I have only two comments. I wonder if you agree.

The very professional writer has decided that cost is important and has therefore crammed his letter on to two sides of one sheet. Apart from the fact that it looks cramped I think it would have been worth investing in a little more paper to give some quotations from people who had read his publication and profited from it.

I also think that putting 'date as postmark' on the top right hand corner is pointless. It doesn't tell the reader the date – if that is important anyhow – but merely underlines the fact that this is a mass-produced piece of direct mail. Either put the date in properly, or omit any reference to it, I would suggest.

Should be able to sell – but don't

The arguments in favour of giving examples in your letters are, I hope, clear by now. Perhaps they will be made even clearer if you study the Institute of Directors' letter on page 202.

It has quite a pleasing heading, and the sort of offer that always makes me sit up – free wine. (Revealingly, this offer also works to just about *every* business audience better than anything else.)

I should be a good prospect for them. I'm a company director; I do a lot of entertaining; their club is neatly situated between my flat and my office; and a good walk through the park on the way appeals to me; indeed, I often walk that way anyhow.

But look how the letter fails to give examples of the benefits you would derive from having all these resources, information and advice; this network of high-level contacts that they allude to. Who and what exactly are they?

Worse still, there is nothing whatsoever about the 'prestigious' – a dreadful word – club you are invited to join. Having been there many a time it is a splendid club, but neither the letter nor the accompanying brochure, which was pitifully sparse, shows you any pictures, gives you any details or even attempts to sell you. The whole thing lacks guts.

When you reflect that this comes out from people who are supposed to know all about business, selling and the like, it's a bit worrying isn't it?

Now let's examine the letter from my bank on page 203 which, once again, has no guts. Once again, I could be a good prospect because I *hate* paying tax. I also talked about this letter in Chapter 5.

What would you do with this one?

Read this letter carefully. Then pause for a couple of minutes and think how you would have improved it – in particular to bring forward the benefits of what is being offered – before you read on.

Now let me tell you the sort of thing I would have suggested.

IOD
Institute of Directors

20th January 1994

Our Ref : IOD DM326D

70811

How to gain a distinct business advantage in 1994

Dear Mr Bird

How would you like free access to some of the best business resources, information and advice? How would you like to expand your personal network of high level business contacts? How would you like to enjoy free membership of London's most prestigious business club?

Join the Institute of Directors and you will gain all these benefits and more - wherever your business is located.

The IOD is a professional and international business organisation which plays a key role in representing the views of business to government. The Institute is dedicated to working for senior executives like yourself. It provides directors from all types and size of organisation with the support and services they need to help in planning, decision making and their future personal and business development.

The enclosed brochure tells you more about the IOD and the many benefits available to members - from exclusive discounts on training courses, conferences and events to a wide range of free publications. I am sure you will agree that for less than the subscription to a daily newspaper, the IOD provides exceptionally good value. But there is more...

Join the IOD in February and enjoy six bottles of wine with our compliments!

You will find full details about joining the IOD on the enclosed application form. I look forward to hearing from you and to welcoming you into membership soon.

Yours sincerely

Mike Bokaie
Marketing Director

F1A   02946

Institute of Directors Mountbarrow House Elizabeth Street London SW1W 9RB Tel 071 730 4600 Fax 071 730 6335

A letter lacking guts.

 **Lloyds Bank**

Lloyds Bank Plc
Covent Garden Branch
22/24 Southampton Street
Strand
London WC2E 7JB

Telephone : 071-836 3045
Extension : 170
Network : 4152
Fax : 071-836 8353

Your Ref :
Our Ref : SDPR/14
26 June 1993

Dear Mr & Mrs Bird

Recognising your interest, as a Gold Service customer, in financial affairs, I have pleasure in offering you a free copy of The Lloyds Bank Tax Guide in advance of the 1 July publication date.

The authors, Sara Williams and John Willman, are independent financial advisors and make sure the Guide is kept up-to-date each year. In particular, the Guide will:-

* Help you check your PAYE Code
* Show how to verify your personal tax bill - and how you might be able to negotiate a reduction with the tax inspector
* Provide 50 valuable tax-saving tips

If you are interested in receiving a free copy of our Tax Guide (which normally retails for £7.99), please contact this branch by 31 July - or fill in the reply slip attached and return it to me at the address shown.

Yours sincerely

R J Ramsden
Manager Personal Banking

C1514.009 (001)

Lloyds Bank Plc is registered in England no 2065
Registered office: 71 Lombard Street, London EC3P 3BS
Member of IMRO

A dull letter with no mention of real benefits.

1. The first thing would have been to work out the sort of savings that people could make if they discovered their PAYE code was wrong.
2. Second, along the same lines, I would try to find out how big the savings could be if you negotiate a reduction with the tax inspectors. I imagine that in such a case you will probably find out you have been paying too much tax for quite a long time. I would be very surprised if with a little diligent research, one would not have been able to come up with some fairly spectacular figures about what this little guide could do.
3. What about some real-life examples? Surely they must have something to quote from all these experts – about whom more in a moment.
4. When somebody talks about 50 valuable tax savings, the first thing a normal person wants to know is: like what? So I would have wanted to enlarge upon that.
5. The guide which is being offered is worth £7.99: I would have brought that up much earlier in this unnecessarily brief letter, which I would also have had prefaced by some sort of heading or series of headings as in the letter for Acuma shown on pages 186 and 187.
6. And, just a small point but an irritating one, it refers to my wife and I as 'customer'. We are also people.

All in all this is a perfunctory, dull letter to sell something potentially extremely interesting, with no attempt to get at the real benefits of the guide, or to put a value on them or the guide itself.

Poor start; unanswered questions

Even the start is flabby. You can say that almost always any opening where the first word of a letter, a paragraph or even a sentence is the present participle of a verb – as in 'recognizing' or 'realizing' – is weak. It is not *active*.

Equally, 'financial affairs' is not a strong phrase.

If I am typical of most Gold Service customers I am not all that interested in financial affairs; indeed I find them confusing and boring. The phrase implies too much of the theoretical.

I have never laughed all the way to the bank. The thought depresses me. On the other hand I am very interested in *money* and *saving* money. That is why I became a Gold Service customer: my bank manager told me it would cost me less. So I would have constructed an opening that said much more about savings.

The second paragraph is another lost opportunity. What I am most interested in is: who do these people advise? Any millionaires? Financial institutions? Do they advise the bank itself? It doesn't make it clear. Give me some information that convinces me they are genuine authorities.

The fact that they keep the guide up to date every year is of no interest to me whatsoever. I would expect them to. What I might want to know is: does this year's issue reveal some fascinating news last year's issue didn't contain?

Just from looking at these letters I hope you will appreciate how the body of the letter makes all the difference – and that even seemingly small details can be made interesting and important if you make the effort – and if you think about what matters to your readers. Now let's turn to the climax of your letter: getting the reply.

12

Close That Sale!

'If there's one absolute rule for direct mail copywriting it is: always write the Order Form first.'

Dick Hodgson

You may recall that in Chapter 6, I said the offer, the opening and the close were the critical elements in a good letter. And in Chapter 4 I stressed that good letters are like good salesmen.

If you ever employ salesmen or have to sell yourself – and I have done both – you soon learn one lesson. The most difficult part of the job is asking for the order. That's when you are most likely to be rejected and repeated rejection is hell.

So the best salespeople have courage. They excel at asking for the order, often despite being pretty indifferent at other aspects of their work their bosses consider important – like keeping proper records. Similarly, the letters that do best are often those that go for the order most effectively. And those that fail often don't.

The order form is your target. Writing it first is an excellent discipline. It tells you where you want to end up – keeps you on track. If it has been properly written – ie includes everything relevant – it's a splendid reminder, as you go along, to make sure your letter contains everything it should.

A good example of what happens if you *don't* pay attention to the order form occurred as I was drafting this very chapter.

I subscribe to a weekly magazine of which I am inordinately fond. It has made my life a much greater pleasure. It is beautifully written for the most part. Its editorial views coincide largely with my own prejudices. So I have been reading it with great pleasure for 24 years now. It's called *The Spectator*.

The Spectator wrote reminding me my subscription was due for renewal. There were many things wrong with the letter, but one in particular was very simple. It mentioned an offer of favourable terms if I renewed, but didn't say what they were. Having more than a touch of the miser in my nature, I immediately turned to the order form to see what the deal was. It wasn't mentioned.

This confused and irritated me so much that I didn't get round to renewing at all, but wrote dolefully to the publisher; and what happened next is no part of this story.

Now you may think that is a foolish mistake; but such things are quite common.

A BORING CHORE

The order form, unfortunately, is often treated as a rather irritating excrescence or afterthought. 'Oh well, I suppose we'll have to put in an order form' seems to be going through the mind of the writer. And a tatty scrap of paper is stuffed into the envelope saying 'Send for more details'.

In fact, there is some evidence to suggest that when people receive something through the post which is clearly commercial, the *first* thing they look is at is the order form. They want to know precisely what somebody is asking them to do. It's natural.

Furthermore, very often people will throw away the rest of your mailing and keep the order form, intending to send it back later. So you'd better make sure you've done a good job on it.

Why *are* people so slapdash about asking for the order? I suspect because it's normal for you to feel very pleased at having successfully thought up a good opening and developed a convincing argument. Having done all this hard work, you feel any intelligent reader will automatically reply.

People who write direct mail for a living have another problem. They realize early on that there is a pretty limited repertoire of ways you can ask for the order and they simply get bored. Both sorts of thinking lead to very limp endings, of which the most common – and weakest – runs something like: 'I look forward to hearing from you'.

The reason why the request for the response is so important is because people are lazy and preoccupied. Your prospect may read all the way through the letter, be ready to act – then be put off because it seems too much effort or something else more urgent comes up. Making it easy to order will often have dramatic effects on your results. Even making it *look* easy to order has a dramatic effect.

In the mid 1980s one of my biggest clients, a huge US-based firm with intense competition, increased the replies to some of their letters by as much as 31 per cent one year largely by making the order form appear easier to fill in. Not by omitting any information requested previously, but by laying the form out in an attractive open way that made it seem simpler.

21 WAYS TO GET MORE ORDERS

Here are some suggestions, starting with something so obvious most people never do it:

1. *Make it complete.* Make sure the order form explains *in full*, though with no unnecessary words, what you are offering and what people are committed to. That way, even if they've mislaid the original letter, they can see immediately what they were interested in.
2. *Put in a reply-paid envelope.* Nobody likes to pay unless they have to. And nobody likes to go looking for a stamp, let alone an envelope. If you want to get the most possible responses, have a *real* stamp on the envelope. (Don't, for goodness sake, make the mistake of an 'expert' sales promotion agency which prepared and sent out mailings for a client with no reply envelope at all.)
3. *Have the name and address of the person you are writing to already filled in in the order form.* Why should they do it if you can? It's the equivalent of the waiter serving you as opposed to self-service. More to the point, it should increase your results by a good 15 per cent.
4. *Feature the phone.* The telephone has now been around for a few years. Use it. Some sort of telephone answering facility can make the difference between profit and loss in a direct mail operation.
5. *A free telephone reply service usually pays.* Failing that, there are several variations, where customers pay all or part of the cost such as 0345 where they only pay the cost of a local call.

6.   *Feature e-mail.* This is easier than any other way of replying except the phone.
7.   *Remember also: many people will read your letters out of office hours.* Make sure that there is an answering service. If your business is large enough, it should be a 24-hour, 7-day-a-week service with real operators, rather than computerized voices which put a lot of people off – but are better than nothing.
8.   *Sell the offer.* If you are offering some literature or free information, a free appointment, or some sort of gift or incentive, make sure all these are properly described – and *sold*. Many small things have been proven to increase replies.
9.   *Don't just settle for 'free booklet'.* Give it a title, say how many pages it has, and how many pictures, say it's in full colour where true. In the same way, describing the gift to make it sound as alluring as possible pays.
10. *If possible, show an attractive picture.* A photograph is better than an illustration. Say how much it's worth, if you can. Guarantee it if possible.
11. *Describe it as a 'Free Gift'.* This may be grammatically wrong; but says one thing your prospects like twice.
12. *Have a person to reply to.* If you are asking somebody to reply to a department with a code number – which you should to count the replies and see what works and what doesn't – don't just say 'Reply to Department BCM6 for full details'. People like to deal with other people. Give somebody's name: 'Write to Ann Jones, Company Secretary'. Don't just settle for the title or, worse still, nobody at all.
13. *Clarify ordering options.* Give as many possible ways of ordering as possible. Can they use their credit cards? Can they order on the phone or via the Internet? Can they try the product free? Do you offer easy terms?
14. *Try several incentives.* Don't forget: it almost always pays to give your prospects an incentive for ordering, an extra incentive for ordering quickly – within ten days, for instance – with yet another incentive for ordering a larger quantity.
15. *Try a temporarily lower price.* If you are starting a club, say: 'Become a charter member, and we'll give you a special rate.' For many years American Express used to waive the normal enrolment fee if people would reply quickly.

My local golf club gave a lower price subscription for those who were prepared to join during the three months before the club officially opened.

16. *Try a time close.* The golf club offer was dependent on *time*. This is both a positive and a negative incentive: i.e. something you will lose if you don't reply now – which we have touched on before. I have seen this approach increase response by 12–50 per cent.

17. *You can promise your readers will belong to a special group if they reply quickly.* An alternative way of doing this is to say: 'We only have so many left: hurry!' The letter from the Institute of Direct Marketing I illustrated earlier has this implication.

18. *Make people feel important.* Make people feel you are going to treat them specially. Notice in the Solarbo letter for the kitchens, I stated we would give their order a special number. Stamping 'Priority' on the order form will lift response. Saying people's applications are 'Pre-approved' will do the same.

19. *Check for comprehension.* Get somebody else to read the letter and the order form and ask them if they know what to do. The person you choose should not know much about your business but ideally might be a prospect, and has never seen the letter before.

20. *Get them to read it aloud.* People read things out loud in their heads. In so doing they sometimes stumble over words or phrases. Someone unfamiliar with the subject is far more likely to make the mistakes the recipient would than you are.

21. *Ask if they have any questions about the product or what has been written.* Those are likely to fill in any gaps in your story.

A PERFECT EFFORT

There are other obvious things you have to remember such as allowing people enough room to write in the order form, and showing how to fill it in.

If you want to know how this is done, get the form from a big mail order catalogue firm and study it carefully. Two good examples follow.

One is an order form from The Collin Street Bakery, who sell cakes all over the world. Their order form, shown on page 211, does an excellent job.

However, I don't know of any company which takes so much care over making sure they get the maximum possible number of orders as the Wyvern Business Library in England.

This famous fruit-and-nut fantasia

BAKED TO ORDER

FOR YOUR CHRISTMAS

For 90 years we've guaranteed our Original Deluxe to be the best fruitcake ever baked, bought, or eaten — or money refunded to the buyer. Sure enough, last year alone DeLuxe Fruit Cakes were shipped to every state and to 194 foreign countries as well. The cakes you order will be loaded with choice, imported fruits, crisp, new-crop pecans (27% by wt.), and no "fillers" or preservatives of any kind. They're hand-decorated, custom-baked, shipped fresh from our kitchens — just say when you want 'em to arrive. And the bottom line isn't only DeLuxe's incomparable goodness — it's your discovery that a hefty slice contains only 180 calories! So order now, and eat hearty during the holidays.

ORDER TODAY BY TOLL-FREE CALL OR BY COUPON (CHECK OR CHARGE CARD)

1-800-624-5041 PHONE CREDIT CARD ORDERS EXT. 536 ANY HOUR

Holiday-packed, cake's colorful history enclosed. Postpaid: Reg. (1⅞ lbs.) $10.15; Med. (2⅞ lbs.) $14.65; Lg. (4⅞ lbs.) $23.95. Discounts on 25 cakes or more.

ORIGINAL
DeLuxe
"that famous Corsicana, Texas Fruit Cake," since 1896

NEVER SOLD IN STORES

COLLIN STREET BAKERY
Box 536 Corsicana, Texas 75110

Please ship ____ Reg. ____ Med. ____ Lg.
☐ Ship to me   ☐ Ship to attached list, showing addresses, sizes, desired arrival dates.
☐ My check enclosed (For card charges see below)

Name _____

Address _____

City _____

State _____ Zip _____
Or charge to my ☐ MC ☐ VISA ☐ AE

Card # _____ Exp. _____

Signature _____

A perfect effort.

Their meticulous approach to business enables them to succeed at something many mail order operators would not even try: selling books which are freely available elsewhere at full price off the page.

Their buyers are mailed once a month with a selection of cards selling some of the many books they offer. And it is the attention to detail in these mailings I particularly like here. I have never seen anyone take so much trouble.

I have illustrated some of the cards you receive in one of their mailings, because each one contains something to learn from – starting with the front of a card selling *Harrap's Book of Business Anecdotes*, on page 213.

10 days at your desk to decide

Yes! please send me the book overleaf at the price shown plus £2.95 towards post and packing (£3.95 for two or more books).

Guarantee: I have 10 days from delivery to decide. After that I can keep the book and pay the price (+p&p) shown or I can return it and owe nothing.

Signature _____

Name Mr/Mrs/Miss _____
BLOCK CAPITALS PLEASE

Position _____

Company _____

Address _____

_____ Post Code _____

Tel No. _____ Fax No. _____
(in case of query)

VERY URGENT ORDERS
Telephone: 0353 665544
Have your credit card ready
Please quote ref: AK7

For several books please use an envelope or staple the cards together. Remember to sign each one. Full details of offer in accompanying letter. Offer subject to acceptance
A B C D E F G

TO:
Wyvern Business Library
FREEPOST CB 511
Ely
Cambs
CB7 4BR

If you pre
out this a

Harrap's Book of BUSINESS ANECDOTES
Peter Hay

How to turn an OK speech into an excellent speech.

A well chosen anecdote can work wonders for your speech, your report, your sales letter and even your conversation.

Whether you are addressing an audience of hundreds or just two or three colleagues, you will make your point so much better and more memorable if you use anecdotes.

£12.95
+p&p

Anecdotes are interesting. They lighten the tone, emphasise important points and can break up long passages of technical or unexciting information.

But to work really well, they must be relevant, they must match the topic, the speaker and the audience.

Harrap's book of Business Anecdotes contains over 500 stories, ranging from a few words to a whole page. They are all relevant to business and conveniently sorted by subject. Money, selling, managers, politics, advertising, rewards - these are just some.

They can be used in speeches, in seminars, in reports, in sales brochures - anywhere, in fact, where you want to make your point vividly and easily.

296 pages Hardback 1899 UK   *See the book before you buy!*   **878** AK7

Wyvern
Business Library   *Practical books for business*

Valuable lessons.

HAVE WE GOT IT RIGHT?

(Please tell us if we have got it wrong)

Use this card if you want us to amend your name and address. Feel free to give us a different address if you prefer, or a different name if the person we have addressed this cardpack to has moved on and you are now dealing with their mail.

REMEMBER, WE NEED THE OLD NAME AND ADDRESS AS WELL AS YOUR NEW DETAILS TO ENABLE US TO AMEND OUR RECORDS.

Print the OLD details in the space below and your new information overleaf.

OLD DETAILS

Name Mr/Mrs/Ms _____
BLOCK CAPITALS PLEASE

Position _____

Company _____

Address _____

Post Code _____

The Full Wyvern Service

When you buy a book from us you automatically qualify for our full updating information service. This service is free. It incorporates regular cardpacks from the Wyvern Business Library keeping you up-to-date books available. It also includes additional information other companies who have asked our permission to contact of their products and services.

For customers wishing to receive just Wyvern mailings, we "Wyvern only" service. You can request this limited servi appropriate box below.

☐ Tick here if you require the reduced "Wyvern only" serv

☐ Tick here if you wish to be removed from our mailing lis

PRIORITY ORDER

I wish to order the following books:-

Book Title	Book Price
1.	£
2.	£
3.	£
4.	£
5.	£

*P&P =
£2.95 for 1 book
£3.95 for 2 or more

+ P&P * £

Total £

(To order more than 5 books please continue on a separate piece of paper)

☐ I enclose my cheque for £ _____ made payable to Wyvern Business Library or

☐ Please debit my ☐ ☐ ☐ ☐ ☐ ☐ ☐

Card No.

Signature _____ Expiry Date ..../..........

Name Mr/Mrs/Miss _____
BLOCK CAPITALS PLEASE

Position _____

Company _____

Address _____

Post Code _____

Tel No. _____ Fax No. _____
(in case of query)

For your security. For cheque payment or to keep your credit details confidential, simply copy out our FREEPOST address onto an envelope. Otherwise you may simply pop this card in the post. It is already addressed and no stamp is needed.

AK7

INTRODUCE A COLLEAGUE

Do you know a friend or colleague who would like to receive our Wyvern Business Library cardpacks?

Simply give them this card to fill in and post back to us. There is no obligation to buy.

To your friend or colleague

The Wyvern Business Library selects and recommends the best business books available. We publish no books ourselves, so we are free to filter out only the finest new business books from the deluge sent to us by hopeful publishers.

Good business books are unique. They are the only books which can be expected to pay for themselves every time. How? It takes:

* Just one profit-boosting idea
* Just a few minutes of professional advice saved
* A tiny improvement in your own business effectiveness

We provide a free recommendation service, keeping you up-to-date with the latest and most practical books available.

To receive our Wyvern Business Library cardpack, simply fill in your details overleaf and post this card to us. There is absolutely no obligation to buy.

We will send you our latest cardpack and in our next mailing.

PLEASE TURN OVER TO FILL IN YOUR ADDRESS DETAILS

HOW TO MAKE MONEY FROM IDEAS AND INVENTIONS
R. Rogers

You are already an inventor. Why not become a rich inventor?

This remarkable book by a full time professional inventor takes you step by step from the idea to the money.

You have had more good ideas in your life than you think. Many of them you used to solve a problem of your own and thought no more about it. Others you assumed were not original - someone MUST have thought of that already.

£16.95 +p&p

Hundreds of thousands of people have good ideas every day. But only a handful bother to do anything about them. And they get rich.

The ideas don't have to be spectacular, highly technical, breathtakingly innovative or even all that new. They just have to be unregistered for Patent or Copyright.

For years housekeepers have picked fluff off upholstery using the sticky side of Sellotape. But only recently has anyone used the idea to make a special roller that is selling like hot cakes in supermarkets across the Country.

This report shows you how to create new ideas out of thin air, how to develop them, register them, find manufacturing and marketing expertise, even how to license them without getting ripped off.

Sample Royalty Agreements, Design Registration, full Patent Specifications, business plans, Declarations of Trust are among the many practical features of this book.

114 pages Hardback 1992 UK
(first published as a special report 1989) See the book before you buy! **B04 AK7**

Wyvern Business Library — Practical Books for business

Valuable Lessons

The first card has a lot of lessons for copywriters – indeed, you could probably reset the whole thing in the form of a letter and do reasonably well. Notice that he sells the benefit – the ability of anecdotes to improve your speeches – not the anecdotes themselves. But we're talking about order forms and details here.

This merchant appreciates what many do not: it is not his business to tell his customers how to order – he should adapt himself to suit them, and make it easy. He also appreciates that once people have decided to buy, it is the best time to get them to do a number of other things – like ordering several, and giving the names of other potential customers:

- Notice 'see the book before you buy' written in script at the end of the copy. He's telling you this is a free trial offer.
- On the reverse, see how carefully the copy in the coupon is phrased and that the free trial promise is explained in more detail (10 days at your desk to decide).
- Read the box headed 'very urgent orders'. Telling people there is a way of getting their order in a hurry will always increase response.
- Notice, too, the small type next to the box telling people what to do if they want several books.
- Another card in their pack is devoted to ensuring address details are up to date. A common and simple problem many people ask me about. Here it is dealt with perfectly. (The publisher considers, quite rightly, this to be so important that he features it again, on the envelope.)
- Look how they deal with another important problem. How do you tell people they're likely to receive regular direct mail? As you see under the heading 'The Full Wyvern Service', the answer is, don't apologise: sell it as a full *updating* service. But give readers the opportunity to be taken off the mailing list, either entirely or partially.
- Apart from the order form on the back of each card, a separate card is headed Priority Order. Here is the publisher trying to move people from the 10 day free trial offer to paying in advance. On the back is a model order form.
- They are carefully reassured that they get the same protection, because if they just send the book back they can have their money back without question. This point is made elsewhere, too.

● In yet another they try to recruit new people as well as doing an excellent selling job on their service and, once again, giving people on the reverse under CARDPACK REQUEST the chance to say 'Please put me on your mailing list'.

The details I am talking about may appear to you to be dull, petty affairs. But I have rarely seen such a clear example of how attention to detail pays off. I would estimate that it probably increases the profitability of the business by at least 30 per cent.

ABOVE ALL, MAKE IT URGENT

Here is the way a marketer offering a money-making proposition in the 1930s ended his message:

Let nothing, absolutely nothing, interfere with immediate action. A change for the better justifies no delay. Don't watch others make money which you can make. Be up and doing now. Some other time may be too late. Place your order and application this very minute. Take the action now which means more money next week, independence next year.

There are many ways in which you can raise urgency at the end of a letter. Suppose you're selling a business course. Here is the sort of thing I've found works:

```
I'm sure you'll agree there are few occasions in life when you
can so dramatically transform your future without risking a
penny.

Let me re-emphasize: there is absolutely no obligation. No
salesman will call. All you have to do is reply in the next
seven days. You'll get your guaranteed 20% discount, and I'll
rush you your free book by return.

Don't forget, if you don't like the course, for any reason — or
no reason at all — just send it back to us. We'll pay the
postage and refund your money in full. So you can't lose, can
you?

Why not act now, while the matter's fresh in your mind? You
know how easy it is to put things off when you're busy. Just
hand the order form to your secretary, and get her to fill it
in and send it off today. It will only take you a minute, but
the rewards will benefit you for many years to come.
```

So, as you see, you restate the proposition when you ask for the order. This is the moment of truth – particularly if the letter has been at all long, i.e. two pages or more. Just remind people, as they're making up their minds, what they get if they respond – and what they lose if they don't. What the deal is.

In particular you should always emphasize the fact that there is no obligation. This is the moment when people are debating with themselves whether they really thought to go ahead or not.

USE A PS

It seems appropriate to end this chapter by mentioning the postscript.

When people receive letters they almost invariably turn to the end to see who has written to them – that's why you will find so many professional sales letters contain a PS. Research has discovered that is what readers recall most, *on average*, in a letter. That's because they look to see who has written to them.

The PS should say something important – generally it should re-emphasize the basic proposition or offer and underline the need for urgency. Here is an example.

PS. Don't forget, if you want to enter the contest, you must do so before 15 April. You don't have to buy anything: simply send in your entry form.

Next, let us move on to consider the business of writing.

13

How To Write Better

'Easy writing's vile hard reading.'

Richard Brinsley Sheridan

Good writing comes from two things. The right *ideas* and the right *technique*. Decide what you want to say; then say it as well as you can. I have already observed that the idea is more important than how well you put it across, but, no matter how good, if you don't convey that idea properly your letter will fail. As the great pianist Paderewski said: 'Technique comes before art.'

I used to conduct a seminar for the UK Chartered Institute of Marketing on writing sales letters. This was a numbing experience for all concerned. In one day I tried to reveal everything I am trying to tell you in this book; then each of my victims had to draft a letter, on which I commented as helpfully as I could.

Finally, I gave up the struggle, exhausted – though perhaps not as much as many of the participants. My excuse was the organizers didn't pay enough, which was true. But it was more that I was utterly drained at the end of each day by the fearful task of reviewing up to 20 letters – many on subjects I knew little about – in about an hour, while trying to be intelligent and not offend anyone.

The most difficult thing to convey to my students was how to write properly. I wish I had read at that time a splendid essay by George Orwell, who you may recall wrote *1984* and *Animal Farm*, with the rather dry title 'Politics and the English Language'. In it he gave six rules for good writing which, had I read them out, would have been a great help to all.

Here they are.

1. Never use a metaphor, simile or other figure of speech which you are used to seeing in print.
2. Never use a long word where a short one will do.
3. If it is possible to cut a word out, always cut it out.
4. Never use the passive where you can use the active.
5. Never use a foreign phrase, a scientific word, or a jargon word if you can think of an everyday English equivalent.
6. Break any of these rules sooner than say anything outright barbarous.

Those points are wonderfully simple: obeying them is not. In this chapter, I shall try to cover them, as well as a number of others, starting with the biggest problem many writers face.

This was not how to write grammatically – in most cases my intervention would have been too late. Nor how to incorporate the right content in the right order, which is an almost mechanical process. Nor even the rules for writing correctly which (if you know English grammar) is largely a matter of discipline, as Orwell suggests.

No: the big challenge was to make people write naturally and thus convincingly – *as themselves*.

A MYSTERIOUS CHANGE

You are, I am sure, familiar with the scene in *Dr Jekyll and Mr Hyde* when the benevolent Jekyll swallows the potion and turns in a few seconds into the bestial Hyde; a trick which, in my youth, used to take me several hours and eight pints of Chester's robust bitter beer on a Saturday night.

Such a transformation often overtakes people the minute they have to write something. From being friendly, down-to-earth souls, they are suddenly transmogrified into dull, impersonal automatons or pompous, boring old farts, who communicate in a strange, formulaic fashion.

In some cases they resort to expressions only found in antique business correspondence: 'We are in receipt of yours of the 15th inst.' and 'Assuring you of our best attention at all times'. How much better to say: 'Thank you for your letter of the 15th'; and 'We're always happy to help'.

Such extreme manifestations of the problem are fairly rare nowadays. Nevertheless I am sure you often receive letters which seem to have been put together by a business phrase-making machine rather than written by one human to another.

An example of what I mean came on the very day I started drafting this chapter in a letter from the people who made my cooker. They were writing to say there might be a problem with the hood.

Instead of saying 'Please', they used the archaic expression: 'We would ask that…' and 'We would apologize…', when what they meant was 'We're sorry'. This sort of thing, apart from using too many words, takes the humanity away from your writing and makes you sound insincere.

BEWARE OF CLICHÉS

I saw when preparing this chapter a letter from a credit card company, the end of which read: 'Apply now for your free no-obligation interview' – a phrase this company had used, no doubt, in their literature so often it had become like a ritual chant. It had become a cliché.

This is what Orwell was talking about in the first of his six rules: an expression which has been used so many times it has lost all its freshness and power to involve. It slides into your mind and out again without even being noticed.

Instead of trotting out the formula I've quoted above, isn't it so much fresher and more personal to say: 'Call or write now for an interview. There's no obligation'?

Your writing loses power when you use too many clichés. Some words become a sort of fashion, included without thought. Often they are thought to make something sound more serious, but they add no real meaning. One is 'strategic' – usually applied to anything more important than going to the toilet. Another is 'basically', which is almost always unnecessary.

A good place to collect clichés is in popular newspapers – particularly on the sports pages. You can rely on politicians to trundle out a fair quota, too. But the cliché flourishes in the sales letter as in few other places.

Is it really *exciting?*

How many times have you seen something described as 'exciting', 'fantastic' or 'fabulous' in a sales letter? I still recall with a frisson of disbelief a letter sent to my wife about an 'exciting range of loans'.

A good way to get rid of that sort of thing is to ask yourself: 'Would I say that to someone I know?' You and I know we would never dream of talking to a friend about a loan being 'exciting'.

It is, I think, impossible to write without using clichés at all; but you should *try* to avoid them. A good way to spot a cliché is to take one half and see how easy it is to put the other half to it.

For instance, *size* and *portions* are practically always *generous*; *rates* are almost invariably *highly competitive*; while *reliability* tends surprisingly often to be *tried and tested*. *Differences* are usually *significant* and *values* are generally *core*, whereas *issues* are always *key*. A remarkable number of *decisions* will be made *at the end of the day*. And there are few occasions indeed when *expertise* is not *unrivalled*.

Perhaps the most common cliché in sales letters is not a word at all. It is the exclamation mark, which bad writers use to whip up fake enthusiasm. In a recent letter from a record company I counted 15 on a single page. Unless what you are saying is really worth shouting about, don't use them. The less you do, the more impact they will have.

BE CAREFUL WITH JARGON

Don't use expressions which are clear to you, but mean nothing, or even something quite different to your readers.

Jargon is almost as great a sin as cliché. People in industries and organizations – especially successful ones – develop their own jargon. Such jargon is a way of distinguishing the insider from the outsider. If you recognize the jargon, you're 'one of us'.

So eradicate jargon unless you are talking to people with a special interest, in which case it may usefully convey to your readers that you are on their wavelength. An example of this is in the letter on pages 222–23 which I wrote for a famous European business school.

But even with jargon aimed at specialist readers you must be careful. Sometimes it is so impenetrable only a cryptologist could understand it and you may be excluding many of your prospects. Here is something I read a while ago in the US publication, *Advertising Age*:

INSEAD

January 1996

**A Partnership or Alliance can prove a fruitful marriage - or a
costly mismatch. How will yours turn out?**

Dear Mr Peng,

As you will certainly know, alliances and partnerships - even with competitors - can be
enormously beneficial. They can help you enter new markets, achieve scale, pace and
competitiveness, gain new skills and technologies - even renew your business.

But you probably also know they can be risky - though few appreciate just *how* risky. In fact,
a US study of those undertaken between 1975-85 found that 57% failed. One reason could be
that managing an alliance may well take twice as much effort as managing a subsidiary.

If you help manage a partnership, or are about to - particularly if you are responsible for its
outcome - our groundbreaking programme *Managing Partnerships and Strategic Alliances* is
essential.

It takes place on 19-24 May 1996- a few short days out of your schedule: but long enough to
shift the odds significantly in your favour. The programme reflects INSEAD's pioneering
work in this field. The distinguished faculty is led by Professor Yves Doz, who has conducted
seminal research in this area, has written extensively on strategic alliances and advised many
major multinational companies.

> You discover which partnerships are more likely to create value; how you
> manage them to maximise that value; what to look for and learn from; and how
> you manage networks of partnerships to build long term competitive
> advantage. Participants gain a unique global perspective - as comments from
> firms such as the Xerox Corporation, USA, testify.

To give you an idea of the depth and value of the programme, let me briefly detail two typical
case studies. In one you explore the history of a partnership between a large and a small
company - from its origins and the structure of the agreement, to the way it functioned, to the
time when it was dissolved after eight years - and what its consequences were for the two
companies.

The European Institute of Business Administration

Boulevard de Constance, 77305 Fontainebleau Cedex, France

Telephone (33) 1 60 72 40 00 Fax: (33) 1 60 72 42 42 Telex 690389 F

Institut privé d'enseignement supérieur,

Association loi 1901 Code ape:804 D

Code siret 775 703 390 000 10

**A little jargon is quite enough – even when dealing with highly technical
subjects.**

In so doing you understand far better why partnerships occur, what causes conflicts, and how they can be sustained. What can be done to make them work more fruitfully? How do you design a structure for partners to collaborate better? What problems occur when terminating a partnership?

You gain a remarkable insight, because participants look at the partnership from three different perspectives: that of each of the partners, and as objective observers. And this is intensely practical. You address such issues as: what problems do you see in the partnership? Why did they come about? What do you think of the way they were approached? What would you have done differently?

You can imagine how involving and instructive that is. It contrasts with a second case in which you review the actions of a world-leading company with a new CEO who takes over in a difficult turnaround situation. This company has managed joint ventures extremely successfully for over half a century and now makes them central to its strategy.

One intriguing issue discussed is: did this in fact improve the company or just make it different? And you assess specific decisions: for example whether the company should allow a foreign company to take a 50% share in one of its core divisions, reflecting a common dilemma: allies have different priorities, which can give rise to problems.

You will get particular value from the programme if you arrange for managers from different companies in a partnership to take part. This naturally creates mutual understanding and can lead to joint solutions to common problems, thus significantly enhancing the likelihood of success.

In this programme you benefit especially from exchanging ideas with those from other industries and cultures, as well as a wide range of nationalities (typically around ten). Because the potential rewards from sound alliances are so great, yet the downside is so daunting, I feel it is a particularly wise investment.

To receive a comprehensive brochure, just call Janet Burdillat on 33 (1) 60 72 42 90, e-mail execed@insead.fr or return the enclosed reply card. You could fax it if you prefer on 33 (1) 60 74 55 13.

Yours sincerely,

Arnoud De Meyer
Associate Dean
Executive Education

P.S.   *Because this programme has such wide relevance, I would advise you reserve a place early. You may use the reply card to do so.*

> Mission marketing operates on companies' vision platforms and uses these commitments to drive a totally integrated corporate communication program both horizontally and vertically.

It is just possible, if you have read the rest of the article in question and you are extremely determined, to understand what the author means. But that sentence is what I call syllabic machismo: bad writing, posing as intelligence. Even I, who have worked in marketing for decades, found it hard to tease meaning out of it.

The worst offenders

Unfortunately, the businesses which use more incomprehensible jargon that most also send out the most direct mail – sellers of financial products. In his book *Dear Sir or Madam* (NTC Publishing), Tom Rayfield records the following opening to a letter:

> 'Investments which provide a geared play in the stock market offer the investor a distinct advantage.'

This was as far as he got in that letter. Also in this book – which is a very educative record of how advertisers respond (or fail to) when you reply to their advertisements – Rayfield comments on another mailing:

> 'I don't understand a word of it. That is, I understand many of the individual words, but not the way they are arranged to conceal any apparent benefit for me from buying these things. Do financial mailings have to be so impenetrable?'

This is part of a letter that raised his ire:

> Last August we predicted the very low interest rates with which we are having to come to terms. Since that time we have constantly followed interest rates down, in an attempt to obtain the best products available before they were withdrawn. During the last three months we have concentrated our efforts and strongly believe that now is the time to act ...

In this instance, not jargon, but sloppy thinking transferred perfectly on to the page is the problem. No doubt engaging brain before putting pen to paper would have helped. As I have already suggested, it's good to get someone who knows nothing about the subject to read what you have written and see if they understand. That would have been wise in this case.

WRITE THE WAY YOU TALK

All these business and marketing clichés, all this vague waffle and strange jargon are bad – in sales letters or anything else. The ideal is to write *more or less* the way you talk. Not exactly, because if you ever read transcriptions of speech, you will see we all talk in a most disorganized fashion.

So good writing is, as I have already observed, simply well-organized speech. In fact, if you know a good writer, you will notice that when you read something they have written you can almost hear them speaking.

Writing is not, of course, exactly the same as speaking; you will often use dramatic effects to make or repeat some point; it is a heightened form of speech, to my mind. But good writing is often *personal* just as speech is; and certainly this is true when we are talking about that most personal kind of communication – the letter.

The secret is to fight off this strange feeling that comes over some of us when we start writing, whereby we almost say to ourselves: 'Now I am *writing*' and tuck an imaginary quill pen behind our ears before starting to communicate in a way we would never do if we were actually speaking to someone.

Just as it's wise to get someone to read your letter for comprehension, that's why it's a splendid idea for you to read the letter out loud yourself. If it sounds like a local by-law or a tax demand or a party political broadcast, it's wrong. Rewrite it so it sounds like natural speech.

'We' is not likeable; 'I' is more personal; and 'you' is perfect

One example of unnatural writing – especially common in business letters – is the use of the word *we* rather than *I*. Unless you are the Queen of England, or a particularly conceited pop star, or you really *are* speaking on behalf of an entire team or corporation, wherever possibly say 'I'.

You are trying to build a relationship with another person – to make them like you enough to do what you want. People find it very difficult to relate to companies or corporations. But they find it very easy to deal with people. They are much more likely to react to a letter written to them from another individual than from some corporate colossus.

In fact, as you might expect from all you have read so far, the word that is most important in a letter is *'you'*. This was discovered by an American researcher called Rudolf Flesch, working 50 or 60 years ago on what makes writing easy to read.

He learned that if you wish people to read what you write, then the words 'you', 'your', and variations like 'yours' and 'yourself' should appear twice and preferably three times as often as words like 'me', 'I', 'our', 'we' and the like.

This, of course, fits in with our theme of talking about what interests your reader, rather than what interests you. Flesch learned a number of other things which are included in what I shall now reveal on the techniques most likely to get your reader to start – and keep – reading.

TRICKS THAT MAKE READING EASY

Orwell, in his six rules, says short words lead to better writing. Consider the following alternatives:

Emolument	*Cash*
Complimentary	*Free*
Affection	*Love*
Expectation	*Hope*
Sanguinary	*Bloody*
Transportation	*Car*
Servicing	*Helping*
Purchase	*Buy*

Short words are usually of Anglo-Saxon rather than Latin origin; they are easier to take in because they don't take as long to read and they pack more emotional punch. This is important. People are swayed more by their hearts than their heads.

Simple words hit the mark

Such words work better for another, practical reason, well put by Winston Churchill: 'Use simple words everybody knows. Then everyone will understand'. In his famous speeches during the Battle of Britain, the words that hit the mark were all short: 'I have nothing to offer you save blood, sweat, toil and tears'.

Now consider these phrases:

Miss out on	*miss*
An additional element	*something else*
At this time	*now*
Female personnel	*women*
Conclude discussions	*end talks*
Deposit waste materials	*put rubbish*
Terminate momentarily	*stop soon*

Get the idea? The same principle applies to sentences and paragraphs. To be easily read, Flesch learned, no sentence should contain more than 32 words. The easiest length of sentence to read was 8 words long. The average for easy reading is 16 words.

A paragraph that is easy to read and understand contains just one thought. And the first paragraph in your letter should definitely be short, because that's the most important – the one that gets the reader started. Don't make all your sentences and paragraphs the same length, though; that would be very dull, just like someone talking in a monotone.

HOW BEST SELLERS ARE WRITTEN

If you think these prescriptions might restrict your fancy, spend a little while reading the two best-written books in the English language, both of which are very persuasive: the King James Version of the Bible and the Book of Common Prayer. Both follow these rules.

If they sound daunting, pick up a best-selling novel. Everything is usually short, lively and easily understood, often even the chapters. And there is another characteristic which makes reading easy: lots of dialogue.

Brevity is always admirable – a good example being the instructions Roosevelt gave Eisenhower in 1943: 'Please assemble a force for the invasion of Europe'.

Two words in particular are often unnecessary: 'that' and 'which'. Take the following: 'There is something else which is'. This can be recast as 'Something else is'. Similarly, in 'Bill tells me that we are going to have problems', the word 'that' is not needed.

But achieving brevity is hard work. I compare cutting unnecessary or overlong words to pruning a garden. I revise my first draft *at least* ten times to get it to my satisfaction – and even then I always read my work after it's been printed and realize I am too easily satisfied.

One thing you will also notice in the Bible and in best sellers is the common use of the active rather than passive sentences. Active sentences are, as you might expect, more lively as well as shorter and often more personal.

Here are two examples to show you the difference, the second taken from the paragraph before last, showing how I actually altered a sentence.

Esau was slain by Jacob (**passive**)
Jacob slew Esau (**active**)

Cutting unnecessary or overlong words is something I compare to pruning a garden (**passive**)
I compare cutting unnecessary or overlong words to pruning a garden (**active**)

Apart from using the right sorts of words, phrases, sentences and paragraphs, there are other things you can do to keep readers with you. Some may conflict with what you were told at school, though, once again, you may well find them in the Bible.

Use carrier words and phrases

There are many ways to tell people there is more to come. At the beginning of a sentence or paragraph, words like 'And', 'Also' and 'Moreover' do this, as do phrases like 'In addition', 'What is more', 'For example' and 'For instance'.

Ending a paragraph with a question which has to be answered in the next helps, too, as does a phrase like 'Let me explain'. Here's an example showing how you might link the two effectively. Suppose you have just made a very bold claim or seemingly over-generous offer. Then you write:

Does this sound too good to be true? Let me explain.

Try not to end a page at the end of a sentence or paragraph

Always break in the middle of such a sentence or paragraph, preferably at a point likely to encourage people to read on. Thus, a page of your letter could end: *'To take advantage of these remarkable savings you simply have to...'*

If the letter is longer than a page, at the end of the page tell people what to do. Use a phrase like 'please read on' or 'next page' or 'please turn over'. If you want to be more imaginative, you could write: 'Read on for more good news'.

Psychologists know that if you tell people to do something they are more likely to do it – which, like a lot of things they say, is blindingly obvious when you think about it. You can use more than words to encourage readers, as you will see in Chapter 15 on layout, where a charity letter uses the tracks of an amphibian to keep people reading. This leads to my next suggestion.

Write your letter so as to encourage an interesting layout

A good letter should have shape. This is a matter of layout, clearly. But layout starts with the way you compose the letter. So as you write consider how what you are writing will appear on the page.

In the next chapter I shall make a number of suggestions on how your letter should look – indented paragraphs, numbered points, dashes, changes of typeface and the like. Bear them in mind when writing, but remember it is best to be sparing with these devices.

A FEW MINOR PROBLEMS – LIKE HOW TO BEGIN

You have probably noticed I have carefully avoided what may be the first thing that comes to mind when you think about writing. How do I get a good idea? Not to mention a few other small details – like, how do I set about the writing itself?

Should you lock yourself away and stare at a blank wall until inspiration smites you? Or resort to stimulants of one kind or another? Are you supposed to sit down and scribble away in an inspired frenzy? Or write down notes and expand upon them?

The answer, I'm afraid, is that it depends largely on you – and on chance. Work in the setting and at the time you find suits you. But always be on the look out for good thoughts. Ideas obstinately refuse to come when you call, but obligingly surface when unexpected. You can sit thinking with screwed up brow for hours – nothing. Then you wake up in the middle of the night and – bingo!

Ideas occur to me when walking or riding my bike. The odd drink seems to open doors for me – but not too many, Some get ideas in the bath or when shaving. Some find them very early in the morning (I often do). Gibbon conceived *The Decline and Fall of the Roman Empire* when ruminating, appropriately, amidst Roman ruins. The philosopher Descartes dreamed up 'I think, therefore I am', when sitting in an oven in Poland. I assume it was large and unlit at the time.

One sure recipe is studying great practitioners – in your own field or in others. It inspires you to do as well. Beethoven was walking in the street with a friend. They heard someone playing Mozart. 'You and I will never write anything as good as that,' he said. He had something to aim for – and he succeeded.

Often a good thought will come from a most unexpected source. But the mine from which your ideas must be quarried, whenever or wherever they come, is always the same. From being well briefed.

I won't labour that point, save to say that when you come to write one source is particularly valuable: reference material. You should start to build a file of letters or ideas that you find interesting. Rather like the list of 100 headlines mentioned earlier, they will often prove a good starting point.

And I would add that having a rich source of knowledge – a well-informed mind – is valuable.

Note all first ideas, however vague

When you have studied all the information available to you, write down any notes that occur to you, however vague, incomplete or even wild and irrelevant. Never 'censor' yourself; indulge your wildest fancies; look favourably at this stage on any interesting thought, however improbable or far-fetched.

At this point, it's a good idea to jot down what you think the letter should contain – the elements, in no particular order.

By 'elements' I don't mean the AIDCA formula I mentioned earlier. I mean all the points you think necessary to your argument. The reasons why people should reply; the objections they might raise to replying; how you would overcome them; proof that what you say is true; examples that make your point – everything you need for a strong argument. Pay special attention to any ideas you have on offers, envelope messages, involvement devices and openings.

Always think of as many ways as you can of how to begin. Is there some relevant saying or story you could use?

Give your subconscious mind time

At the end of this process you should have a good jumble of thoughts on paper. Don't worry if they don't point to a clear solution. Now is the time you allow your subconscious mind – the source of all good ideas – to work on that material. Give it two or three days. Then return to the task and start writing.

It is not generally good to write a short letter and then try to lengthen it. Better to overwrite and then edit. Imagine you have that prospect sitting in front of you and you *must* persuade them. Write with passion, correct with care.

If you have that passion, that determination and you have done all the other things I mention, you will do well, as long as you remember one other maxim, sometimes given in a rather different context: use it or lose it. To write well, you must write often. It is like everything else. Practice does tend to make perfect.

Paderewski, whom I have already quoted, put it this way: 'If I don't practise for a day, I can tell the difference. If I don't practise for two days, the critics can tell. If I don't practise for three days, the audience begins to.'

Let's now consider how you might do more than write a good letter: how you might write an *outstanding* letter.

14

Writing that Charms

The eighteenth-century wit John Wilkes was famously ugly;
he squinted horribly. He was also famously successful with
women. *'It takes me five minutes to talk away my face'*, he
confided to a friend.

You can divide sales letters into three categories.

First, there are those which are plain bad – and most are. As we've
learned, there can be all sorts of reasons for this. It's probably a good
idea to remind ourselves of some of the common ones now.

Perhaps the writer hasn't done enough preliminary work and so is
talking about the wrong thing to the right person or the right thing to
the wrong person. Maybe the letter is wrongly constructed, or it
doesn't make the right offer, or that offer isn't introduced quickly
enough.

Or is there something essential missing; perhaps testimonials or a
compelling urge to action? Is the letter just poorly aimed, so the
wrong readers are being addressed? Often the unfortunate writer
simply doesn't know how to use the English language.

Well, such letters, for all those reasons, are obviously failures from
the start.

But let's suppose the letter is well aimed and the writer *understands*
all the technicalities of effective letter writing – the right order, the

right offer, the right tricks to keep people reading, vivid language as opposed to dull language, attention to talking about *you* rather than *we*, and so forth.

In this case we have our second category of letter: the workmanlike; the adequate. But what makes the difference between a letter that's OK and one that's brilliant?

Adaptability is often critical here. And that means the ability to vary the tone of what you write, depending on the audience and the sender. This ability makes your letter, apart from anything else, more believable.

By 'believable', I mean the tone does not jar; the reader is not pulled up short by feeling: 'I don't believe that person would write to me like that.' This is one aspect of what is meant by the right tone; but assuming the tone is appropriate, if it is carefully handled it can have great impact on the performance of your letter.

WHAT IS TONE?

In the direct marketing business, you will often see a client look at a letter and say: 'I don't like the tone'. This message is then taken back to the copywriter – the poor soul who actually wrote the letter – and he or she is reduced to gibbering fury for two reasons.

First, because writers believe anything they write into which they have poured their heart and soul, is perfect anyhow – so how can the client presume to criticize it? Second, because saying something has the wrong 'tone' is a pretty vague way of criticizing it. Yet the client knows what he or she means, even if it is not easy to explain why the 'tone' is wrong.

In this, as so many areas of our subject, it's a good idea to liken the situation to a face-to-face confrontation. We all know of occasions where we meet somebody and we say: 'I didn't like his manner'. Or: 'We didn't get on well – it was just a matter of personal chemistry'.

What are you really saying in such a case? That the person you met – as far as you were concerned – didn't speak in what you felt to be the appropriate way. This jarred on you. Exactly the same thing occurs in direct mail. In some respects I liken it to *charm*.

We all know people who are charming. People who seem to get on with almost everybody. How do they do it? Quite simply. They take the trouble to study the person they're talking to and approach them in a sympathetic manner, based upon that study.

That is what a good letter does.

Think of it. You may like to go to a particular restaurant or patronize a particular shop. But mostly, apart from the quality of the product being sold there, what makes all the difference is how pleasant the people are to you. They treat you in a suitably agreeable fashion.

This is one reason why big corporations have recently been investing enormous amounts of money into trying to persuade their surly minions to behave in a reasonably pleasant manner.

A classic example most British people are familiar with is British Airways. They were doing a very poor job of making money until they introduced a programme called Putting People First, which transformed their business.

THE SECRET OF CHARM

Your ability to adapt the tone of your letters will make your letters *charming*. It will give them personality. A good example is the letter opening reproduced opposite. You almost feel that the writer is a friend.

Competent letters – the second category I referred to earlier – have everything *except* that magic, that conviction, that charm such mastery of tone gives. The writers who produce this adequate stuff write exactly the same way, no matter who they are addressing.

But the outstanding writers disarm their prospect in just the same way as a charming individual can disarm somebody he or she is trying to persuade to do something. And is this something you can learn? I believe that to some extent it is, just as if you make an effort you can be charming in person.

The first secret of personal charm is easy to master. You have already been told it in this book. You study the person you're talking to. How often have you heard it said of someone known to be charming, 'She seemed so interested in me'?

This is not false. You have to be genuinely interested in people to get them on your side. Relating to your prospect and then linking the needs of that prospect to what you want does the trick.

A RELAXED APPROACH

Charmers, of course, always appear relaxed and confident because they *do* relate to their listeners. In the same way the knowledge you

Operating Through THE UNITED STATES MAILS Exclusively Since 1925

HABAND COMPANY FAMOUS FOR TIES

M. HABERNICKEL, JR   *Men's Wear*   PARCEL POST ASSN

PATERSON, N.J.

For the Man Who Has Everything
(Plus Everything His Wife Can Think of!)

Dear Haband Customer:

We have come up with something new that you haven't got. And we are not talking about a nuclear reactor to heat the chicken coop. We are talking about something that you can get for less than a thirteen dollar bill. And we are talking about something that every man had in the good old days. In fact, one of the things that made the good old days good.

I am talking about Sunday Pants. Are you old enough to remember that institution? Sunday was the day everybody wore their "Sunday Best". Like for some folks Sunday meant an extra hour in bed. Others were waiting for the next adventure of The Katzenjammer Kids. Or remember Hearst's "scandal section"? And Sunday Noontime dinner! Soup, meat, potatoes, vegetables, and heavy on the bread and butter. Then Dessert! Men collapsed afterwards for a nap. Almost everybody spent a couple of hours in church before or after, or both.

But everybody, young or old, always got dressed up in their Sunday Best. Including the women cooking dinner and Pop on his stroll through the park. For front porch and backyard visits. Or for the family trolley ride out into the country. (How I longed to ride on the outside running board like my father.) Every man had his Sunday suit and nothing was guarded and cherished more than his Sunday Pants. It was all so nice!

Miss Feeney, my secretary for 25 years, differs a little bit on this phase of the old-fashioned Sundays. She thinks that the Sunday Pants were

A letter with charm.

have amassed enables *you* to be relaxed and confident. To put the reader at his or her ease. Not to alarm them in any way.

Selling, I suppose, is a little bit like catching wild animals. You mustn't make a wrong move, otherwise they will be able to scent you and feel threatened. I think there is some analogy here when talking about a good letter. I do not believe you should ever make the reader feel threatened. And the secret is in this easy, relaxed approach.

And what other characteristics do charmers have? They are a pleasure to spend time with. They are thoughtful and polite, not abrasive, cold or obviously commercial.

A good example of how *not* to be pleasant is the pensions letter on page 80 which I have referred to several times. That letter is written in a manner entirely suitable to the internal demands of an insurance company, but no thought has been given to my feelings as the customer. They haven't even addressed me by name – though they've had tens of thousands of pounds off me over the years.

Naturally, charmers vary what they say according to the listener – and to their relationship with that person – as the writer of the letter should have done. This is something the run-of-the-mill writer is very bad at, often not even attempting any variation at all.

HOW SHOULD YOU VARY TONE?

Marketers divide their world into consumers and businesspeople. Should you speak to consumers in the same way you speak to businesspeople?

There is some disagreement about this, as you can see by reading the direct mail you receive yourself. There seem to be two extreme views on the problem. One points out, rightly, that businesspeople are human beings – or even, to go further, that businesspeople are also consumers. Therefore, you should speak to them in exactly the same way as you would to an ordinary consumer.

This leads to letters identical in tone to those one would send out to sell a housewife a kitchen product. Clearly wrong.

Others believe the businessperson should be approached in a totally different way to the consumer. That businesspeople undergo some strange transmutation when they leave home and go to the office or the factory.

This approach leads to letters written very stiffly, almost as though by a Victorian clerk scratching away with a quill – rather like the one my cooker people wrote to me which I quoted at the beginning of Chapter 13. Just as clearly wrong.

I believe that in this case, as in so many other things in life, extremes are unwise.

Of course the businessperson is a consumer when not working. But in the office, although motivations may be *parallel*, eg the desire for self-improvement, or the need to belong to a group, or to be admired by one's peers, they are not identical. That's because the *context* is different. And I do not think people talk at business in entirely the same way as they do when at home.

The trick is to understand their motivations – as demonstrated in the letter on pages 238–240 to sell a new service on the Internet. This letter, unaccompanied by a brochure, got a response rate of 19.5% of which 51% were either 'yes' or 'maybe'. Many of the 'maybes' were persuaded to see a demonstration after a phone call followed them up.

My advice is very simple. It is: write to people in a business-to-business letter just as you would if you were speaking to them on business.

You would not be quite so casual with them as you might be when talking in the pub. You would perhaps be a little bit more serious for the most part – though this does not mean to say you cannot be witty: many of the most successful businesspeople you meet are extremely entertaining.

When writing to *consumers*, you should talk very much as though you might talk to somebody in a leisure setting – at a restaurant or in somebody's home. So it should be with your letter.

BE A CHAMELEON

So, as you see, to write really convincingly, you must not only be a bit of a psychologist; you must also be something of a chameleon. This is certainly true if you are not writing under your own name, but on behalf of someone else.

Thus, you may have the task of writing letters which will go out with your managing director's signature under them. Or in the name of your sales manager, or possibly somebody who manages one of your shops or branches. In all these cases you have to adapt.

If you work for a firm which creates communications for other companies – eg a direct mail house, direct marketing or advertising

WEBCAST

live internet broadcasting

9th October1996

Dear *Mr. Bird,*

<u>**Now, at last, the Internet is delivering what it promised...**</u>

"Through the remarkable technology of live Webcasting, **half a million people** around the world took part in Apple's **Live** Worldwide Developer's Conference last May - though **only 2,000 were actually there** in San José"

All business involves risk, but I think you'll agree that some things can keep you awake at nights a whole lot more than others.

For instance, launching a new product or service, giving a live demonstration or holding an important conference.

Your company's future - and sometimes yours - may depend on it. You must convince many audiences it will be a winner. Your customers. Retailers and distributors. Suppliers. Financial institutions. Journalists. Opinion formers. Your salesforce. The rest of your staff. Maybe even your colleagues. Not to mention your competitors!

And you must convince them fast. Because in those first few critical days and weeks, they will form views - good or bad - which you won't shift easily.

I'm sure you can think of other examples of events that must succeed - or else. Your annual conference. A major exhibition you're showing at. A shareholder's meeting. At all of them, you have to get as many people as possible together to explain, persuade and enthuse. The more you can get on your side simultaneously, the better you'll do.

This letter is about a form of technology which has been proven not only to increase but **transform** your likelihood of success.

WebCasting enables you to **multiply** the audience for a range of messages and events which are utterly time critical to your business.

And all for a **fraction** of the cost of previous technology, like satellite transmission.

128 Cleveland Street . London . W1P 5DN . Tel: 0171 388 4100 . Fax: 0171 388 3366
e-mail: mail @ webcast.co.uk
WEBCAST LIMITED . Registered No: 3220067

This letter selling a highly technical service got responses from BAT, Royal Bank of Scotland, Reed Healthcare, Mars Confectionery, Calvin Klein and Unilever.

Here's a simple example. A couple of years ago an interactive learning system connected by satellite helped Mercedes Benz familiarise 4,000 employees in Germany with its new model in just 20 days, The cost was pretty huge, as you can imagine. **We could well have cut that cost by 75%.**

Essentially, WebCasting is live broadcasting over the Internet. In addition to "real" attendees, it gives you a much larger number of "virtual" delegates. In effect you can have the whole world attending your next important event. Or you can talk to select groups that matter to you.

They experience what those on site do - as it happens. **Sound, pictures, movement: everything.** But in addition, your WebCast can do some things that aren't even possible at an ordinary conference or exhibition. You'll appreciate some of those possibilities.

- Your WebCast participants can **direct questions to experts** at a conference. So you know what concerns them; what they understand and don't; what turns them on; what they have doubts about. And they enjoy the involvement.

- You can **track** which parts of your event attract most interest, and how individual delegates make their way round the WebCast. (Haven't you often wondered whether attendees were really as keen as they said - or were just being polite?)

- You learn as much, and maybe more about delegates as if you met them in person. You can **link demographic profiles with "interest paths'**, to see what attracts particular types, or even individual delegates. Just like following them around.

- **How about instant market research?** They can **vote** on particular ideas or issues -- so you know how they feel about your concepts or products. You learn what your audience thinks, as they think it. You don't have to undergo that familiar nail-biting exercise after most events: "how did we do?"

- You can learn an extraordinary amount about **who** "attends" your event. You can call up demographic data at any time on how many people have logged on, and their Internet addresses.

- "Virtual" delegates can **talk to each other** over the Web during the event - just as if they were there. Very important because as you know delegates love to exchange ideas and gossip with each other.

- And delegates themselves can get further information or **expert advice** on any product or service of yours that interests them.

I don't want to get too technical because buzzwords confuse more than they illuminate. But frankly, this **is** a breakthrough. You don't have to know the jargon to appreciate the rewards.

Now you can get thousands, tens of thousands. or even like Apple, hundreds of thousands of extra participants at your next event. Moreover, compared to previous technologies the costs are very modest. And many major firms are exploiting this approach to communication.

A recent business school advertisement noted that this type of technology helped **Andersen Consulting** reduce staff training time by 50% whilst saving $2 million on payroll and $8.5 million on delivery a year. Rupert Murdoch's **Fox TV** in the US uses the Internet to learn what viewers want - it even led to the name of a hot new TV programme, "Models, Inc."

Today approximately 30 million people have direct access to the World Wide Web. And they are special people. In the UK there are over 2.7 million, with average salaries of over £35,000 a year and over 50% educated to degree level. Many companies now use the Internet as an indispensable business tool.

A letter - even a fairly detailed one like this simply cannot reveal all the possibilities WebCasting offers, **whether communicating within or outside your business.** I'd like the chance to show you. If you have an event large or small that matters to you coming up in the next 12 months, we should talk.

A demonstration only takes an hour. You'll find it intriguing - and fun. There's no cost or obligation. But that hour could make a remarkable difference to the results of your next event - and the future of your business.

I have only written to a small number of companies. including yours, who I thought would have the vision to appreciate this. I don't expect you to say right now "let's do it." But I am suggesting this is something you can't ignore. You really should be getting in on it before the competition.

You're busy, I'm sure. But I hope not too busy to look at something with such huge possibilities for your business. I think you'll be pretty staggered by the potential. Why not return the enclosed reply-paid card today? Better still, why not call me now? I look forward to hearing from you.

Yours sincerely,

Moira Thomson
Business Development Director

P.S.   If what you have read has whetted your appetite, I should tell you the lead time for planning a WebCast is six weeks. Don't hesitate to let me know if you are not interested, in the space provided on the card. I don't want to waste your time in future.

agency – you will certainly find yourself writing on behalf of different clients, each with their own personality.

You must adapt *your* personality to fit the firm you're writing for, and the individual who is signing the letter. That, in turn, requires you to be keenly aware of the nature of the firm and the appropriate tone.

It requires you (as you should have done when briefing yourself) to study previous material sent out by them. To see what their customers are used to hearing from them. The sort of things they would or would not say. Anything out of place will arouse suspicion.

Let me give you a few examples. The chairman of a bank writing to people who had a great deal of money on deposit would adopt a very different tone to the manager of a local off-licence suggesting you come in and buy some extra wine for Christmas. Not only would the tone of voice be slightly different, but the sort of examples and allusions in the letter would be very different.

It would be quite appropriate for the bank chairman to open his letter with some interesting pronouncement upon the state of business in Britain or on the state of the investment market. Readers might well be interested in the views of someone who should be well informed. On the other hand the manager of the off-licence could quite reasonably open by giving his customers a recipe for making mulled wine.

The latter would obviously be a much more down-to-earth individual than the former, who could afford to be a little more grand.

VARY WORDING

Again, if writing to a list of junior people in a company, then you would not only adopt a slightly different tone to the one you would use if you were writing to Managing Directors; you might vary the wording.

Young assistants tend to be aware they don't know as much as they ought to because they are relatively inexperienced. They will be thirsty for helpful information as a general rule. They will be interested in furthering their careers. They will be interested in moving up the ladder.

Managing directors often (wrongly) think they are rather important. They may require a little bit more flattery.

So you impart the same information to these two groups in a slightly different way. To the junior executive you might say: *'Did you know*, the customer you already have is up to eight times more likely to buy from you than a similar person?'

To the managing director you might well write: '*As you know*, the customer you have is up to eight times more likely to buy from you than a similar person.' Had you said to him, 'Did you know…' he might have regarded it as an affront. And even if he doesn't know, the assumption on your part that he does flatters his self-esteem.

When talking earlier about understanding your prospect, I pointed out that even a simple list of addresses may tell you a good deal about people. Take a simple example. Suppose you find a very large percentage of these addresses are in low income areas. Then you will obviously adopt a different tone of voice to the one you might adopt if you find they dwell in the wealthy suburbs.

Down-to-earth or formal?

If they are business people, and you see a high percentage of them come from industrial areas in the north of England, you might decide to use a more down-to-earth approach than if you see they are all in the City of London. You can adopt a bluff, no-nonsense manner rather than a more suave and sophisticated approach.

For instance, you might say something like:

```
'You're a busy person, so I'm not going to waste your time. And
I'm not going to try and pull the wool over your eyes. You prob-
ably want proof. Here it is.'
```

Overleaf is a rather self-serving example of a letter to just such a group.

Earlier I discussed the Royal Viking Line letter I wrote a few years ago to a list of people whom you may recall were very wealthy. Compare the tone with that used in the letter illustrated in Chapter 10 to mail order agents.

Another example of what I mean occurs in the letter illustrated on pages 245–46 from the London tailor to American customers. This is particularly interesting because the *look* of the letter has been changed to fit the audience, by the use of handwriting.

Moreover, the language is very carefully tailored (sorry – I couldn't resist that) to suit both customer and writer in the context of the US. The wording is genteel, even archaic, to match Americans' rather picturesque views of Savile Row formality. If

John Heath & Co. Ltd.
Crest House
Progression Centre
Mark Road, Hemel Hempstead
Herts, HP2 7DW
Telephone: 0442 66400
Facsimile: 0442 231877

Dear Customer,   1st September 1994

The good old days we reminisce about have gone forever in our business. You know it. I know it. We can't ignore direct sellers like Viking. We can't ignore "sheds" like Staples. But what should we do? Weak spirits think nothing can be done; that we are outdated. That we should just give up.

I don't believe it. I believe our industry will follow what has happened in the U.S., and in other industries – the best of the new will co-exist with the best of the old. Those of us who adapt will continue to thrive; those who don't, won't.

Yes it is tough. But to adapt a familiar saying – when the going gets tough, the tough keep going.

For you and me, the way to keep going starts with thinking, then doing. You have to look at how you really compare with your competitors, then decide how to make the most of it.

> What you can offer through us is a wider product range than the
> direct sellers; a warmer, more personal and knowledgeable
> service than the sheds; and far more competitive prices across
> the board than many customers realise.

But all this is useless unless you communicate it. One way is to do so directly. That's why our mailer programme is becoming more and more important. We've now reached an all-time record circulation – and that's linked to more and more individualisation.

And that's why we've retained one of the world's leading direct marketing experts and his team to advise you how to do it well.

> *Drayton Bird is the writer of the standard text on direct
> marketing – "Commonsense Direct Marketing" – an international
> bestseller published in ten languages.

/contd.

The down-to-earth approach.

* He and his team have helped – and continue to help – companies like IBM, Rank Xerox, Digital, Polaroid, American Express, Inmac, Misco, British Telecom, Toyota – in fact over the past twelve years they've advised marketers in <u>literally</u> scores of countries around the world.

So Drayton knows what he's talking about. But more importantly, he communicates it in a down-to-earth, memorable way.

As a first step we've asked Drayton to prepare the video that accompanies this letter. I think you'll find it fascinating – and extremely useful. But it's only the beginning. It's just one in a series of initiatives we've planned with him and his team to help you, a member of the 'Brand Value Alliance', succeed in the testing, but exciting times we face.

In coming months, you'll see significant changes in what we send out, and a stream of ideas to help you do better. We have invested heavily to help your business win.

I hope you find what he has to say as interesting as I did. But most of all, I hope you are enthused to <u>act</u> on it, because I know it works.

Yours sincerely

Terry Blyth
Chief Executive

P.S. When you watch the video, you will see we have a special offer for you.

ELSON & NEILL LIMITED

33 PARK LANE LONDON W.1. 01-499-3529
Manchester Office:
45 FAULKNER STREET MANCHESTER M1 4EH 061-236 5271

Our ref. D.E.

7th November 1972.

Dear Sir,

I hope you will not consider it an impertinence of me to write you this Personal letter. I do so because I am shortly planning to come to the East Coast to measure a number of other gentlemen in your vicinity for suits which we shall have the Pleasure of making for them in England.

It has been suggested to me that you too might be interested to hear about our service and to have me call upon you and show you our latest range of fine English cloth. Then, if you wish it, I should be glad to measure you for a suit in the material and style of your choice. Needless to say, seeing me will not put you under any obligation to place an order.

Although we are traditional English tailors, you may rest assured that we are well aware of the special requirements of American clients with regard to style, make-up and fit. In any case, every one of our suits is of course individually made to each clients personal requirements.

Example of the tone adapted to fit the market.

So that I can plan my visit carefully in advance I should be most grateful if you could complete the enclosed airmail letter form letting me know whether or not you wish to do me the honour of allowing me to call upon you. If you decide to do so, I will get in touch with you later to let you know the precise date of my visit so that you can give me a time which will be convenient for you.

I have the honour, Sir, to remain

Yours faithfully.

George Neill

such a letter were sent out in England it would probably be greeted with disbelief.

And, on a higher note, the letter on page 248 sent to the Duke of Edinburgh has equally been carefully drafted to fit its exalted reader.

Sometimes your reader may not be just concerned with wealth and position, but also with intellectual status. In Chapter 13, when discussing jargon, I mentioned the letter on pages 222–23. Here I am masquerading as a professor, using far more long words than I might to an ordinary audience. (To be honest, this is to a degree in deference to my client's rather than my own views.)

MORE THAN CHARM: THE RELEVANT SURPRISE

Now at this point I hope you are saying: surely there's more to an outstanding letter than the right idea and the right style. You are quite right. In these two chapters I have been talking largely about the tricks of the trade.

I don't want to come out with too much theory in this book but perhaps you'll allow me to make some comments on the 'creative process'. This essentially is taking various elements and combining them in different combinations to make a striking effect.

The best ideas seem to be those that are completely unexpected but absolutely right for the job at hand.

A good example is the letter I've quoted many times already 'Quite frankly, the American Express Card is not for everyone…'. You normally expect a letter to encourage *everybody* to reply. This one did the opposite, which comes as a surprise to the reader. On the other hand it is absolutely appropriate for a company which is only trying to attract certain types of individual.

Bill Jayme, to whom I have referred several times, is famous for his striking envelope lines, of which my two favourites are one I illustrated, 'Do you lock the bathroom door behind you even when there's no one else home?' for a magazine about psychology; and 'How much should you tip when you're planning to steal the ashtray?' for a magazine about travel and entertainment.

You will see quite a few examples of what makes an outstanding idea in these pages. I believe the only one for which I have been responsible is the letter with the burnt top on page 128. I suspect readers were surprised to see the burnt top and even more surprised

Registered Office:
274 BANBURY ROAD · OXFORD OX2 7DZ
TELEPHONE: 0865 56777 · TELEX 83610

His Royal Highness The Prince Philip,
Duke of Edinburgh,
Buckingham Palace,
London SW1.

Your Royal Highness,

This is a unique kind of appeal letter because we are not asking you for money. Incredible but true!

What we would like you to donate is your best after dinner story. It may be a joke, or a serious anecdote, fact or fiction; in fact the best story you have ever heard or told at a gathering where speeches are made. We want to publish your contribution in a book containing the 1000 best after dinner stories contributed by famous people.

The book will be attractively produced and sold with all profits going to Oxfam. Because your contribution will lend the book a unique attraction, you will be donating more than money. You may be sure that the proceeds will be put to good use and there is surely no need to tell you about the work done by Oxfam around the world. We shall naturally send you a specially bound complimentary copy on publication day.

Even the idea for the book was donated to us. We hope you will think it an amusing one and will send us your contribution as soon as you can.   We enclose a stamped, ready addressed envelope for your reply.

I have the honour to be, Sir, Your Royal Highness's most humble and obedient servant.

Brian W. Walker

Brian W. Walker
Director

A company limited by guarantee · Registered in London No. 612172
Chairman: Michael H Rowntree MA · Vice Chairman· R J Mullard MA · Hon Treasurer: R S Jenkinson MA
Director· Brian W Walker

A fitting Royal tone.

that I suggested they set fire to the bottom – but as you see, it was relevant.

But a good letter doesn't just use the right words in the right order or the right style and the right idea. It can also have visual appeal, if it is laid out carefully – which is what we consider next.

15

How Should Your Letters Look?

'Faultily faultless, icily regular, splendidly null.'

Tennyson

The odds are you and I have never met, so I don't know your hobbies. But one of mine, perhaps because my parents owned a pub and restaurant, is eating and drinking.

The most successful restaurants not only cook and serve good food. They have the right ambiance. In some cases the decor is rather better than the food. It can hardly rescue dreadful cooking, but it is important, sometimes lifting an ordinary restaurant out of the pack.

So it is with sales letters. The words obviously matter most. But the look can contribute greatly. And this look should not be 'icily regular' as Tennyson put it.

I am sure you have often received letters which don't look like letters at all. By that I mean they are printed, using the sort of typeface you normally see in an advertisement, brochure or book.

Of course, unless you are mailing on a very small scale using an old-fashioned typewriter and duplicating copies (and there's no need to be ashamed of that – it works) then your letter *is* printed.

So it is natural to say: 'Gosh, this letter has to be printed, anyhow. So I'll have it printed in a proper typeface and make it look more expensive and important.' That may sound logical, but it is wrong. A letter should look like a letter.

The presentation should match what your reader might expect to receive from you. The sort of letter you would normally send out in the course of business – though there are a few tricks you can use which will make it more appealing and easy to read.

If you are a small business, people expect a typewritten letter, I believe. If you are a larger business, perhaps a word-processed letter makes sense. But to be on the safe side, stick to the typewriter face. It is what people are used to. More to the point, as far as I know in every case where the two have been tested against each other, the typewriter face gets more replies.

MAKE IT LOOK PERSONAL

The more personal your letter looks the better. Many direct mail letters which were handwritten and then reproduced have worked extremely well. Indeed, you can now have a 'typeface' which resembles handwriting.

My erstwhile partner Glenmore Trenear-Harvey wanted to buy a flat in a particular building in London some years ago. None appeared to be for sale, so he handwrote a letter, had it copied and stuck it through every door. He had his flat within weeks and I believe he has hated it ever since.

He had a distinct advantage: beautiful handwriting, a talent we put to use when writing to titans of industry who might otherwise never even have read what we sent. He handwrote the letters individually and we had the nerve to send them to these people at their home addresses.

We got replies from everyone we wrote to – but no business, perhaps because I drafted the letters, but more probably because the people we wrote to were far too senior to worry about who should do their direct marketing.

The handwritten look can work like a charm for charities, where for no logical reason it gives donors the reassuring feeling that the charity works on a shoestring and is not squandering their benefactions.

It also does well to unsophisticated recipients. Years ago, I worked for a catalogue company who wanted to persuade sales agents who had dropped out to come back into the field. A shrewd colleague suggested we send a letter signed by an agent who had returned to the company, explaining why she had done so.

We used a photograph of the writer holding one of her children in her arms (we wished to emphasize that although she now had a young family, she could still make money, which she probably needed more than ever, through the catalogue) and the letter itself was hand-written.

This worked, not merely because of the personal touch, nor even because we knew that pictures of mothers with babies are compelling, but because having a real person talk to the prospect is almost invari-ably persuasive. Mind you, I seem to recall that the letter copy wasn't bad either.

More recently a letter using the picture of the writer in the top right hand corner increased response by 30%. And, of course, you have already seen the handwritten letter from a tailor which shows how effective this style can be.

TRICKS TO MAKE LETTERS WORK BETTER

In *The 100 Greatest Direct Mail Letters*, which I mentioned in the intro-duction, Dick Hodgson, rightly seen as one of America's best experts, comments on what he calls 'squiggling'.

By this he means all the little emphases you often see in profes-sional direct mail letters. Examples are: putting a word in capital letters, underlining a word, putting 'handwritten' notes in the margin and the like. The letter for Omaha steaks is a good example.

Do they work? I suspect so, but I have no proof. I have never seen or conducted a test comparing the results of a letter with these things against one with the same wording but no squiggles.

I have, however, seen more than one test where a particular visual element had been added or rearranged with substantial effect. Thus, for one letter sent out in France, a stamp saying 'Priority: we guar-antee to accept your application' was placed at the top left-hand corner of the letter, and an increase of over 10 per cent in response was produced.

JUDGEMENT IS ESSENTIAL

In this question, as in so many others, people seek a definitive answer.

Unfortunately there's no such thing in what is, however modestly, a creative process.

You have to use your judgement. If you were writing this sort of letter to the sort of person you are writing it to, from the sort of person you are supposed to be, would you have all these things on the page?

I think if you were a lawyer, a bank manager or the chairman of a big company, you would not be likely to do this sort of thing. Or, if you did, you would so do only very sparingly. Perhaps you might underline something, or put two lines in the margin next to an important point, or have a handwritten PS – but no more.

On the other hand, if you were a sales manager writing about something that *was* a little sensational – perhaps an unusual new product – you would certainly resort to that sort of thing. Indeed, if you were known to be an ebullient sort of person, you would do that. A good example, I think, might be Sir Freddy Laker, who though a company chairman, was hardly bashful. Dick Hodgson observes, rightly, in his book that this sort of technique often tends to be used when something is being presented as a bargain.

This is all an aspect of tone, but a good analogy, once more, is with salesmen. Ask yourself: what sort of a salesman would my letter be, if it were a salesman? A salesman in a street market will be brash and loud, unafraid of heavy emphasis and exaggeration A salesman selling door to door might use it, but to a lesser extent.

It would depend on what he was selling. If it were insurance I suggest he wouldn't overly exaggerate. Money is a serious matter. If it were a new vacuum cleaner, maybe he would be a little bit more emphatic. If, on the other hand, he were going to an office selling pensions to managers, I suggest the salesman would adopt a very sober demeanour.

But the little additions – the squiggly bits – are only one of the elements which make a letter work harder.

MAKE IT LOOK INVITING

A good letter has shape and variety, just as a good newspaper page does. That is what ordinary people prefer to the clean, uncluttered, dull rectangle of type many designers like.

This is especially true of a long letter, which otherwise looks like a long trudge through a grey desert. This is one reason why I also think it is a good idea to indent all your paragraph beginnings.

Here are some of the things you can do to add interest.

1. You can indent sections of the letter and, if you have several points to make, you can number the paragraphs.
2. You can, as mentioned above, <u>underline certain words or even sentences</u>.
3. You can also CAPITALIZE or make things **bold**, as well as using all the other squiggles mentioned above.
4. In addition, you can:
   - use dashes to list points;
   - asterisks fulfil the same function;
   - as do letters, (a) (b) and (c) or Roman numerals, i, ii, iii, iv, and so on.
5. You can even *italicize* or use a different colour for emphasis, if you are printing in more than one colour; more on this below.

In fact the limits of what can be done are only set by your ingenuity and your judgement. <u>**NEVER FORGET THAT HE WHO EMPHASIZES EVERYTHING, OR OVER-EMPHASIZES, ENDS UP EMPHASIZING NOTHING.**</u>

Perhaps the most common sin in this respect is the use of exclamation marks, for which there are few legitimate places! Yet they are scattered about with such joyous abandon by bad writers as almost to constitute a visual element!! Which is why I mention them not just in Chapter 13 but again here!!!

So when you indent, underline, capitalize or otherwise emphasize, don't do it on a random basis. The purpose is to draw attention to that which deserves it.

WHEN TO USE HEADINGS

On the subject of drawing attention, this is a good place to consider the matter of headings. You will see that in some of the letters I have given as instances there are headings at the top; and in others there are not.

I find it impossible to lay down a hard and fast rule on this. It really is a matter of judgement, largely depending on how long the letter is and how much you want to give away about the subject.

The purpose of a heading at the top of a letter, or headings – for you can have more than one – is to telegraph the main point or points of your message without giving it all way. To sum up what is in store for the readers in the hope that it will keep them reading.

Accordingly, where you have a strong benefit or benefits to offer, or a particularly appealing incentive, and nothing is to be lost by revealing them, then a heading makes sense.

Having said that, with all its advantages of encapsulation and ability to catchy the eye, the heading has one serious disadvantage. Unless it is very discreet, it signals to the reader that this is a 'commercial' message. And while there is no doubt that most people like receiving personal letters, they're not nearly so keen on commercial ones. That fact has to be weighed in your mind when you decide whether to use a heading.

There are three factors, I believe, to consider when deciding whether a particular heading is any good.

1. Do you think it will make the reader wish to read on to find out more? This is the most important consideration.
3. Does it, on the contrary, reveal so much that people might be tempted to reject your proposition even before starting to read?
3. Is the letter *long* enough to benefit from a heading? If it is more than one page long, a heading should always be considered.

If you want to be on the safe side, my advice is: use a heading more often than not. Usually what you gain by enticing people into the main text makes it worthwhile. This can even be true in a letter only four or five paragraphs long.

How should your main headings be laid out?

First, they should generally be centred. You can make them bold or underline them – or both. Some people differentiate them even more by having them, unlike the rest of the text, set in a printed display type.

I do not like this in high level business-to-business letters. I would not use it in a letter to senior executives on an important subject but I have no evidence to show it lowers response. It just seems inappropriate to me.

You can set headings and, indeed, other important points in your letter in a different colour. More on this in a moment.

One device is the 'Johnson Box', whereby you put your heading within a box composed of asterisks. This is usually a good way to convey more than one point. That is the sort of approach – though without the asterisks – used in the Acuma letter I have already discussed on pages 186–87.

George V Place 4 Thames Avenue Windsor Berkshire SL4 1Q

CRAIG HERRON
MANAGING DIRECTOR

"Don't buy a thing until you phone us first. Here's how you can save £40·23 ... £84·08... £134·99 or more on your very next purchase." *

Dear Reader,

<u>To introduce you to DISCOUNT HOTLINE Plus – an important money-saving service of Comp-U-Card – you're invited to try our new shopping service FREE for three full months.</u>

For the next three months, you've got 'instant' access to the lowest prices in Britain on over 19,000 top-name makes and models.

<u>HERE'S HOW IT WORKS TO SAVE YOU £££s ON ALMOST EVERYTHING YOU WANT AND NEED.</u>

What do you or your family need right now? A new washing machine or tumble dryer? A lawn mower? Furniture? A new cooker or fridge? Sports equipment? Or a new TV, video or home computer?

Check in your newspaper, high street shop ... even discount stores in your area, and decide on the makes and models that interest you most - and jot down their prices. — *read the product brochures too*

<u>THEN REACH FOR YOUR PHONE ... AND SEE IF WE CAN'T GIVE YOU A BETTER PRICE!</u>

Your call is answered by one of our friendly Discount Hotline shopping consultants - specially trained to find the best buys for you.

Say what makes and models you want, and a price check is quickly made from a list of over 19,000 products - with the lowest available quotes.

Compare our price quotes with others you've found, and almost without exception, I can promise you ...

*See our Price Challenge leaflet enclosed.
COMP-U-CARD LTD. REG. NO. ENGLAND AND WALES 1908797 REG. OFFICE EASTCHESTER HOUSE HARLANDS ROAD HAYWARDS HEATH SUSSEX RH16 1TG.

D R A Y T O N   B I R D   D I R E C T

"Don't buy a thing until you phone us first. Here's how you can save £40.23... £84.08... £134.99 or more on your very next purchase."

Dear Reader

To introduce you to Discount Hotline Plus - an important money saving service of Comp-U-Card - you're invited to try our new shopping service FREE for three full months.

For the next three months, you've got 'instant' access to the lowest prices in Britain on over 19,000 top-name makes and models.

Here's how it works to save you £££s on almost everything you want and need.

What do you or your family need right now? A new washing machine or tumble dryer? A lawn mower? Furniture? A new cooker or fringe? Sports equipment? Or a new TV, video or home computer?

Check in your newspaper, high street shop ... even discount stores in your area, and decide on the makes and models that interest you most - and jot down their prices.

Then reach for your phone ... and see if we can't give you a better price!

Your call is answered by one of our friendly Discount Hotline shopping consultants - specially trained to find the best buys for you.

Say what makes and models you want, and a price check is quickly made from a list of over 19,000 products - with the lowest available quotes.

MCB House 133 137 Westbourne Grove London W 1 2RS Telephone 071 243 0196 Fax 071 229 0426

I think you will agree that, even if overdone, the use of shape and emphasis makes the layout on the left more interesting.

Through the adroit use of headings, you can communicate more than one message pretty quickly. On page 259 is the opening page of a very successful letter I wrote some years ago to sell a series of seminars put on by my partners and me.

As you see, the headings quickly convey a series of messages. Notice that they do not fight with each other, but lead the reader into the opening in a logical fashion.

When to use other headings

Apart from the main heading you will also notice that some letters – the longer ones – often have subsidiary headings – crossheads is the technical term.

One reason is obvious: they break up a long text. For example my letter illustrated on page 259 was four pages long. But a second reason is that when people first pick up a letter, they do not start at the beginning as you planned. They start anywhere they please.

Usually they will scan it pretty carelessly, noting any odd visual features and also who signed it. Their eyes alight naturally around one or two paragraphs down the page. If you can have something interesting there, all the better. Crossheads are there to entice them into reading properly, just as a main heading should.

If you want to know how headings and crossheads should be devised, you could do worse than note the chapter headings and the crossheads in this book. They are designed to give you a clue, quickly, as to precisely what each chapter and section is about. That is because you have no time to waste.

Note that they are not cleverly written, to entertain. That is not the purpose of this book. You are reading it because you wish to learn. It is perfectly possible that among you there are those who also wish to be entertained, but that is not my main aim.

In the same way, though the readers of your letters probably like to be entertained or amused under other circumstances, that is not what they read sales letters for. They read them to find out what benefit they can gain or what misery they can avoid.

Headings tell the story in brief

Your headings and crossheads should quickly reveal precise benefits and offers. Read them all in sequence. Do they present a condensed version of your story? If a reader scans them, he or she

THE PRINTED SHOP

7 Langley Street, Covent Garden,
London WC2H 9JX
Telephone 01-836 4145
Telex 269920

PLEASE DON'T
DISCARD THE ENVELOPE.
IT IS VALUABLE.

```
* * * * * * * * * * * * * * * * * * *
*  THE ENVELOPE THIS LETTER ARRIVED  *
*  IN COULD BRING YOU A BUSINESS     *
*  EXPERIENCE WORTH £772.50.  DON'T  *
*  THROW IT AWAY!                    *
* * * * * * * * * * * * * * * * * * *
```

Dear Colleague,

How one evening of entertaining reading - total investment under £20 - could give you enough tested ideas to transform your business. For example:

- A china and glass retailer in Cornwall sent out a simple one-sheet duplicated mailing to his customers, which he wrote and designed himself in minutes.

 For every £ he invested, he got back £30, in a sale that lasted only 5 hours. He got the idea from a book.

- A giant mail order company spent 5 years following the principles outlined in this book ... five of the worst years the British economy has ever seen, when the value of the £ halved, and today's depression set in.

 They pulled in more customers every year for the same cost per recruit ... i.e. their cost of recruitment halved in real terms, whilst their business base expanded dramatically.

- The Managing Director of an insurance company read this book and tried out its ideas one by one. In a 12 month period, every idea they tested was a success - and one resulted in them being "flooded with banker's orders."

- A company selling D-I-Y tools spent 18 months following these principles, and multiplied its turnover tenfold. Whilst a leading U.K. finance company attracted four times the amount of money they expected from one promotion in Reader's Digest. The secret was the offer they made.

If you seek tested marketing ideas that bring in results you can measure ... if you want those results in weeks, not years ... then welcome to "Commonsense Direct Marketing", by Drayton Bird. The first U.K. book to reveal the secrets of the world's fastest-growing marketing discipline.

If you're already a Direct Marketer, you know the power of this most accountable form of promotion. Even if you're not, you probably already use some

- 1 -

Please read on ...

Headings can be used to communicate a number of messages.

should be able to get a good idea of what you are offering – just enough to create the desire to know more.

To give you an idea of the full panoply of things you can do with headings, squiggles and the like, I illustrated the first page of a letter I blush to admit responsibility for on page 256. I wrote it for a new discount buying service a few years ago.

It worked pretty well, but I think it looks like a dog's breakfast. We overdid all the devices – to say the least of it. But note the picture of the head of the company on the letterhead. As I have just observed, this works – and the reason is that people look at people.

Of course, the headings are designed to drive you into the text. But you can also lay out your letter to keep people interested and reading. A good example is the letter for the Sea Turtle Rescue Fund shown on the next page.

An even simpler example was demonstrated by Bill Jayme in a private letter he wrote to me recently. He simply put an arrow at the bottom of the first page, like this.

It worked.

WHAT ABOUT STYLE, COLOUR, TEXTURE?

In visual style, like many things in life, exactly what you do is a matter of taste. But I believe that, essentially, when writing to people who are wealthier, writing in a business context or about something serious you should be more conservative.

When writing about something frivolous, or to less wealthy and pompous groups, be freer with the emphasis. For example, if you were selling a coach trip to rugby club supporters, this calls for colour, cartoons and quips, not gloomy punctilio.

I cannot recall any formal research on what happens if you change the colour of the paper in a letter, though if you change the colour of an envelope it certainly has an effect.

However, I well remember when I started to write sales letters, being told by a sage and experienced American writer that colour certainly could make a difference. He had found the colour of paper called 'gold' – a sort of rich yellow – had increased responses for him.

Clearly, anything which adds variety to proceedings can prove successful. A different colour of paper within a mailing pack can make

Sea Turtle Rescue Fund
Center for Environmental Education, Inc.
624 Ninth St., NW   Washington, DC 20001

August 8, 1986

Dear Florida Neighbor,

    Will you take a moment to consider the desperate plight of the
baby sea turtles to your right?

    Imagine, if you will, that this piece of paper is a Florida beach.
And imagine that it is a dark and moonless night.

    At the top of the page is the shoreline -- the Atlantic Ocean. At
the bottom is "civilization." Condominiums. Highways. Hotels.
Parking lots.

    To the newly hatched sea turtle, heading towards the top of the
page means heading towards safety. <u>Heading towards the bottom means
heading towards death.</u>

    These baby sea turtles have just scratched their way out of the
sandy nest where they've spent the past two months incubating in the
warm sun. It took several days and it was hard work, so they're close
to exhaustion. But the worse is yet to come.

    JUST FOLLOW THE LIGHT

    Instinctively, the tiny hatchling knows to wait until dark before
making his break from the nest. The sand is cooler at night, and
there are fewer predators looking for an easy meal.

    But he has a serious problem.

    A sea turtle is terribly nearsighted on land. And on a dark night
like this one, he can't see the shoreline, even though it's only a
few feet away.

    Fortunately, after a hundred million years of evolution, Mother
Nature has provided the hatchling sea turtle with instincts on how to
find the ocean:

    <u>Follow the light.</u>

    Even on a moonless night , .the wide expanse of sky over the sea is
much brighter than the dark horizon on the landward side. And the
little turtle knows that if he follows the light he will find the sea.

    He starts out in the right direction. But wait ...

over please

How to keep the reader interested.

sense. The gold mentioned above was used for a sheet of testimonials within a mailing I used to send out.

If you have sent out several mailings on white paper, then sending out one on another colour is bound to attract attention. But the colour must be fitting. A pale grey would be appropriate for a fashion designer, perhaps. A pink would suit a fragrance. A cream might suit a professional. A blue might convey prestige.

Your own judgement is important here. And don't forget: you must allow not just for how you, the writer, should appear, but also what is appropriate to your audience.

A second colour of ink? Textured paper?

People often ask whether it is a good idea to have a second colour of ink in a mailing. This has been tested (no doubt many times) in America. And the pundits there say that it works.

However, I would urge caution, just as with some of the other techniques covered here. If you were writing to wealthy people and trying to be as personal as possible, a second colour would seem to me inappropriate.

Once again, the rugby club outing seems relevant. In such a case the letter should be fun. Any mailing where you feel a carefree atmosphere is right calls for colour. This is usually true of overtly commercial mailings where there is no attempt to masquerade as a genuine personal letter.

There is no doubt that textured paper can increase results. When discussing envelopes, I mentioned one case, where a paper manufacturer, Suecia Antiqua, conducted a series of tests to prove it. In one case, response rose by over 90 per cent. Since the first job your mailing has to do is gain attention, anything which makes you stand out from the crowd, unless it is foolish, can pay.

One mailing worked very well where the only significant difference was that the letter was longer and narrower in shape than usual. It did significantly better than one with identical wording, but the usual A4 shape.

WHAT USE IS YOUR LETTERHEAD?

I mentioned when discussing envelopes that there may be occasions when you wish to camouflage your identity in a mailing.

You will sometimes see letters which do not actually have a letter-head in the accepted sense of the word. There is no mention of their company's name at the top of the letter, it is put at the bottom of the page – the top being devoted to a selling message.

The reasons for this may be two. One I have already given. You don't actually want people to know who you are. The other may be given by the answer to a simple question: Which is more interesting to your reader? Your company, or what you have to offer?

Gary Halbert, whom I have quoted twice, believes you should give your prospect no indication that your letter is of a commercial nature. He believes that ideally the envelope should be handwritten and when you get inside all the commercial material – the order form and so forth – should be in a separate envelope, with the message: 'Do not open until you have read the letter'.

In this way, he believes, people are beguiled into reading the letter and don't realize you're trying to flog something to them.

I suspect he is partly right and partly wrong. Any injunction not to open something inevitably has the reverse consequence as I pointed out when talking about this previously. But I think that his ploy should get the envelope opened in the right frame of mind, because everyone likes to get personal letters.

However, how do they feel when they realize they have been sent a sales letter? This is where Mr Halbert's skill as a writer helps him get away with it. And, I imagine, people are so intrigued by the envelope with its hidden content that they pay attention.

The other reason for not having your company's name on the letter-head is that it is unknown; or so little known that it carries no weight; or, worse still, has a poor reputation. A well-known and reputable company name, however, can *double* response.

Where you do not think your company name is of sufficient impor-tance, you may think, rightly, that the benefits you are talking about should be emphasized at the expense of not even mentioning the company at the head of the sheet.

In short, I believe that where you have no previous relationship with the reader and your company has no 'name', then featuring it at the top of the letterhead is completely pointless.

A good example is given in the opening of the letter to sell the book *The New Mail Order*. The writer, Eugene Schwartz, sold more books through mail order than anyone else in the world. Thirty five years ago he offered me a job as copywriter. I decided I had no intention of competing with somebody as good as him.

You can see why by studying the envelope, which is calculated to get any businessman very interested, without revealing what the subject is, followed by this letter opening.

There is of course another case where you might not want to reveal the company's name: that is where you have written to people several times before and they have resolutely refused to reply. The no letter-head ploy was once employed by American Express in a splendid piece written by my former colleague, Pamela, one of the best copy-writers in London. The letter told how Pamela was out one day when she met somebody she'd always admired but had not seen for some years. This person, a young and successful executive invited her out to lunch. Then he discovered he'd forgotten his wallet. Pamela proudly produced her American Express Card with a flourish.

This letter did pretty well, and would have done distinctly better had the dullards responsible in the marketing department had the sense to keep the Amex name off the envelope and only send the mailing out to the young people it was intended for.

I have written in Chapter 13 about all the verbal techniques you can use to make your writing easier for people to read. The points I have made in this chapter are about the equivalent visual techniques.

However, they are also to be looked at when considering the matter of tone – dealt with in Chapter 14. The right look and the right language can together lift a letter out of the ordinary. Indeed, I have seen cases where no real change has been made to the content, only to the presentation, with remarkable results. In the next chapter we consider a number of the other questions that come up when consid-ering the planning and organization not just of your letter, but of its objectives too.

16

Common Questions

'What men seek is not knowledge, but certainty.'
George Bernard Shaw

You have no doubt heard the old Chinese saying, 'A journey of a thousand miles starts with but a single step' – a good reminder that most people never get anything done, because they don't begin.

A compendium of uncertainties may confront you before you start to write. They can reduce you to a paralysis of indecision. Sometimes this is welcome; as I confessed earlier, writers will use any excuse to avoid getting down to the task.

You must have nothing whatsoever clouding your mind, so that you can really concentrate. So I shall now answer some of the questions not covered in earlier chapters.

There is one question I'm going to deal with in this chapter which is particularly relevant to those of you who are interested in more than sales letters (which I hope means most of you; confining yourself to one medium such as this is not very smart).

The question is: how do you fit your sales letters into any other activities you are conducting; and the answer I will give you immediately: you should do so whenever you can. The reasons for this and the benefits that flow from it I shall discuss later.

For instance, do I need a brochure? Who should sign the wretched thing? What is the best way to address the prospect? How long should it be? Should it be personalized?

Some of these will depend on another question: what exactly am I trying to achieve with this letter – what do I want the reader to *do* after reading it? If I get a response, what next? How do I respond to replies? Indeed, how many replies should I expect? How do I keep track?

LONG LETTER OR SHORT?

The question of whether your letter should be long or short is one of the hoariest ones in this business. Most professionals say long letters are *always* better. Most amateurs can't believe it.

Some while ago, Pamela Craik, to whom I referred in Chapter 15, and I wrote between us a letter for American Express. It was three times longer than another letter making the same offer. It out-performed it on every list mailed – much to the surprise of the senior executive we were dealing with.

As a matter of fact, he didn't believe changing the letter in the mailing would make any difference at all to the response. He thought the brochure was much more important. That's another subject I shall come to.

But, returning to long versus short, let me quote the man many people believe to be *the* outstanding direct mail exponent in America. Richard V Benson has 31 Rules of Thumb. These are things he has discovered over a 40-year period which he believes *always* apply.

Here's his rule 18: 'Long copy is better than short copy.' Yes; he puts it that simply.

In 37 years of writing, I have never known a short letter *making the same proposition* do better than a long letter. The last time I tested it, a four-page letter making the same offer as a two-page letter got 52 per cent more replies.

This does not mean that you should strive officiously to have longer letters. Despite my personal experience, I do not agree with Mr Benson that long letters will *always* do better. Good short letters are better than indifferent long ones, obviously.

However, generally the long letter seems to do better. But why?

Anything we are doing is simply multiplied salesmanship. Or, as American advertising man John E Kennedy put it 85 years ago: 'Salesmanship in print'.

Ask yourself: 'What would a salesman do?' And the answer is: he would never dream of going in to see somebody to sell something, coming out with three short paragraphs (however well phrased) and leaving. It would be nonsense.

It is as though you had paid somebody to get in their car, drive out to see a prospect at considerable expense, drive back again – maybe taking several hours – and only stay at their appointment for a minute.

The question is: *How* long? *How* short?

Length depends on the objective

The answer is: it's just like real life: it depends on what you're trying to *achieve*. If all you want to do is to get a simple, unqualified enquiry, you probably don't need many words. If you are trying to get a sale or a major commitment, you need to say more.

As I pointed out earlier, a product which is extremely well known will generally not require as long a letter as one which is not. One case, you may recall, was the very short letter which worked in America to acquire new Cardmembers. Remember, in other markets where American Express is not well known, that short approach did not work.

However, it is worth reflecting that your letter is not written as an artistic endeavour on its own, it is part of everything you do to build your business. Normally your business will be furthered more quickly by letters which *achieve more*: which get people to commit themselves as much as possible; to put in a strong enquiry, rather than a weak one; to buy more rather than less.

There's one good way to be sure you're doing it right. Methodically write down all the sensible reasons why anybody should do what you want them to do; and all the excuses they might give you as to why they shouldn't. Every one of these should be covered in the copy (and the pictures, for that matter).

Once you have covered all the relevant benefits, and overcome all the likely objections, you will have more or less the right content to get a sale.

To get an enquiry, all you need do is cover the benefits, with less attention paid to the objections. These can be dealt with in the follow-up (unless, of course, they are objections that might discourage enquiries). For example, 'No salesperson will call' is often a vital line when seeking an enquiry.

Of course, there are other important things you have to do to have effective copy.

You need an appealing opening; you have to edit to eliminate unnecessary words, make sure your argument is in the right order, emphasize benefits before features – all the things we have already covered.

Incidentally, research conducted by McGraw-Hill in the US in 1988 into the readership of *advertisements* indicated that advertisements with more than 1000 words in them are read significantly more than advertisements with less than 1000 words in them. This is a fact even most people in advertising are unaware of.

So you will not be surprised that I believe the same principles apply to letters and, for that matter, brochures.

A good example of a long letter is the one by David Tetther on pages 269–72, written for the Franklin Mint. There is nothing new about this business; for centuries works of art of one kind or another have been created to commemorate famous events and people.

This letter, rich with detail, accompanied a brochure which it presents as a sort of art exhibition. I've never seen this done before but the skill of the writer enables him to get away with it.

Here you see the storytelling which makes a lot of letters successful. Indeed, there is more than one story in the letter: the story of the origins of the sculpture, Cavallo; and then the story of how the present day recreator of the sculpture became involved in the project.

As often with the Franklin Mint the message is laid on thick – maybe too thick – as on the last page, with the phrase 'truly a "timeless" work'. There is no need for the inverted commas round timeless; and you should beware of the word 'truly'. It is one of those adjectives – 'basically' is another – which are nearly always unnecessary and often weaken the impact of the word they qualify.

PERSONALIZED OR NOT?

Only in relatively recent years has technology made it possible for us to personalize communications cheaply and easily – even to introduce personalized pieces in the body of the message. When first introduced this actually increased response by as much as 50 per cent.

Of course, it will not have escaped your attention that technology has also given us great opportunities to get a personalization subtly wrong. Or totally wrong. Or even hilariously wrong.

A high point in the technological revolution which I shall long

FRANKLIN MINT LIMITED

<u>The 500-year-old dream of a genius becomes reality ...</u>
<u>creating a unique, unrepeatable collecting opportunity</u>

(And – for registered Franklin Mint Collectors exclusively –
at a valuable privilege price.)

Dear Collector,

It was five centuries ago that Leonardo da Vinci created drawings for a
great sculpture, 'Il Cavallo' ... commissioned from him by the Duke of
Milan.

Life-size – showing the Duke's father mounted on a horse, in full armour,
preparing to charge – it was an enormous undertaking. And Leonardo, determined
it should be the greatest equestrian sculpture ever seen, worked on it
with immense enthusiasm.

But it was not to be.

Just when he was ready to cast the bronze, the turbulent politics of the
Renaissance – the era, after all, of Machiavelli – took a hand. His patron
was defeated in battle. Leonardo had to flee from Milan. The impressive
clay model he had fashioned was shot to pieces by the arrows of invading
soldiers. Nothing of 'Il Cavallo' remained.

<u>Except the original drawings</u>. These survived for two hundred years in
Italy and other European countries until, towards the end of the 17th century,
they were acquired for this country where they are preserved to this day
in the Royal Library at Windsor.

And now, what I feel I can best describe as a 'miracle of art' has happened.

> Five centuries after Leonardo da Vinci put
> pen to paper, Gianni Benvenuti, the great
> Italian sculptor of our own time, born in
> the same region as da Vinci, has brought
> 'Il Cavallo' into being. A magnificent
> bronze sculpture, completely authentic –
> completely faithful to the artistic vision
> of Leonardo himself.

How it came about is, I think you'll agree, a fascinating story.

Gianni Benvenuti – though aware, of course, of 'Il Cavallo' – discovered
the full historical details while on a visit to Spain two years ago.

FRANKLIN MINT LIMITED BROMLEY ROAD LONDON SE6 2XG TELEPHONE 01-697 8131
Registered in England No 357382
Brussels · Copenhagen · Grimstad · Hong Kong · London · Melbourne · Munich · Paris · Philadelphia · Rotterdam · Salzburg · Singapore · Stockholm · Tokyo · Toronto

A good example of a long letter.

He read da Vinci's own extensive notes (it was as recently as 1967 that seventeen pages in the artist's own hand were discovered in the National Library in Madrid).

He studied his drawings - admiring their power and vigour, undimmed by the passage of time.

And slowly, over a period of months - without really being aware of what was happening, he has since told me - the idea, the question grew in his mind. Could <u>he</u> complete what Leonardo da Vinci had begun ... bring to fruition the Renaissance master's dream?

<u>Franklin Mint helps a great artist to triumph</u>

For a while, doubts - about his own ability, about the 'rightness' of the endeavour - held him back. Until one day, after visiting an exhibition in Paris with his friend Georges, the head of our sister company there, he mentioned what was in his mind.

Georges was not only enthusiastic; not only swept away Benvenuti's doubts by reminding him of the quality of his own work; of his high international reputation and his status as a founder of the world-famous annual sculpture show at Pietrasanta. He also acted as his 'Duke of Milan' ... as a traditional patron ... obtaining for the artist the commission from Franklin Mint to create 'Il Cavallo'.

If it were possible to discover the result of this commission only in one exhibition, in one place, that exhibition would, in my opinion, be worth travelling many miles to see. And I believe every collector who appreciates the special three-dimensional beauty sculpture brings into a home, will agree with me that 'Il Cavallo' is indeed a triumph of art.

Fortunately, you don't have to travel to see the work. As a Franklin Mint collector, the 'Il Cavallo exhibition' is brought to you, personally, by way of an illustrated, full colour brochure.

<u>The convenience of your own private view</u>

So you can easily see for yourself, at your leisure, the powerful, exceptionally life-like quality of this classic sculpture. Admire the perfect proportion and grace of the horse ... the detail - historically authentic - of the rider's armour with its intricate decorative work.

And notice especially an unusual <u>dramatic</u> touch, particularly appropriate to a work rooted in the spirited times of the Renaissance. The <u>highlights</u> distinguishing the rider ... the bronze being carefully hand-polished to create this intriguing contrast with the darker tone of the horse.

But I will not describe further the appearance of the work in this letter.

As some one who appreciates sculpture, you will easily discern for yourself the many remarkable qualities that make 'Il Cavallo' so appealing.

A genuine, traditional bronze – rich in hand-craftsmanship

I would, however, just like to make one thing absolutely clear to you. This is indeed a genuine, traditional bronze sculpture, crafted in the time-honoured way followed by great sculptors over the centuries.

First, the artist creates a detailed, fully three-dimensional clay model. From this a mould is made and carefully finished by hand. Hot wax is forced into the mould so that it reproduces every tiny detail of the original. Once this mould has cooled it is painstakingly hand-finished. Then a ceramic liquid is poured around the mould and fired in a kiln at high temperature. This causes the wax to melt. (Hence the ancient name for the process – 'cire perdue', lost wax.)

What is left is a perfect casting mould into which molten bronze is poured. After the bronze has cooled, it is hand-chased. Special acids and fire are patiently applied to achieve the lustrous patina that is one of the chief glories of bronze.

Finally, the sculpture is carefully rubbed by hand to bring out individual details and the full richness of colour. And in the case of 'Il Cavallo', particular care is lavished on polishing – to bring about the beautiful 'highlighting' I mentioned earlier.

Available solely by individual commission

But beauty is not the only criterion by which this outstanding work is judged. The status, the permanent significance, of this unique sculpture by Gianni Benvenuti ... fulfilling the dream of Leonardo da Vinci after five centuries ... is clearly recognised in the strict limitations applied to its issue.

> 'Il Cavallo' is being made available solely by direct, individual commission. No sculptures will be created for original sale through any gallery or dealer. No collector may commission more than one sculpture. And once all the individual commissions have been fulfilled, the moulds will be destroyed. 'Il Cavallo' can never be issued again.

The price is modest for such a major work

The 'direct commission' arrangement is, of course, extremely good news for all collectors. It has a quite dramatically favourable effect on the price. As you probably know, if you visit any gallery where comparable

works by major sculptors are being shown, you will find prices typically
in the four figure range. But 'Il Cavallo' offered only <u>direct</u>, to individual
commission, and <u>not</u> through any gallery or dealer, is able <u>to be</u> made available
for substantial<u>ly less</u>. £650 – and as a registered Franklin Mint Collector,
you will also be entitled to make use of an attractive subscription plan
which allows payments to be conveniently spread over a ten-month period.

<u>In your home – beauty that will not date or fade ...</u>

I have little doubt that you will be able to see straight away in your
mind's eye a perfect setting for 'Il Cavallo' in your home. For this is
indeed a classically beautiful bronze ... truly a 'timeless' work inspired
by the original drawings of Leonardo da Vinci and created by Italy's
internationally acclaimed master of today, Gianni Benvenuti. Its beauty
will not date or fade; and future generations also will appreciate its
unique significance and rare artistic distinction.

<u>In your own interests, apply promptly</u>

If you wish to acquire 'Il Cavallo' you will find a Commissioning Authorisation
enclosed. This is for your personal use: it may not be transferred to
anyone else. In your own interests, the return of this Commissioning
Authorisation is requested as soon as possible – and certainly no later
than 10th April, 1987.

I say this for a particular reason. As I'm sure you'll agree, the casting
and finishing of a bronze like this should not be rushed. And 'Il Cavallo'
certainly will not be. <u>Hand</u>-cast ... <u>hand</u>-finished ... every detail will
be 'right' before it is released to you. It may take two or three months
to complete the work. However, orders will be filled in sequence of receipt
and the <u>earliest ones will be despatched within six to eight weeks</u>.

That's why, if you already know you wish to acquire this magnificent bronze,
you may wish to put your decision into effect promptly. In any event, I
am confident you will always be delighted to be the owner of 'Il Cavallo'.
And I am pleased to have been able to bring you news of this outstanding
opportunity personally, in advance of any announcement to the general public.

I look forward to hearing from you and, as a fellow collector, I send you
my best wishes.

Yours sincerely,

M.R. Ellis

M.R. Ellis
Managing Director

cherish was reached when a supplier to my own agency managed to send out a message a few years ago to somebody called HM Queen. (It happened that the person in question was already a customer, believe it or not. And we got a very polite reply.)

Another fairly startling case occurred when one of my clients in Switzerland received seven letters from *The Economist* in one week, asking him to subscribe. Each address was slightly different. Maybe they thought they were saving money by not having the duplicates in various mailing lists checked. Sounds like lousy economics to me. On the following page is a montage of some of the openings: it's easy to see how things went wrong.

The question is: What is the purpose of personalization? And what effect does it have?

Quite clearly, you can only be writing to two types of people: people who are prospects and people who are customers.

There is no particular reason why somebody who is a prospect should expect you to know his or her name. Under those circumstances, I have found more often than not that paying the extra money involved in personalization does not result in an incremental response that justifies the cost.

The frequent exception to this rule is where the personalization is employed as a sort of entertainment device to gain attention.

Typical examples are the person's name in huge letters on the order form. Or scattered all over the envelope or used in capitals in the letter itself. A typical example was an envelope, once again for a cookery course, addressed to Mr Teper.

This is, obviously, an aspect of show business and none the worse for that. It works in attracting the attention of unsophisticated prospects. Even sophisticated people respond to the sight of their name.

Personalize to customers and enquirers

Where you are writing to customers, the evidence suggests that personalization certainly pays. A good example of the sort of thing that shouldn't happen is the letter on page 276, which demonstrates *im*personalization. It is 'newsletter' written in the form of a letter.

It was sent by the people we use for bicycle dispatch. Note the date. It was actually received by us on 30 November 1993. It would take a finer mind than mine (or indeed my secretary's – for we both puzzled over this long and hard) to discover how it took so long to reach us, maybe they should have sent it by bike.

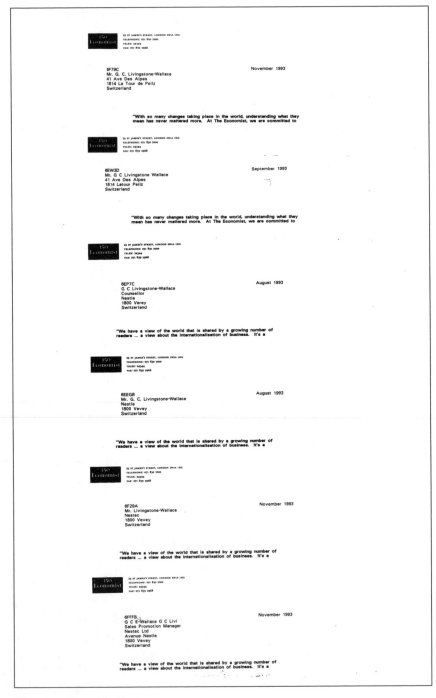

Sloppy personalization.

Clever personalization.

Probably it was just a mistake – but perhaps you can spend a little time looking at it and write down what you think of it.

This is what I think.

1. Not very personal, is it? I'm one of their existing clients; and not only that, what they sell is quite expensive. They definitely should have addressed it to me.
2. The opening paragraph is like a bad speech delivered by the chairman of Amalgamated Consolidated to his suppliers (apart from which, for those interested in grammar, the change from 'our' existing clients to 'your' current needs is incorrect).
3. The simple listing gives me no idea whatsoever of what the benefits are of these nine services they offer. It is just a list which means something to them – but nothing to me.
4. The 'summary' summarizes nothing, since the list itself is a summary; nor is there any indication whatsoever as to why they are so confident as to what they can do.

---

13 December 1991

Dear Client:

We are pleased to announce the following facilities to all our existing clients in addition to your current needs.

1. London hand delivery service for business mail

2. International courier (documents and parcels)

3. Overnight/sameday couriers (documents and parcels)

4. International mailing service

5. Fulfilment service

6. Polywrapped document/distribution service

7. Warehousing/storage delivery service

8. Mailroom staffing.

9. Total facility management.

Summary:

To reiterate, we are confident that we could supply you with the class and type of service you require.

Please call us on 0171 000 0000 for further details.

Naturally we would be pleased to meet with you to discuss your requirements.

Yours faithfully

An example of impersonalization.

The next example, shown opposite, is copy taken from a letter, and illustrates another impersonal effort. The letter was sent to my office with some brochures for office furniture. Neither my secretary nor I have the slightest recollection of having enquired about this, since we already have plenty of office furniture which, cheapskates that we are, we bought second hand.

What do you think of it?

Dear Sir/Madam

Thankyou for showing an interest in our nationally renowned exhibition systems, craftsman built by ourselves in the United Kingdom.

As well as our excellent modular and portable stands, we design and build exhibitions in the traditional manner, which includes storage and hire.

Roadshows, conferences and product launches are a speciality, with major Blue Chip companies as satisfied clients, in fact over 900 of The Times top 1000 companies use these systems.

I do hope that the enclosed information is of interest to you, and should you wish to take advantage of the very special offers that are available for a limited period only, please contact me to arrange an appointment.

Yours faithfully

Here are my comments.

1. They can't be bothered to put a date on the letter – nor for that matter find out what my name is or even what sex I am – it's an androgynous letter.
2. As the writer hasn't even bothered to sign the letter, this is not a promising indication of the service I am likely to receive in the future.
3. Even if this were a good letter, which of course it is not, it would work infinitely better if it said 'Thank you for enquiring on such and such date about our nationally renowned exhibition systems etc'. Then at least we'd have some idea of how we came to be singled out.
4. Statements like 'nationally renowned' are always to be used extremely carefully since what may be very famous to you is not famous to me. In this case I'd heard of neither the company nor what they make.
5. The whole thing is written from the point of the view of the writer, not from mine.

6. An opportunity is missed in the only interesting line in the letter: 'over 900 of *The Times* top 1000 companies use these systems'. Surely some of them must have said something complimentary at one time or another about this company's products. This could have been incorporated.
7. Many other things could have been included about matters such as price, benefits as compared with the competition, and so on and so on.
8. It is infuriating to be told there is a very special offer for a limited period only when no details of that offer are supplied or indeed of the period to which the writer refers. Altogether an abysmal letter.

Both these letters would have benefited from personalization. In one case, I am a customer. In the other I am an enquirer. As in so many others ways, when considering personalization, the sales letter mirrors a conversation. If you were talking to somebody and you had already dealt with them, they would expect you to be polite enough to address them by name.

HOW DO YOU ADDRESS PEOPLE?

This is a subject which comes up surprisingly often – unnecessarily in most cases, to my mind. What should you call people if you can't personalize?

I've often listened to discussions as to whether the letter should begin 'Dear Reader' or 'Dear Friend'. Particularly in England, there is an enormous amount of concern about whether people's delicate susceptibilities are going to be offended by being wrongly addressed.

Some experts believe you are better to begin with something like 'Good morning!' – which is fine, I suppose, if your readers don't save the letter till later in the day.

The attitude of the reader, unless he or she is a rare human being, is much more likely to be influenced by what benefit or offer the opening of the letter reveals than what the salutation is. Tell me I can get slim or happy or win a million pounds and I don't care what you call me as long as it's polite.

If you have something that interests your readers, believe me, they will soon get over any preliminary squirmings about being addressed as a friend by somebody they don't know. If what is being offered is of sufficient appeal, then they will keep reading.

There are other times when you are likely, if not to be offended, then at the very least to be irritated. These are those occasions when your name has been spelt wrong, or your title wrongly described, or some other details like your company's name is incorrect.

These sort of things are important. They not only irritate; they erode credibility. In the first place, people look at their names and addresses very carefully. If somebody can't take the trouble to find out who you really are, what are the odds that they will get everything else right?

There is one wacky list I am on in which the company name is both wrongly spelled and out of date. I don't work there any more. Even if I did, the title they have given me is wrong, as is the name of the building and even the street. Yet there is no attempt to ask me to correct the name and address.

Sexual confusion and other oddities

Perhaps the most common example of this sort of thing is where somebody gets your sex wrong. Though for my money the most infuriating salutation is 'Dear Mr/Mrs' or 'Sir/Madam', which as I have just pointed out belongs to the sexually indeterminate school of letter-writing. When I receive them I am convinced the people sending them are just plain damned idle.

One salutation bound to offend, but which nobody has found a solution to, is one that addresses somebody who has died. As I pointed out earlier, this caused quite a problem in my letter for Save the Children.

One English company claims to have developed a capability to screen these names out. It is, however, quite impossible unless you can get every funeral director in the country to agree to give you names of their customers as they become known. And even then there is bound to be some sort of delay.

We can, however, take a certain morose comfort from the fact that very few deceased recipients have complained as far as I'm aware.

The safest appellation is 'Dear Reader'. This should apply to almost all those receiving the letter. It cannot cause offence, and those who, due to the erratic quality of our educational system, cannot read won't understand what you're saying anyhow.

Some people believe it adds to the effectiveness of a mailing if, when writing, for instance to those who like collecting things, you write 'Dear Collector', so as to make them feel part of a special group. I can't believe it makes a jot of difference. The same thing, I strongly suspect, applies to such salutations as 'Dear Investor', 'Dear Professional' and so forth.

One solution – certainly when you are mailing people you have never mailed before – is to have no salutation whatsoever, but simply begin the whole thing in the same style as you would begin any letter. That seems to work pretty well, too. Some even think a salutation is never necessary.

In short, you should be much more concerned about making sure you've got the name and address and title right than anything else.

Business salutations

When mailing people in businesses, on the first occasion mailing to the *title* of the individual rather than the *name* makes more sense.

This is because people change their jobs so frequently nowadays that the odds are more than 50 per cent that the name on a rented list is wrong. So the extra trouble and expense you may have gone to so as to personalize the mailing does not pay. If you are dealing with existing customers, whose names you clearly ought to know, you should personalize.

One original way of handling the salutation which some people have used is to start a sentence and put the person's name in halfway through. For example, 'Since I last wrote to you, Mr Bird, something rather unexpected has come up, which I thought I should tell you about.'

I find this approach rather appealing.

SIGNING OFF

I haven't heard nearly as much debate about the right wording to end the letter – the sign off. Rightly so: I think this even less worthy of debate than the salutation.

However, having been taught in an old-fashioned English school that you should never say 'Yours sincerely' at the end of the letter unless you are writing to somebody by name, the use of that phrase always irritates me. I shouldn't think it bothers most recipients, though.

You should give thought, though, to who signs the letter. Getting a message from the assistant deputy marketing officer does not bring a lift to the average person's day. Getting a letter from the Chief Executive Officer does.

I learnt this in a surprising way when, over 20 years ago, I wrote a letter to sell some very expensive villas in Portugal. We got the letter signed by the chairman of Costain's the builders. We were inviting people to attend the screening of a film about the property at the Hyde Park Hotel.

Several people wrote back to the chairman, Sir Richard, apologizing that they could not come. The mailing sold more properties in two weeks than they had managed in the previous year through national advertising.

Get the most important person you can to sign the letter. If that person objects there are three possible reasons:

1. They have some objection to the tone of the letter – this is not unusual. They may wish to fiddle with some of the phrases on the grounds that 'this isn't the way I would write'. As long as any changes they propose don't do serious harm to the content, let them have their way.
2. They may object to the content – such phrases as 'It's too commercial' are not uncommon from pompous idiots who have forgotten where their salaries come from. If you have written the letter properly you should be able to explain the reason for everything in it.

    To tricky clients I often used the expression 'Everything in here is here for a reason. If you want to know what it is, just ask.' This was surprisingly effective in disarming silly objections before they came forth.
3. They may be worried about getting complaints from customers. In that case, they should improve their product or, better still in some cases, resign. If you can't stand the heat, stay out of the kitchen.

The mere fact that the chairman puts his name on something gives it added credibility. One Australian company which had had a lot of complaints about poor service sent out a letter from their chairman with a cork doll portraying him and a pin for customers to jab into it.

The chairman gave his direct line for complaints. Although the service barely improved over the following 12 months, research showed the customers thought it had.

DO I NEED A BROCHURE AS WELL?

Amateur direct mailers (and this includes many otherwise sophisticated companies and even some who claim to be direct mail experts – particularly direct mail handling houses and sales promotion companies) frequently mail brochures with no letter.

As I have already noted, 99 times out of 100, this is wrong. The great virtue of direct mail is that it is personal. It is a unique opportunity to single someone out and speak to them as an individual. People like receiving letters. And when they get an envelope through the post, they *expect* a letter.

A brochure, generally speaking, is an impersonal communication. Certainly less personal than a letter. Often, when sent out without any advance indication that it is coming – a 'cold mailing' – it gets the response 'What's this about?' For this reason, if you have a choice of sending out a brochure or a letter – probably because you can't afford to do both – a letter is almost invariably better.

I have recently conducted tests for a client which showed significant increases in response – between 9 and 28 per cent – when mailings of brochures – even very detailed ones written in a very personal tone of voice – had letters added.

Indeed, in more than one case *eliminating* a brochure from a direct mail shot and letting the work be done entirely by a letter and order form has increased response. In a test for the Bank of Scotland I found that taking out a brochure increased return on investment by 90 per cent as the response was almost the same, but the cost far less.

This is not to say, though, that brochures are a bad idea. If you can afford it, almost invariably a good brochure will help.

Five factors to consider

When considering whether you ought to send out a brochure, five things should be borne in mind.

1. Is the brochure doing something the letter isn't? Covering something the letter is not covering? Showing attractive pictures of what you sell, if looks are important? Or demonstrating some benefit or aspect of the product the letter can not? In that case, it is probably a good idea.
2. If the product depends for its appeal on its looks, but you can't afford a brochure, you could put pictures in the letter. I have seen this increase replies by 17 per cent.

Generally, photographs are more credible and therefore more persuasive than drawings. Astonishingly, I once saw the change from drawing to photograph *double* response to an advertisement.

3. You will often see very professional direct mailers use a brochure which appears to be saying more or less exactly what the letter said.

    If you study these mailings carefully, you will see that what the brochure is usually doing is saying the same thing in a different way or looking at the problem from a different angle. This frequently pays. The pioneering British direct mail expert, Christian Brann, likens this process to that of witnesses in court, each describing an event from a different perspective.

4. Remember: when you send out a letter, you have already paid for the postage and (if you're renting the list) the list, and the handling.

    Accordingly, you have substantial fixed costs before you start. Often it does not cost you a great deal more, relatively speaking, to send out a brochure which will improve response and thus make the mailing more profitable overall. So, if you already have a brochure printed, there is an argument for using it.

5. If you are trying to sell something very expensive, or get a substantial commitment, you may need the extra power a brochure brings to your mailing, just as you will probably find you require longer copy in the letter itself.

Don't forget, when talking about brochures, that there are many other possible enclosures you might find worth including with your letter. A sheet of testimonials is often very effective, particularly if it shows pictures of the people and reprints their comments in their own hand-writing or on their own letterhead.

So, where appropriate, is an elegant invitation – with an RSVP, perhaps, as with the Royal Viking Line letter shown earlier.

What about letters to accompany brochures?

Now that we have established that the letter is more important than the brochure but a brochure is often a good idea, you may well ask what sort of letter?

The answer is: not the kind you generally get with a brochure. Most of them suffer from one or both of the following faults:

1. They are brief, unenthusiastic announcements of the fact that a brochure is enclosed;
2. They are sometimes not separate letters, but actually printed inside the brochure so that they cannot stand out.

The purpose of the letter under these circumstances is indeed to introduce the brochure.

But there is a world of difference between a man who introduces you by saying: 'Meet Jim Jones' and somebody who says 'Here is Jim Jones who is the leading expert in the world on airport design. I have worked with him for 15 years and if you have a serious project to consider, he's the man for you…' followed by examples of the wonderful work Jones has done in the past and how well others speak of him.

It is the latter sort of introduction that we are looking for in a letter. The letter is, as I pointed out above, like the salesman showing you round the store. Poor salesmen let you get on with it without offering any help or guidance. Good salesmen, in a polite, helpful way, ask if you have any questions, answer them and advise you on how you can make the best possible decisions. They also point out the new stock that has come in, special bargains and so forth.

That's what a letter going out with a brochure should do.

A GOOD EXAMPLE TO ANALYSE

On page 285 is a brochure sent to me which incorporates the letter.

The letter should either be completely separate or, if you are sending out a catalogue, try attaching it to the front so it can't be missed – as is sometimes the case where you open an envelope and pull out the catalogue leaving the letter behind.

What other comments would you have about this letter? Pause a moment and think about this letter and, indeed, the page which is reproduced with it.

Here are my observations:

1. The shape of the brochure is good. It will stand out in its envelope from the morning mail.
2. The design on the front is well judged from the sense of stability one wants to feel from somebody training.
3. The quote from a satisfied customer at the bottom of the right-

Good layout and shape, but what about the letter?

Dear Client,

As the rate of change in business accelerates, it is ever more important to equip people at all levels with the knowledge and skills they need to keep you ahead of the competition.

You have the choice of open training, giving your directors and managers a valuable opportunity to get out and look back in; or in-house training – designed with you to satisfy team training needs.

Throughout the recession we are proud to have gained an average of one new client a day, mainly as a result of recommendations, for which we thank you.

We look forward to continuing to be of service.

Yours sincerely,

Ron Coleman
Managing Director

---

hand page is a good idea. Indeed all that page tells you everything that you want to know.

4. The most interesting thing in the letter is at the end where you learn the company has gained new clients constantly in the recession.

5. The first paragraph of the letter is pretty pointless because it makes the sort of statement with which one can either agree or disagree. If one agrees one doesn't need to be told what that paragraph tells. If one disagrees it is not all that persuasive. Had it been in the body of a longer letter it probably would have been a helpful piece of substantiation.

6. The letter is too brief – which it had to be because it has been placed inside the front cover.

7. I'm not keen on the old-fashioned phraseology: 'look forward to continuing to be of service' – in itself a clumsy sentence. In short this letter lacks meat and persuasion. The quote I referred to originally probably does more for the company than the letter, particularly because the brochure is peppered with such quotes.

WHAT SHOULD I ASK PEOPLE TO DO?

Nothing hard. Don't forget what I said when discussing the close of your letter and the order form.

Research in 1992 showed – to no intelligent person's surprise – that if advertisers pay for telephone calls or postal responses, customers prefer that to paying themselves. Of course, many companies aren't intelligent and about half still make customers pay. God knows how much money they lose by this.

Only ask people to pay if you are getting too many replies from people who aren't likely to make good customers. *This is very rare.* Always make it as easy as you can for your prospect or customer. They don't want to do your work for you.

In addition to the points I made in Chapter 12 this means three simple things:

1. Answer all questions, no matter how apparently stupid, politely.
2. NEVER say: 'There's no call for it' or the like, when people ask for something. You just *had* a call for it.
3. Listen to customers – and give them what they want.

One of my partners spoke to a British Telecom employee on the phone wanting information about a particular service. She offered to send a salesman. My partner said he just wanted a brochure.

She didn't send it, but rang *three times* asking when the salesman could come. Dumb. And deaf.

All this, you will rightly think, adds up to: *don't take enquiries or customers for granted*. They're too hard to get for you to give them away. And they cost you money to acquire. Cherish them.

We have now considered the obvious questions that arise when planning your letter and which you need to have clear before beginning. Next, let's turn to what happens after your letter has gone out. First, how many customers are you likely to get?

HOW MANY REPLIES CAN I EXPECT?

A man in New Zealand, after I had finished making a speech, said: 'Well, you seem to know all the answers; you should be able to *guarantee* results.'

I replied that if that were so, I would have stopped working a long time ago and be snoring on a beach somewhere. The most I would claim is that I know most of the mistakes to avoid and most of the questions to ask.

Nobody can tell you how many replies you will get, but here are some good questions to ask, beginning with the obvious one.

1. Have you sent out a similar letter before? That is the best guide to likely response.
2. How difficult is the task? Just as a more difficult objective requires longer copy, so you will clearly get a lower response. The criteria are the same, really.

   Thus, if you are writing to your customers to ask their opinions, then a good 50 per cent should reply, especially if you offer them a small incentive. If they don't, then the letter is bad or your service is.

   If you want someone you have never had any relationship with to buy something expensive, 0.5 per cent might be a likely response.
3. A good rule of thumb: if the result you think you'll get would make you rich overnight, you are being unrealistic. Life ain't that easy.
4. Keep an eye on the pattern of replies you get. Your replies don't all come in immediately. They start slowly, build to a peak, then

tail off over a period. How long will depend on the nature of your product, but a pattern will emerge.

You have to keep your eye on what mail order people call *'double day'* – that's the day when as a rule around half your replies come in. It could be ten days to two weeks after your letter produced its first reply. Knowing that, you can predict likely eventual response.

How do I record results?

The answer is simple. Meticulously. And you record *everything that could be relevant.*

That means you should have a code on the order form so you know where a reply came from. You record the replies, day by day. You note any relevant factor that might have influenced results.

These include what your competitors are doing, what's happening to the weather (good weather, lower replies; bad weather, better replies) and sometimes even the news. When there is heavy news – a big war scare, for instance – replies slump unless you're selling something relevant, like weapons. Clearly, too, new taxes or the announcement of the budget could affect your replies; people might be delaying a purchase for that reason.

Measure the results of *every* activity. If you are inviting people to attend a show or come into your shop, give them a leaflet offering a small gift or an invitation card that they have to bring – and code it.

What to do with replies?

I spent many miserable hours in the Boy Scouts, being unable to tie knots, which as far as I recall was the main talent required. The only thing I remember about it all was the motto: 'Be prepared'.

Be prepared when replies come in. If you have got people answering the phone, be sure they know all about the letter going out and know what to say. If you have promised literature, have it ready to go out. If you have said you'll come and see the customer, get out there fast.

Sounds obvious? It isn't to most business people. In the book I have already quoted, *'Dear Sir or Madam'*, the author records how poorly most companies respond to enquiries.

Results were as follows: 3.5 per cent took more than 27 days, by which time I imagine most of those who replied had forgotten what the subject was; 27 per cent took between 8 and 26 days, which hardly shows intense enthusiasm to get the business; 61 per cent achieved the modest aim of replying within a week.

But 8.5 per cent never replied at all! They might just as well have taken their money and thrown it out of the window. Worse: they actively put people off them.

In fact, I recall figures some years ago which showed that every day you delay replying cuts 1 per cent off the response you would have got. That is, 1 per cent of the likely percentage; so if you might have got 20 per cent, then a day's delay reduces this to 19.8 per cent.

HOW TO GET THEM SPENDING

It is sometimes the case that a customer has agreed to deal with you, but has not yet bought anything. This is often so where somebody has established an account.

The moment they sign the form and give it back to you saying they want to become a customer is very important. How you then handle the relationship is critical. They are ready to do business with you, but they have not yet actually done anything apart from join the club, as it were.

In fact a good example is if somebody has joined a book club or a wine society but not bought anything. In marketing jargon, making these people do something is known as 'activating' them.

If they have actually been buying for some time and then stopped buying, then we talk about *re*activating them. The RSVP letter I illustrated earlier from British Telecom is a good example of this. The principles in the latter case are much the same as with a new customer – and you might like to know that the best list of prospects you will ever get is a list of such people.

Get the customer to act

Let me deal first with an instance where a company has done an exemplary job of marketing and got my custom, then done nothing whatsoever for far too long to make me act.

First Direct offers – as the name implies – a direct banking service which I was persuaded to join, because my secretary told me that they delivered a much better service than anyone else. First Direct get most of their business through people who ring up in response to advertisements or mailings.

Since you conduct all your business on the phone with a minimum of correspondence and no personal contact whatsoever, the telephone is the logical way to start the relationship. My enquiry was dealt with courteously and promptly. I was asked for a certain amount of information which was filled in on the form by them before it was sent to me to be signed. So far, excellent.

Then, what happened? I received a series of communications to me as a customer. All very polite and well written. What I did not receive was a communication saying 'I see you have applied for an account, but you have not put any money into it'.

A pretty critical step one would have thought. I do not know what it costs them to acquire a new customer. Probably not less than £50 on average. That £50 they spent on acquiring me is money down the drain if I don't act.

In fact it took about a year before they wrote to me – and the letter was quite good; it's reproduced overleaf. The point is, I had not fallen out of love with First Direct and lost interest in having an account. No, I had done nothing, for the reason a lot of people do nothing: sheer *sloth*. I have a lot of other things on my mind and opening this account is something I may or may not get round to eventually. So far, ten years on, I retain an account but barely use it. They should have persisted. Especially as a little data analysis would have shown them I am a valuable prospect. Dumb.

Contrast the First Direct approach with that of Mercury, the telephone company in the UK. I was allured by their claims of lower prices than British Telecom – accordingly I spoke to a friend who told me that the best thing to do was go out and buy a Mercury phone.

I went out and did so. Inside there was a form to fill in. I did so and received by return the letter which you see on page 294. Notice, not only do they want me to start using my Mercury number; they have gone to the trouble of offering me the chance to win £100 just by making a telephone call. Very intelligent.

AFTER THEY'VE BOUGHT, HOW DO I STRENGTHEN THE RELATIONSHIP?

The answer is, of course, write and say 'Thank you'. It is polite – and, as we have already learned, research shows your sales will go up subsequently. This will be even more true if you plan what you say carefully.

Our ref **PRG/M610/610031/A**

Firstdirect
Millshaw Park Lane
Leeds
LS11 0LT
Telephone 0345 100 100

first direct

25 February 1994

Dear Mr Bird

Are you missing out on the rewards that should be yours as a Firstdirect customer?

I tried to contact you some time ago about making the most of your Firstdirect Cheque Account. As I have not heard from you, I am concerned that you are missing out on the rewards that should be yours.

From regular research conducted with our customers, we recognise that moving your salary and account from one bank to another is perceived to be a troublesome experience. However, we can help you make this process very simple and straightforward. We have established a trained team of people - the Account Transfer Team - who are here to help you.

We could be paying your bills for you

Have your salary paid into your Firstdirect Cheque Account and you will never again have to worry about paying bills. No need to write out cheques, fill in Giro forms, find a stamp, catch the post or queue at the bank. Just call Firstdirect, tell us who to pay, when and how much, and leave the rest to us.

We could be adding to your bank balance

Are you earning a good rate of interest at the moment? Firstdirect pays good interest rates on your Cheque Account .... consistently higher than the current accounts of our major high street competitors. The more you have in your account, the better the rate of interest you earn as interest rates are tiered - yet another good reason to have your salary paid straight into Firstdirect.

You enjoy free banking on your Cheque Account - with no charges for processing cheques, standing orders, direct debits or monthly statements. If you should slip into the red, you will find that we do not charge fees for overdrafts up to £250, just interest on the amount you borrow.

We could be making life easier for you, every single day . . .

Your Firstdirect Card guarantees cheques for up to £100 - twice the amount of many other bank cards and it also lets you pay by Switch. It allows you to withdraw up to £500 in cash per day from one of the largest bank cash machine networks in the UK. You can pay money into your account at any Midland branch (free of charge) or, if you prefer, post cheques to us direct.

Continued . . .

L318 - A
(20/07/93)
Firstdirect is a division of Midland Bank plc Registered in England, Registered number 14259, Registered office Poultry, London EC2P 2BX
A member of the Investment Management Regulatory Organisation

---

Get the customer to act.

Of course, Firstdirect also offers a wide range of other financial services, including loans, savings accounts, Visa Card and sharedealing services, to name but a few. For all your banking needs - from checking your balance, to transferring money, to opening another account - you can call Firstdirect at any time of the night or day. We are always open and ready to help you. There are no answering machines at Firstdirect, just friendly, helpful people who are genuinely proud of the service they offer. Remember, no matter where you call from in the UK, you pay only for a local rate call.

So, why not take advantage of all the benefits that are waiting for you at Firstdirect?

.... starting today.

To make the most of your Firstdirect Cheque Account, all you need to do is transfer your salary and existing bank account to us. This straightforward procedure takes very little time and we can help to arrange the transfer on your behalf.

An independent National Opinion Polls (NOP) survey revealed that 82% of Firstdirect customers are very or extremely satisfied with our service, 92% think our service is better than that offered by their previous bank and 89% of customers recommend Firstdirect to their friends and relations. Now let us show you why opening an account with Firstdirect was the best move you ever made.

If, however, we are unable to convince you of the benefits of using your Firstdirect Cheque Account, then you may wish to consider closing your account. This is to enable you to keep your financial arrangements simple and to avoid the risk of fraud. If you do want to keep your account open, please contact us as soon as possible.

Call us anytime

To begin to enjoy the benefits of banking with Firstdirect, call us any time on **0345 100 100** and ask for the New Accounts Team. We will be pleased to help make your move to Firstdirect as smooth as possible.

I look forward to showing you what Firstdirect can really do.

Yours sincerely

Paul Gratton
Customer Sales Director

PS   I have enclosed a leaflet which compares Firstdirect's interest rates and services with those of some of our major competitors. If you have any questions about any aspect of banking with Firstdirect, please do not hesitate to call us.

Mercury Communications Ltd.

Sales Enquiries, PO Box 49   Telephone: 0500 500194
Birmingham B1 1TE

Mercury
COMMUNICATIONS

Customer Billing Number: 0664266

19th July 1993

Dear Mr Bird,

Thank you for ordering the Mercury 2300 Service.

Within the next 7-10 days you can expect to receive your Mercury PIN Code which for security reasons, will be sent to you in two separate parts. If for any reason you do not receive your PIN Code, please call Mercury Customer Assistance free on 0500 500 194.

When you receive your PIN Code remember to programme your equipment as soon as possible. You may find it helpful to refer to the enclosed programming guide. However, if you still have difficulties please call Mercury Fault Reporting, free of charge on 0500 500 193, who will be happy to help you.

<u>MAKE A TEST CALL NOW AND YOU COULD WIN £100.</u>

After you have programmed your PIN Code, simply make a test call, and you could enter our Free Prize Draw with a chance to win £100!

Take a look inside your enclosed Welcome Pack for more details of this and other exciting ways you can benefit from Mercury.

Thank you once again for ordering Mercury's 2300 Service.

Yours sincerely

C Holgate

Christine Holgate
Manager, Consumer Marketing

PS. As of 10th August 1992, the Mercury PIN Code annual charge is £11.75 (inc VAT at 17.5%). This price is correct at time of writing, and may vary in future without notice.

Reg in England No 1541957 Reg Office New Mercury House, 26 Red Lion Square, London WC1R 4HQ    A CABLE & WIRELESS COMPANY

The intelligent approach.

One secret of success, as I pointed out earlier, is that if you're going to write to somebody anyway, it's often a good idea to do more than one thing. A good example is where you send people regular statements. You have to pay the postage on them so it's an opportunity to sell people something extra.

When you send merchandise to people, it's a good idea to include a thank you letter and leaflets selling other merchandise. In the same way, if people are phoning to order something, it will often be on freephone which you have to pay for. When they call it's an opportunity to sell them something extra.

There follows an example of how one company, Inmac, who sell computer paraphernalia, say thank you. Why don't you read through the letter and see what you think? Make some notes on how you would have improved it. Then read my comments.

As you see, they take the opportunity not only to say thank you but also to ask people to evaluate their service. They also make two special offers if you will place a second order, the offers dependent upon the value of that order; and in addition, they ask people if they would like to get free regular copies of their catalogue. All good stuff.

The emphasis on placing orders within two weeks, featured in the flash on the sheet showing the free offers, is bound to have a good effect. It's also a good idea to have a picture of someone looking out of the page at you. This increases the attention value of the letter, because people look at people.

This is only inappropriate when you are trying to make the letter look as close as possible to a personal one. In this case it doesn't matter, because this is a clearly commercial letter sent out in the context of an existing commercial relationship.

What else could they have done?

1. The style of the letter is somewhat dull and repetitive. For instance, the use of the adjective 'exciting' in the heading is one of the clichés in copywriting I have talked about elsewhere in this book. I doubt if it will add anything to the sales. There are a number of other clichéd expressions elsewhere, such as 'with your order details'.

2. It might have made sense to explain that we are making the free offers to thank you when you place a second order. This gives the reason for the offers.

3. In the first two paragraphs the writer makes the same point twice in slightly different ways – here at Inmac etc and we at Inmac etc.

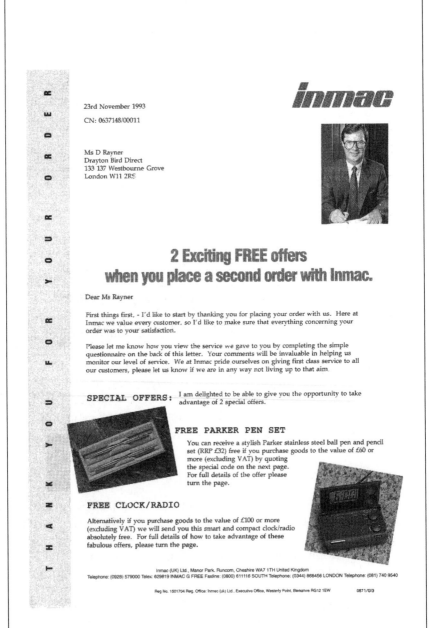

Thank the reader first. But what an ugly layout!

A WIDE RANGE OF CATALOGUES TO SUIT ALL YOUR COMPUTING NEEDS.

Our General Computer Users Catalogue contains a very broad range of widely used products, including computer and printer supplies and accessories, furniture and the less complex data communications products such as cables, switches etc.

We also have the following catalogues:

HARDWARE/SOFTWARE
All the market leading PCs, printers, faxes and software.

HEWLETT PACKARD SUPPLIES
Comprehensive range of HP branded supplies

SYSTEMS & NETWORKING
This contains the more specialised networking and data communications products. Ideal for MIS/DP and Buying professionals.

If you wish to subscribe to any of the above catalogues, please either telephone our Subscription Hotline on 0344 860606 or complete the subscription request on the back of this letter.

TAKE ADVANTAGE OF OUR SPECIAL OFFERS TODAY!

Just call us on any of the following numbers with your order details, remembering to quote the special code to ensure you receive your free gift.

081 740 9540 London
0344 868456 South
0928 579000 North
Free Fax 0800 611116

Hurry, to take advantage of these offers you must place your order within 2 weeks.

Yours sincerely

Peter Hill
Managing Director

4. The second page of the letter to my mind tails away into a sort of laundry list of what they sell. I suspect they could have said more about the items they are selling, eg perhaps they offer more Hewlett Packard supplies than anyone else or they offer better prices. Obviously without knowing a lot about their business it is hard to say.
5. Almost certainly the last paragraph in the latter beginning 'Hurry', should have been in the form of a PS.
6. More could have been made of the free gifts. For instance, the 'stylish' – again a cliché – Parker Pen set is worth over half the value of the minimum purchase of £60. This really is a very good offer. Far more impressive things could have been said than 'exciting' about an offer like that. However, the recommended retail price is quoted. This is a good idea because it establishes the value of the pen set; but we are given no idea of the value of the clock radio.

On the next two pages is an example of how not to retain customers – from a firm that desperately needs to.

THE EASIEST SOURCE OF NEW BUSINESS

One other thing you must ask your customers to do is recommend you to their friends. Not just when they first buy from you, but as often as you can within reason. You've heard many times the expression 'Word of mouth advertising'. This exemplifies the truth that nothing is more persuasive than a friend saying to you: 'Why don't you try it?'

So it's logical that getting your customers to recommend their friends is generally the best way to get new business. You can do this with a small message on your order form or a very brief letter after people have bought.

This is hardly what I would call a big letter writing challenge. The principle is simple: you offer your customer a gift for introducing a friend or more than one friend; and you are usually wise to offer the friend a gift. You should always explain why you are doing it. A typical letter might run as follows.

Dear Sir

<u>Free gifts — for you and your friends</u>

Would any of your friends like our widgets? If so I have a free gift for you — and for them.

You know better than anyone else the quality of our widgets and I find that the recommendation of satisfied customers such as you is our best source of new business. Apart from anything else, it saves expensive advertising and helps us keep our costs down.

If you have any friends who would like to try our products, why not list their names and addresses on the little form I've enclosed below? For every one who becomes a customer we will give you a free gift — and we will give each of them a free gift as a thank you for trying our service.

Clearly, you should 'sell' the free gift, whatever it is, and put a value on it.

WHAT IF THEY HAVEN'T PAID?

Hardly surprisingly, the person I learned most from on the subject of extracting money from people who owe it to you was a money-lender. He described himself as a private banker, but as far as I was concerned he only banked on the willingness of those who really needed money to pay what seems to me to be extortionate rates of interest.

He really was a rat, but I learned quite a lot from him. Among the techniques he used which I do not recommend are the not entirely subtle ploys that he used in his last two attempts to extract money from people before he actually sent somebody round in person to collect it.

The first was simply to send a request for money in the form of a postcard which could clearly be read by the postman. This was used in the hope of shaming people into paying up. If it didn't work, then his last, most fiendish, device was to send a letter addressed to the people next door, as it were by accident.

SOUTH WESTERN ELECTRICITY plc

Priorswood Office
Priorswood Road
Taunton TA2 8DD

Telephone 0823-259721
Fax 0823-259471

our ref 6229 5990/CP01   *date* 1st December, 1993

Dear Mr Bird,

I refer to your outstanding account of £313.19.

IF PAYMENT HAS BEEN MADE IN THE LAST FEW DAYS PLEASE IGNORE THIS LETTER AND
ACCEPT OUR THANKS.

If you have not paid, you should now:

   1. PAY THE AMOUNT IMMEDIATELY IN FULL.

or 2. HAVE A KEY BUDGET METER INSTALLED to pay off your bill and to cover future
      usage.

or 3. PAY THE AMOUNT BY WEEKLY INSTALMENTS, an IMMEDIATE payment of £63.19,
      followed by 5 weekly payments of £50.00 commencing 10th December, 1993.

or 4. PAY THE AMOUNT AND YOUR NEXT 3 ACCOUNTS BY WEEKLY INSTALMENTS OF £30.00 per
      week commencing 10th December, 1993.

or 5. IF YOU ARE HAVING DIFFICULTY IN PAYING PLEASE CONTACT US FOR ASSISTANCE.

Please let us know how you are going to pay, otherwise we will be calling to
install a Key Budget Meter on or after week commencing 20th December, 1993.

However, if for any reason we are unable to install this type of meter we do have
the right to disconnect, which will involve additional costs.

If you have any query about this letter please contact us in the first
instance. If we are unable to satisfy your query you may like to contact the
Office of Electricity Regulation.

Yours sincerely,

J Everett
J Everett (Mrs)
Credit Control Manager

South Western Electricity plc
Registered in England and Wales No 2366894
Registered Office
800 Park Avenue, Aztec West, Almondsbury Bristol BS12 4SE

Sympathise with the reader.

Leo Burnett, whom I have quoted already, once observed:

> In learning to work and live with people, the most important thing I am coming to understand is the simple truth that 'no one makes mistakes on purpose'.
>
> Knowing this should allow us to concentrate on correcting the mistake rather than making life miserable for the mistake maker. If he is the right sort, nothing you can say or do to him will make him feel any worse than he does already.

Being unable to pay money is one of the most unpleasant mistakes one can make. It is always smart for the creditor to try and sympathize and offer you ways of paying the money, rather than simply sending abusive letters.

The letter opposite is to me a good example of how to go about it. As you see, it assumes politely that the matter has slipped the reader's mind. My only criticism would be the opening sentence 'I refer to your outstanding account of £313.19'.

When you don't get a response to something as polite as this, it is often tempting to express your frustration by sending out something pretty aggressive. However the time for that is not yet right. The next letter should be equally polite, but slightly more to the point.

You may recall my writing to you two weeks ago about the sum of £15, due to us as the final payment for your [details].

I have now written to you twice about this, and would appreciate an early payment. [Here you remind the reader once again of all the ways they can pay.]

Because this sum is now two months overdue, I really would very much appreciate your prompt attention to this matter.

If there is any reason why you have not so far paid, please call 0800 xxxx and ask to speak to our Mr Jones who will be happy to discuss the matter with you.

Next letter:

<u>£15, now overdue since 15th</u>

My credit controller is now pressing me very hard about this payment. I do hope you can send it to me by return.

This will save additional cost on both our parts, since I am required to pass the matter over to our collection department if I do not hear from you within 7 days.

If you are having difficulty in paying, please ring 0800 4656 and ask to speak to our Mr Jones who will make every effort to work out an arrangement that will suit you.

Next letter:

<u>Your payment of £15 now due to be passed to our collection department</u>

I have now written to you six times about this payment without receiving any reply. Unfortunately, it is now my duty to pass the letter over to our collection department. This will involve you in additional legal costs.

I do hope this will not be necessary. To prevent the matter going to court, simply send the payment to xxxx.

There are many variations employed by people to get money out of debtors, but the principle outlined here of starting by assuming politely that the matter has been overlooked and progressing slowly through greater degrees of urgency is the one that seems to work best.

Index